FAILED STATEBUILDING

FAILED STATEBUILDING

INTERVENTION AND THE DYNAMICS OF PEACE FORMATION

OLIVER P. RICHMOND

YALE UNIVERSITY PRESS
NEW HAVEN AND LONDON

For information about this and other Yale University Press publications, please contact:

U.S. Office: sales.press@yale.edu www.yalebooks.com
Europe Office: sales@yaleup.co.uk www.yalebooks.co.uk

Typeset in Adobe Caslon Pro by IDSUK (DataConnection) Ltd
Printed in Great Britain by TJ International Ltd, Padstow, Cornwall

Library of Congress Cataloging-in-Publication Data

Richmond, Oliver P.
Failed statebuilding : intervention, the state, and the dynamics of peace formation / Oliver P. Richmond.
pages cm
Includes bibliographical references and index.
ISBN 978-0-300-17531-8 (cloth)
1. Developing countries—Foreign relations—Western countries. 2. Developing countries—Politics and government. 3. Nation-building—Developing countries. 4. Peace-building—Developing countries. 5. Intervention (International law) 6. Nation-building—Philosophy. 7. Peace-building—Philosophy. 8. World politics—1989- 9. Western countries—Relations—Developing countries. I. Title. II. Title:Failed state-building.
D888.W47R42 2014
327.1'17—dc23

2014022295

A catalogue record for this book is available from the British Library.

10 9 8 7 6 5 4 3 2 1

MIX
Paper from responsible sources
FSC® C013056
FSC www.fsc.org

Contents

Acknowledgements

I have been working on the problem of 'failed statebuilding' as a product of international assemblages of intervention, and on its counterdynamics of peace formation, since 2009, when I finished my previous book (co-written with Jason Franks), *Liberal Peace Transitions*. This analysis is underpinned by the concept of 'peace-as-governance' as a culmination of three generations of peacemaking praxis, which I introduced in my book *Maintaining Order, Making Peace* in 2000. This, combined with the critique of liberal peace, as discussed in my later study *The Transformation of Peace* (2005), and the realisation of the requirement for empathy emancipation from an everyday perspective of peace, as I explored in *Peace in IR* (2008), led eventually to an interest in local forms of mobilisation for peace. Everyday peace encounters and their hybrid outcomes have underlain much of my work since and during my PhD on UN mediation in Cyprus, even if I did not begin to express it in this language until much later. It is only recently that I have begun to see the larger picture in which local practices of peace formation have proven a rich counterpoint to much that has gone wrong with the UN and donor system and ultimately with some basic assumptions in International Relations (IR) itself. The analysis I present in this study is most indebted to the many people around the world in conflict-affected societies who have shared their thoughts on the potential in, and obstacles to, the work over the last two decades or so. Without those discussions it would have been very hard to move beyond mainstream peacebuilding and state-building theory. I would also like to thank my editor at Yale, Phoebe Clapham, for encouraging me to write this book; likewise, numerous colleagues for their support, constructive advice and warnings, at the University of St Andrews and HCRI, University of Manchester, where I was based while this book was being written, especially Alison Watson, Roger Mac Ginty and Sandra Pogodda. Thanks also to colleagues and (relatively) friendly audiences at Gothenburg and Lund Universities in Sweden; York University in Toronto; Sabanci University in Istanbul; Kenyon Institute, East Jerusalem; Bradford, Durham, Kent and Warwick universities; ISA audiences in San Francisco in 2013 and Montreal in 2012; University for Peace in Costa Rica; the PACSA-PRIO conference in Nicosia, Cyprus; ECPR in Reykjavík, Iceland; Kyung Hee university, Korea; Javeriana University, Bogota, Colombia; University of Cyprus; University of Otago, New Zealand; Murdoch University, Australia; and UNDP, New York, where various versions of this approach were first presented.

Preface

I HAVE LONG BEEN interested in the nature of the contemporary form of peace, and how the major players in world politics are attempting to build this new peace. Yet it is clear to me that attempts to propagate the new peace are in part responsible for some of the structural violence we see in the world today. A new peace in the twenty-first century, as a consequence, needs to be more sensitive to context and culture, to its own unintended consequences, and particularly to how it is embedded in old patterns of exclusion, discrimination, class, greed and elitism, as well as in ideological prescriptions about states and markets. Peacebuilding and statebuilding in today's world resemble the colonial projects of previous eras when looked at from the perspective of their recipients in far-flung corners of Liberia, Guatemala, Timor-Leste, Afghanistan or Bosnia, for example. The liberal peace and statebuilding derived from them have similar contradictions and tensions within them, as Keynes saw in the Treaty of Versailles.[1]

Many would imagine that war and post-conflict zones are devoid of any component of peace, or any aspect of normal life. They are not. Everyday life continues for most. But it is disrupted, moulded and shaped by the tensions of personal, political and group interests channelled into ethnonationalism, tribalism, religious or ideological extremism, terrorism and fear. Poverty and insecurity are the result for most ordinary people, though elites often continue relatively untouched. I have seen such dynamics from a wary proximity over a long period of research spent on peace processes, peacebuilding and conflict. While I was initially relatively apolitical and disconnected from the world 'out there' thanks to the predominantly positivist methodology the Western Academy dictates, these experiences helped me understand everyday life in such places better, and become more self-critical and aware of how embedded the developed world is in those conflicts. So this reflection is part an exposé of hypocrisy, an uncovering of the inflexibility of peace processes revolving around state power and sovereignty, and part a celebration of the braveness and resilience in everyday life shown by children, women, and men – hundreds of millions of them around the world – who live under the pressure of intractable conflicts. It is an investigation of the processes of peace formation they bring into being, often with external help, but also often by themselves.

Since the Cold War ended, many have waited for policymakers, politicians, bureaucrats, economists, development specialists, military and academics to consolidate peace through peacebuilding and state-building, to tame the violent internal and regional dynamics of state formation. The last twenty years have shown they cannot do this without grounded and embedded legitimacy, which connects to the everyday lives of the citizens of the states they are attempting to create. International law, Security Council resolutions and donor development policies are not contextual or legitimate enough. International institutions are too mired in their own routines of thought, in their own internal hierarchies and, of course, those of international sovereignty – their own paradigms – and in their own comfortable professional situations. They are afraid of context and the local, because they expose their ignorance and lack of capacity. They are thus caught in a trap of their own making.

Agency on the ground in hidden, local and contextual modes – representing little-noticed or little-understood dynamics of peace formation – plays a far larger role in international peacebuilding than has so far been realised, if only in blocking elements seen to be unsuitable for peacebuilding on the ground (and, of course, in challenging the entrenched power of local elites). In post-conflict situations, people are very aware of this, and of the need to find modes of political organisation that maintain their integrity in ways that do not necessarily mirror the West. The liberal international dream has missed peace's absolutely crucial contextual dimensions.

The understanding of peace is often far superior in post-conflict environments than in the developed world, where those who have been through conflict have spent much time thinking and actively working for peace, resisting conflict structures, and building solidarity, social justice and empathy across 'national' borders, ceasefire lines, and religious and linguistic barriers. Everyday life is in this sense about transgression, resistance and solidarity in the name of peace. It underlines the significance of hidden peacebuilding agencies even while statebuilding may be failing.

This has both negative and positive aspects. The post-conflict individual – one of the hundreds of millions of people on the planet who have lived through a conflict – is much more motivated to strive for peace, but has much less capacity, both material and emotional, to bring it about. The West has more capacity to question the current orthodoxy of peace, but less interest in doing so. Despite so much Western philosophising about political liberalism, the acquiescence of the 'dismal science' of economics, development studies and other disciplinary approaches, statebuilding has not produced peace, but instead – for the weak, at any rate – the structural violence (in its Galtungian sense of hidden, indirect violence) of competition, inequality, resource exhaustion, human exhaustion and loss of community. Development, free trade and prosperity might be an answer to war, but they also have a dark side: much of the corruption, arms trade, exploitation and violence we see rests on some complicity from within the Western states-system and global economy. In some cases, the profits of such behaviour are recycled into the Western economy, and conflict may be exacerbated by the strategies of Western institutions, organisations like the World Bank, or non-governmental organisations (NGOs) and humanitarian agencies. The militaries of the US and UK are also themselves often in the difficult situation of being perceived to be fighting ideological wars or for natural resources, rather than defending the rights of citizens – Iraq is a recent example of this. Democracy also has its dark side, especially where it promotes majoritarian behaviour on the part of one interest or identity group over control of a state and its territory.

Behind all of this is a major difficulty with the way in which the developed world's actors, states and institutions, as well as its academics, gather their knowledge, analyse and respond. Many commentators, pundits, scholars and policymakers only talk to each other rather than to local actors below the elite level. They do not travel outside the isolated and secure bubbles that are provided for them 'out there', normally in national capitals, and so tend to circulate among themselves gossip as knowledge and fact, or use very limited raw data. This leads to the creation of theories, concepts, policies and approaches that appear to be relevant when looking from the privileged, metropolitan capitals of the West and the local 'bubbles' they create, but in actual fact tend to avoid issues relating to ordinary everyday life 'out there', and in doing so sacrifice the quality of life of conflict-affected generations. Such problem-solving knowledge resists positions critical of the orthodoxy, which have often been built up via generations of experience, and often mounts its own countercritiques to local complaints. 'Local ownership' is a classic example. This concept was first developed as a World Bank, International Monetary Fund (IMF) and United Nations Development Programme (UNDP) response to local criticisms that they were not allowing local actors ownership of their own poverty reduction and development; but international actors then channelled local ownership into the liberal and neoliberal systems of politics and economics, rather than enabling local choice about which systems to adopt. As a senior UN political officer once told me, 'We should not expose ourselves to local contexts. We risk our ignorance undermining our legitimacy.'

As a consequence of this dominant attitude among many of the world's political and bureaucratic elites, the developing and conflict-affected world has become a laboratory for the unethical experimentation of those who claim superior knowledge from afar, with little local knowledge. Local knowledge is viewed as cant, regressive and valueless, in contrast to the knowledge of those in their ivory towers, offices and ministries far away. This is why an understanding of peace-formation dynamics is so important, and also why it has been ignored. International actors feel it exposes their weaknesses and lack of legitimacy, and so rarely take notice of it. Local life means little in a global context. It is little wonder that the modern liberal state is in crisis and the West has lost some of its store of legitimacy. Even worse, this encourages the bird's-eye, international-level view sometimes expressed in foreign policies or by international institutions that trusteeship and soft forms of colonialism are preferable to allowing local people to work peace out for themselves (with international assistance, of course).

One of my first experiences of these dynamics was in Cyprus during the early 1990s. I arrived with a vague idea that there had been a recent conflict that formed part of a historic, if not primeval, cycle of wars between Greeks and Turks. Much of what I was told over the next ten years spent on the island confirmed this stereotype. It seemed that the will of the people was reflected by politicians whose paranoia about status, territory, sovereignty and security allowed them publicly to decry peace in favour of victory, often referring to justice and international law as the reason for a frozen peace process. International actors were also seduced by this view. It is still repeated by analysts, whether Cypriot or not. This victory was endlessly deferred until some mythical future when a Greek or Turkish 'power' would arise and drive the other into the sea on the island. This was not idle and occasional chatter, but a mainstream, oft-repeated and endlessly recycled view on both sides of the divide that was used to shape just about every political decision taken on the island – and not just those taken in relation to the conflict.

The 'other' of this seemingly intractable conflict – and the all-pervasive dynamics of fear and insecurity that it promoted (along with ethnic cleansing, rape, nationalism, private armies and so on) – was the very small conflict-resolution workshop 'industry'. This evolved under the patronage of a number of US universities and academics, and was the only space where ordinary people who wanted to talk about peace could congregate – and a few of them did so, even though they were often socially and professionally disciplined for doing this. Yet it was isolated and marginalised by the political, military and economic elites of both sides' race for statehood. Statehood and territorial sovereignty had become more important than peace. Conflict resolution had become marginal, even treacherous, in the eyes of many local nationalists. Even so peace formation in Cyprus has – in indirect ways, admittedly – proven to be the only space where many of the conflict's issues have already been settled.

This book extends this argument. Increasingly, if autonomy, local ownership and legitimacy, and a social contract are to connect with democracy, human rights, a rule of law and a vibrant civil society, it is the dynamics of peace formation that need to be understood. Brave groups and individuals, as in Cyprus, can act in small ways, and such agency makes a disproportionately big difference when it connects to key sources of both local and international legitimacy, not merely legality and institutional frameworks. As this is where much legitimacy and capacity for peace, especially at the societal level, lies, it is surprising that relatively little thought has been put into it. This book is an investigation of the political consequences of the liberal peace and its statebuilding turn, and how local actors have taken peace into their own hands in an attempt to *form* a post-liberal peace. Peace-formation dynamics lead to the creation of new and contextual forms out of social, political, economic, cultural and historical forms of peace in local, transnational and international terms, while still remaining cognisant of the liberal peace and its norms, technologies, capacities and advantages. This realisation offers significant opportunities for the reconsideration of emancipatory and hybrid notions of peace beyond the liberal-peace and liberal- or neoliberal-state frameworks. These may lead to the development of forms of peace and related polities that have more contextual legitimacy, relevance and significance, while maintaining international norms, institutions and processes in modified forms.

Abbreviations

BRICS	Brazil, Russia, India, China and South Africa
CES	Center for Exchange and Solidarity
COIN	counterinsurgency strategy
DDR	Disarmament, Demobilisation and Reintegration
ECOSOC	UN Economic and Social Council
IFIs	International Financial Institutions
IMF	International Monetary Fund
INGOs	international non-governmental organisations
IOs	international organisations
IR	International Relations
LTTE	The Liberation Tigers of Tamil Eelam
MDG	Millennium Development Goals
NGOs	non-governmental organisations
OECD-DAC	OECD Development Assistance Committee
OSCE	Organization for Security and Co-operation in Europe

PBC	UN Peacebuilding Commission
RAMSI	Regional Assistance Mission to Solomon Islands
SSR	Security Sector Reform
UNDP	United Nations Development Programme
UNDPKO	UN Department of Peacekeeping Operations
UNMIK	UN Interim Administration Mission in Kosovo
UNTAC	UN Transitional Authority in Cambodia
USAID	US Agency for International Development
WTO	World Trade Organization

INTRODUCTION

The Limits of Peacebuilding and Statebuilding

The lesson of the last twenty or so years of intervention to build a liberal peace and the modern state is that great plans often go awry. Historically, 'from Plato to NATO', intervention has tended to result in relatively poor quality forms of peace. The era of liberal peace after the Cold War rapidly turned into an age of intervention, and perhaps a parallel age of resistance. Peacebuilding, statebuilding, modernisation and development represent heuristic, scientific and political processes of intervention conducted by the global North's dominant states and its institutions, often aimed at the global South, conflict-affected or developing, countries such as Timor-Leste to Cambodia, Sierra Leone, Bosnia-Herzegovina or Afghanistan. They represent the 'rule of experts' – a form of neo-trusteeship often conducted in an authoritarian style contrary to prescriptions about democratic and human rights.[1]

Peacebuilding and statebuilding in particular are based upon a negative understanding of the politics of state formation: that is, that states are formed through violent struggles and so intervention is necessary to mitigate the processes they unleash. Rarely has there been a consideration that there may be an internal and non-violent struggle for peace at the grassroots level that has the potential to bring about a sustainable order – this might be termed 'peace formation'. Thus, the interaction between the processes of state formation, statebuilding, peacebuilding and a concept this book introduces, 'peace formation', is necessary to understand the forms of peace that are emerging in international politics. Different forms of power, authority, legitimacy, rights, norms and identity circulate around peace frameworks in conflict-affected societies.

These processes emanate from different sites of legitimate authority, utilising different types of power, connected to different constituencies that support them. They are aimed at building states in unstable regions around the world, and are thought to represent a significant advance on the practices of peacekeeping, mediation and other forms of intervention that were employed before the end of the Cold War. They seek to modernise, maintain and further develop an international system based on neoliberal states that are embedded in an international architecture of liberal peace (as Jeremy Bentham envisioned when he invented the term 'international').[2] Through the prism of world order these approaches provide, external actors perceive local polities as having 'closed access', hence their fragility, underdevelopment, hierarchical nature, centralised power, patrimonialism and conflict-proneness. Intervention involves the building of 'open-access societies', which are secure, inclusive and supported by the rule of law, development, decentralisation, liberal institutions, equality, a vibrant civil society (meaning one that enables human rights and liberal norms) and economy.[3] Thus, peacebuilding and statebuilding represent the achievement, but also the limits, of intervention and progressive politics in the modern era.

This 'Eurocentric' approach to peacebuilding comprises the United Nations (UN), International Financial Institutions (IFIs), international non-governmental organisations (INGOs) and major state donors. Its architectural blueprint revolves around democracy, human rights, law, free trade and an international community that promotes associated values. The liberal peace aims at producing a secure and consensual international order and states-system based on liberal norms and institutions, much as has seemingly existed since the end of the Cold War. It aims – from the perspective of the global North – at creating a positive peace, where both structural violence (meaning inequality in terms of rights, needs, and access to law and institutions) and overt violence are overcome and emancipation becomes possible, rather than a negative peace, where structural violence remains even after the guns have fallen silent.[4] Following Huntington's argument that authoritarian transitions are more effective than democratic transitions, peacebuilding and statebuilding have come to reflect a compromise between what, on the face of it, would seem to be uneasy partners: democracy and authoritarianism in transition.[5]

Yet interventionary practices (including the use of war, invasion, humanitarian intervention, structural adjustment and conditionality) are required to maintain this system on the part of major states and international donors. The UN system is itself a contradictory product of colonialism and self-determination, but its liberal framework also suggests the elevation of the ancient Greek concept of a commonwealth, and universal values of justice and liberty, over local particularism.[6] This implies that ethnically fragmented 'statelets' should not come to dominate the world order. Yet the UN has presided over a process of colonial and state fragmentation and the affirmation of the modern state as the dominant actor.

This system's interventionary capacity has been tested by a wide range of conflicts over the last twenty-five years, during which time the liberal peace has retreated from the democratisation- and human rights-oriented ambitions of peacekeeping in Central America, sub-Saharan Africa and Cambodia in the early 1990s. It has faded into the more retrogressive *pax* neoliberal, underpinned by statebuilding, a practice that focuses principally on territorial security and free-market reform in a globalising world (as the more recent examples of statebuilding in Afghanistan and Iraq illustrate). Within these frameworks there are minor internal variations but the liberal peace and neoliberal state are the dominant paradigms used in most interventions.

There has also long been an assumption of the paramount legitimacy of the Western norms that underpin the international community, as well as of the authority and legitimacy of the state. Yet liberal peacebuilding and neoliberal statebuilding have perpetuated the tensions between liberal universalism versus culture or identity, individual versus collective rights, and a liberal or neoliberal understanding of citizenship inside modern states. Much of the world's population relates to authority and states merely in terms of being their 'subjects', and often only very distantly.[7]

Consequently, mainstream approaches aimed at ending conflict and making peace through peacebuilding and statebuilding have reached an impasse. They have produced negative forms of peace: sometimes a victor's peace, or else more often a peace resting upon the bureaucratic and economic rationale of state 'governmentality',[8] rather than reconciliation, rights, equality and justice as local political debates might recognise these.[9] While claiming to support a positive and emancipatory form of peace, first, second and third generations of peacemaking – from early peacekeeping and mediation practices of the 1960s, conflict-resolution approaches thereafter and liberal peacebuilding in the 1990s – have often bypassed citizen-subjects' right to determine their own peace, especially where they are from the global South. This evolution is based upon the belief that state-level and local-scale political institutions, under pressure from the need to modernise and develop both internally and externally, have failed to accommodate necessary change and thus require direction from external actors better equipped to reform the state and its peace system.[10] Direct, structural and governmental forms of power do not recognise the contemporary post-colonial world as autonomously evolving so they intervene to reshape the state in their own image. From this perspective, the subaltern (meaning the marginal subject of power, widely regarded to have little agency or capacity) citizen-subject is merely a putative shadow of the modern liberal citizen from the global North.[11] This conflict and post-conflict subject resides in geographic locations outside of the West/North and is therefore assumed to carry no ramifications for the global North. Yet the global 'North' and 'South' are implicated in each other.

The power relations surrounding peacebuilding and statebuilding replicate a subtle form of structural violence. 'Peace' experiments on post-conflict subjects are disguised by concepts like 'development', 'peacebuilding' and 'statebuilding', which maintain the pre-existing international/local or North/South hierarchy of late modernity even as it appears to be dissolving. Some governments, policymakers and bureaucrats in a range of international institutions, including the UN, World Bank and IMF, and from main state donors, jealously guard their authority over these matters. They assume – based on their status and positionality at the top of an international hierarchy supported by 'superior' norms such as human rights – that their partners are elites in post-conflict countries. Yet as a former UN secretary general, Kofi Annan, pointed out, the UN system is notionally run on behalf of 'we the peoples of the United Nations' rather than 'we the governments'.[12]

Exporting neoliberal states and the liberal peace during the last two decades has had a range of unintended consequences. Peacebuilding and statebuilding may support, clash with, or detract from local legitimacy. They may appear to denigrate local political, economic, social, cultural and environmental worlds, while maintaining Northern preferences. Universalism inadvertently encourages particularism, but provides no form of mediation between the two. Peacebuilding and statebuilding encourage democracy but majoritarianism often leads to a monopoly over power and resources. Rational-legal epistemologies for peace and statehood confront neopatrimonialism or custom.[13] There is a gulf between the maintenance of international and local forms of legitimacy in widely different contexts.

What is missing from debates on intervention, peacebuilding and statebuilding is an understanding of how people and communities act to make peace themselves. What sources of agency and inspiration do they draw upon, and why? What prevents them from achieving peace? Sustainable peace rests as much on a social, grassroots and mid-level process of accommodation and reconciliation, as on the technology of the state, with the support and normative preferences of international organisations or donors. Ordinary peacemakers and the 'everyday' are often missing from accounts of the international system, state formation, statebuilding and peacebuilding. Yet wide-ranging empirical and historical evidence is emerging that such actors and perspectives enable innovative and alternative sites for peace to emerge. This process occurs 'in the interstices of a failing state: local society and extrapolitical social networks'.[14]

There are reasons why this activity is missing: partly it is because Western rational knowledge about power, interests and norms leads to a focus on rights, institutions and states rather than people and needs; and partly it is because Eurocentrism indicates that subjects have little to offer the debate on peace. While debates on peace and emancipation are probably more advanced in the global North,[15] it is also true that all societies have developed historical peace processes and institutions, and have their own understanding of the politics of rights, needs and legitimacy, without which a legitimate order cannot be achieved. There is an ongoing encounter between the (neo) liberal-peace system and localised processes of politics which may facilitate new debates about progressive forms of politics, revisions to the state and an evolution of the international system.

Over the years of its existence, the UN – often through the General Assembly or agencies like the UN Development Programme (UNDP) or the UN Economic and Social Council (ECOSOC) – has often compiled and released documents, reports and resolutions resting on a wide global consensus in favour of progressive forms of politics. These have pointed to clear strategies aimed at dealing with the often adverse relationship between political and economic power and peace. They indicate a possible resolution of this difficulty through programmes for 'cultures of peace', rights to peace, the need for 'new economic orders', economic, social and cultural rights, independence, self-determination, development and peacebuilding. Equality, self-determination, participation, cooperation, social justice, development, a right to culture, society and work, and to maintain identity formulations according to context, have been their recurrent motifs. An international states-system, framed in the interests of positive peace rather than interests or power, has been their goal.[16] Such documents were signed by representatives of much of the planet's population, yet such global political and scientific consensus is constantly ignored in practice.

In what follows, this Introduction defines some key terms and concepts used throughout the book.

A range of kinds of intervention, from peacekeeping to programmes to improve security forces, introduce markets and development, and support civil society, have been developed to try to prop up failed states, from Liberia and El Salvador, to Kosovo and Bosnia, and Cambodia and Timor-Leste since the early 1990s. In 2009 alone, more than $33 billion was invested in so-called fragile and failed states by international donors, according to the UNDP.[17] Some of this was invested in 'governance-related projects'. Since then it has become the ambition of the international community to link all aid to effectiveness in peacebuilding and statebuilding. The language of these processes reflects the ambitions of UN peacebuilding in the 1990s: comprehensive and multidimensional peace processes, peace support and stabilisation, and a newer addition, following on from a more recent turn to the state and to governance, of 'whole of government approaches to recovery, reconstruction, and development'.[18] These new approaches represent a genuine learning process – in the past mistakes were made with quick-fix blueprints, hasty peace agreements, a focus on elections and their link with exit strategies, or a scattered approach to funding civil society and state institutions by an uncoordinated range of donors. Attempts to coordinate and 'benchmark' progress in peacebuilding and statebuilding have been made as a result[19] – though these reflect counterproductive managerial and neoliberal technologies used to measure efficiency and productivity rather than the social quality of peace.

Interventions through peacebuilding, statebuilding and development praxes all tend to start with a liberal or neoliberal institutional design and set of norms in mind, and expect compliance from a range of local partners and subjects in post-conflict settings around the world. They assume they must sustain an ongoing world order despite its injustices, inequalities and contradictory assemblages of rights, identities, markets, interests and institutions (say, when comparing Sierra Leone, Nepal, Bosnia or Timor-Leste to most Northern states).

States are embedded in their own ontological, historical and ethical contexts (or positionalities). This creates a local epistemology of peace, security and order, shaping national interests: the need to protect its own territory, boundaries and citizens, and prioritise their needs over those of others. If the state is absent or failed in many countries, how do people support themselves and maintain order and peace in everyday life? Some countries continue to lose huge percentages of their GDP to violence (in Guatemala's case, 7 per cent in 2005, years after the Peace Accords of 1996) or fail to receive a peace dividend.[20] Institutions fail to span social, identity and class divides, as in Northern Ireland before the Good Friday Agreement, and so cannot mediate conflict smoothly, and as in Kosovo today, many years after the NATO intervention in 1999. The different elements of the Bosnian state similarly remain in political deadlock along ethnic lines almost two decades after the Dayton Agreement.

Rapid urbanisation in many developing and post-conflict countries has increased the pressure for reform and equality, but states and donors often cannot, or do not, deliver emergency assistance or 'good governance' and institutional reform, even in their favoured realms. In Cambodia, a subsistence economy is all that maintains around 80 per cent of the population more than twenty years after the Paris Peace Accords. In Sierra Leone, Liberia and Mozambique, significant progress has been made since their peace accords, but local organisations complain frequently about the shortcomings of the state as well as the failings of international donors.

In many states, such as Timor-Leste, historical socio-political frameworks exist around which authority and legitimacy have long been organised. Yet these have been ignored by both statebuilding and peacebuilding processes. The predictable result has been that the state has little everyday meaning in people's lives, other than perhaps as a failure, an absence, or a predator. Public services, infrastructure, law and security are absent. War and conflict provide the reason for externally led modernisation in the interests of broader security, international norms and the development of markets. Agreements that describe themselves as contributing to peace, from the Democratic Republic of

Congo to Cyprus, have often failed to offer security or justice to populations, and lack legitimacy especially from local perspectives.

The list of 'failed state' dynamics and symptoms, despite years of international engagement, continues to grow. Yet each failure in peacebuilding or statebuilding is often taken by international actors to be symptomatic of the unwillingness of local actors to undertake sensible reforms and of the imperfect techniques internationals (meaning the various international actors involved in peacebuilding, statebuilding, and development activities) use, rather than of the imperfections of the underlying models or philosophies they themselves apply. Critiques of the orthodoxies of liberal peacebuilding and neoliberal statebuilding are often repudiated by policymakers and mainstream scholars as a kind of 'Cassandra Syndrome'. They claim that improvements over the last twenty years have been ignored by critics in favour of doom-laden analyses that tend to romanticise the capacity of local actors to achieve peace.

If liberal peacebuilding and neoliberal statebuilding have been the dominant models in the post-Cold War era, and their successes have been so limited, why do they continue to be used and defended in this way? Do an assemblage of liberal norms and the rationalities of governance associated with a neoliberal political economy represent the only way of making peace and fostering development, rights and law? In the face of a mass of evidence that liberal peacebuilding and neoliberal statebuilding have failed to deliver peace in emancipatory form, the defence of these practices looks increasingly authoritarian.[21]

This may partly be explained, first, because the institutional frameworks are externally designed with a European or Northern, developed, individualistic context, security, norms and interests in mind, but they do not provide a peace dividend quickly enough to undercut currents of violence and root causes of conflict. Secondly, the universe the sponsoring institutions, donors or INGOs operate from (New

York, Washington, Geneva, Brussels, Paris, London, Tokyo, etc.) is rarely commensurate with that of the context their frameworks are applied in (currently mostly in developing, post-conflict settings outside the global North, with the exception, perhaps, of a few cases such as Bosnia or Kosovo). Thirdly, and as a result of these problems, both statebuilding and liberal peacebuilding strategies fail to connect with their target populations. It is notable that many peacebuilding and statebuilding ventures in the last twenty-five years have seen even limited forms of pluralist politics collapse into mono-ethnic units, as in the Balkans. The state and the international system are constantly reiterated through forms of intervention, as if they themselves are unproblematic contributions to peace. Fourthly, while analysts and practitioners are keen to focus on the normative or technical processes of such forms of intervention, they are rarely keen to consider the global as opposed to regional or local power structures in which they take place. The statebuilding or peacebuilding agenda does not address global inequality or environmental sustainability, other than in a piecemeal manner. Despite these issues, there has been a common consensus that statebuilding is crucial for broader peace and security, and many theoretical and policy contributions have been made to improving its tools and mechanisms.[22]

Like liberal peacebuilding, statebuilding – a discourse that appeared via the IFIs after 9/11 – appears to be failed by design. Neoliberal forms of state require the communities least able to support themselves to be self-sufficient (or they are expected to be 'resilient', according to more fashionable terminology), with predictable results for peace and development. Such internationally designed artifices (meaning state forms designed in New York, Washington, Brussels and Geneva, where major international organisations or donors tend to be based) have failed to coordinate the assemblage of rights, law, resources, institutions, cultures and identities in a way that produces consensus across post-conflict societies. They have instead become reminiscent of exercises of colonial power to pacify 'unruly natives'.

The 'failed states' discourse emerged in the 1990s to describe states that could not maintain security and order, regional stability, or the rights and needs of their populations. Almost 1.5 billion people currently live in such states, and not one low-income and conflict-affected fragile state has achieved a single UN Millennium Development Goal so far (as of 2013). For example, in the Democratic Republic of Congo the state is absent from most of its territory and local armed groups contest power and resources, despite the UN having had a sporadic peacekeeping and peacebuilding involvement there since the 1960s.

Contradictions are easily detected by the recipients of these interventions. Subjects may respond with a mixture of acceptance, cooptation and resistance, producing hybrid forms of politics. The latter may lead to a negative or positive form of hybrid peace, framed intersubjectively rather than according to 'objective' local or international epistemologies. Hybridity is often a site of tension between local, state and international loyalties and preferences.

Continuing local power relations and unmitigated conflict structures, which lead to exclusion, discrimination, inequality and other forms of structural violence within the modern state and international system, indicate a negative hybrid peace. The replication of older practices of colonial government and trusteeship through intervention may be another aspect of a negative hybrid peace. Mixtures of local state-formation processes, international peacebuilding and statebuilding, and, perhaps most importantly, local peace-formation processes configure themselves in different ways, however.

Hybridity, as with genealogy, represents a site of encounter, and perhaps harbours a potential for a more radical and progressive political struggle for the 'right to politics' and even, perhaps, 'equaliberty' in which liberty and equality are co-dependent, towards which localised processes of peace are often aimed.[23] Such processes, stemming from local networks, may focus on rights, needs and identity issues in the context of a peace process and state reform in an inclusive manner. The outcome of such a process, which can mainly be perceived from below, might be a positive hybrid peace, offering emancipation in an everyday context.

The latter may represent a significant avenue for research and practice, in which peacemaking (meaning agreeing on a peace treaty), peacebuilding (building a broad peace framework), statebuilding (reconstructing the security, institutional and economic framework of the state) and development more closely reflect the accommodation of resistances, differences, socio-historical processes of politics, economic situation and customs. This is not to say that authoritarian, sectarian or quasi-liberal regimes (as in the cases of Angola, Sri Lanka, Cambodia and Rwanda, among others), or locally predatory political, economic or cultural practices, are an acceptable alternative form of negative peace.[24] A congruence between local forms of legitimate authority, the state and the international community has long been recognised as important, even if this has been interpreted in some quarters as meaning that the local should follow state, sovereignty or international principles, rather than vice versa.[25]

Political mobilisation for peace on a mass grassroots scale, or in a more fragmented and hidden form, constructs legitimacy. This should be mirrored in the state and its institutions, and in the international norms the international community recycles as security, development, citizenship, rights and responsibilities. Peace emerges as a political process from the grassroots to the international level. International legitimacy should therefore reflect a far broader post-colonial (meaning derived from subaltern rather than state-level actors) set of norms than the Western-dominated 'cosmopolitanism' that currently exists. That this has not been realised reflects a crisis of legitimacy in the liberal-peace system – and the mainstream consensus surrounding it – from the perspective of its subjects. Such subjects' main role is to be pacified, to produce and consume, to respect private property and to vote in a procedural manner. The subject is subordinate to international expertise, as with the colonial subject's relationship to the metropolitan centre in an early phase of anthropological engagement with political power structures of the early twentieth century.[26] For example, the constitution of the Republic of Cyprus was negotiated with little reference to local preferences in the late 1950s; no Cypriots were involved in independence negotiations. Such subjects may be termed the 'children' of Western colonialism, interventionism, peacebuilding and humanitarianism. Power and interests have contaminated the wider missions of peace throughout history.

Nevertheless, it has become axiomatic that matters of peace and war are no longer solely in the hands of Western officials, policymakers, the military and politicians, but are also engaged by civil society, grassroots actors and citizens. Since the 1980s, it has been widely recognised that civil society, often comprised of NGOs or social movements, is crucial to peace and the state, and that it should be assisted by external actors. This has also made local NGOs visible, and has underlined their need to be connected to the international community.[27] This relationship would inevitably be subject to unequal power relations. Yet this recognition has also ignored – for the most part – the organisations that have worked outside the framework of the modern state as well as Western norms for peacebuilding.

Even so, the state, though undergoing a resurgence since 9/11 for security reasons, is being challenged from all quarters: by global norms and trade, by regional organisations, and by transnational or local actors. Indeed, though the state has been the focus of peacebuilding and statebuilding for the last two decades and more, it is widely accepted – even at the highest levels in the UN system – that many of the resulting 'new democracies' are essentially 'elected dictatorships'.[28] Notwithstanding, calls for accountability and support are most often focused on the state and the international. There have also been increasing calls for local ownership and participation, and for a local-to-international form of the social contract (in which citizens have international representation), as the problems with peacebuilding and statebuilding have emerged.[29] Slowly, awareness is growing that a range of social actors should have a voice and interest in peacebuilding in local contexts. Yet this realisation challenges international models of peacebuilding because such supranational bodies have little capacity to 'see' what occurs on the ground as a result of their biases, distance from the problems they address, and employment of different contextual knowledge systems. Peacebuilding and statebuilding are 'local' to Europe, the US, and the global North in historical, political and cultural terms, though, of course, they have been shaped by a broader history.

Social movements have long been involved in peace matters.[30] Both their transient nature and limited ability to influence political debate have also been noted, yet peace movements – along with non-violent resistance – have often been widely ignored in IR. They play quiet but influential roles in building legitimacy for more cooperative orders.[31] This has taken an institutional form in the UN system, via donors, the OECD Development Assistance Committee (OECD-DAC) frameworks, INGOs and local civil-society partners.

Local agency, expressed through critical, transnational and transversal movements for peace, often connected to religious, customary or social organisations and norms, offers a critique both of the liberal-peace architecture and its Westernised, universal and modernisation-based rationalities.[32] Yet the international peace architecture has not responded conceptually (though it has increased the array of tools it has to maintain itself) because of a mixture of ideological and normative preferences and interests. Thus, it has been subject to both an internal crisis of efficiency and an external crisis of legitimacy.

After it was first identified that the liberal peace was in crisis in the mid-2000s, it became fashionable to search for alternatives. The policy response was to shift from the normative liberal peace framework towards a more minimalist attempt to build neoliberal states. Many critical scholars looked to social forms of democracy and to local customs, cultures, identities, histories or civil societies in their attempt to find a route to the kind of emancipation that peace theory promises. This partly reflected a recognition that the linking of globalisation with peace had produced both a defence of the 'local' and resistance. Nevertheless, even the search for alternatives has tended to operate within Western epistemological parameters. Like the concept of 'poverty', where wealth might be defined in terms of cash in many contexts or cattle in subsistence contexts (as with the Maasai in Kenya),[33] peace is subject to different localised understandings. Whereas in Timor-Leste 'poverty' requires assistance, the thinking about peace has been divided around whether its construction should be minimalist or rest on third-party interests and norms, but not around whether the form of assistance should be determined by its recipients.[34] International actors are unwilling to undertake the acts of translation that would be necessary to engage more appropriately with autonomous local actors embedded within a local-to-global social context.

Northern biases towards the liberal peace may mean localised peace systems are misunderstood or rendered invisible to the Western eye; indeed, they may even introduce new dimensions of conflict by disrupting local systems. Peacemaking in liberal terms introduces alien norms, institutions and expectations to a post-conflict society, while neoliberal statebuilding exposes its people to global markets and a different type of insecurity. Local awareness of such international/local divides encourages both local and international actors to take matters into their own hands, infusing 'peace' with their historical preferences, biases, ideologies and interests while learning from outside models and exploiting external resources. Political reform and change may tackle such problems, but given the hierarchy between international and local actors in post-conflict environments, it raises the question of whose responsibility this is, and where its legitimacy is drawn from. Power, even when expressed through an international peace architecture such as the liberal-peace system, or the conditional creation of neoliberal states, spills over into disciplinary, liberal governmentality and even cruder realist and structural forms.[35]

Thus, an understanding of varying aspects of power as it circulates around its subjects involved in any peace activity is crucial for this study. It deploys three approaches. First, power is direct or structural and directed from its holders onto their subjects in a unidirectional manner, brooking no opposition.[36] Context can also be taken to mean structure, indicating another aspect of structural power. Context raises the age-old issue of structure and agency, or more simply the way power is used for progressive reasons rather than self-interest in the face of a range of material, social and environmental needs and constraints. Secondly, power as governmentality, as defined by Foucault, sees it operating in a more subtle manner, through discourses and knowledge as well as institutions, and defines its subjects by their inability to resist it.[37] This may also be called 'soft power' or 'normative power'.[38] Finally, there is subaltern power, in which critical agency offers discursive political challenges, resistance and everyday patterns of activity are able to some degree at least to subvert both forms of power.[39] Power circulates among all of its subjects and their networks rather than being simplistically unidirectional, bottom-up or top-down, producing hybrid outcomes.[40] This decentring process, which emerges from subaltern power, is essential to the evolution of hybrid forms of peace and post-liberal debates on the development of progressive politics in post-conflict societies.

To allow a better engagement with subaltern agency, a more ethnographic and sociological account of peace has become commonplace. This highlights practices, context and power relations, in addition to indigenous and agential approaches, and the structural and normative visions of peacebuilding and statebuilding.

Power and its circulation produces hybridity and post-liberalism in these terms. Essential to power is legitimacy, which is also essential for any positive hybrid peace. This can be seen in varying ways, from the legitimacy gathered at the international level for the liberal-peace system and for the neoliberal state as the epicentre of modernity, epitomised in the UN system and supported by humanitarian and international law, and international human rights.[41] This version of how authority is exercised to produce peace reflects a view from IR. Next, there is the legitimacy of the legally recognised state and its right to rule (Weber called this normative legitimacy) via its control of the means of violence and its constitutional framework and conformity with international norms. This rational-legal version reflects a view from the state of its own authority and legitimacy. Then there is the more grounded legitimacy of the polity in its context, drawn from historical and socio-political sources, in which any political, social or economic institutions are the result of negotiation between a wide range of interests, identities and objectives. Shared beliefs, needs and objectives are key, meaning reciprocity. This level of analysis reflects a view from the community and society, in other words, an ethnographic and sociological view, and is sometimes called empirical, traditional, customary or local legitimacy. There is also the well-known 'charismatic' legitimacy of elites and leaders, as well as the legitimacy that arises from process or performance.[42]

These forms of legitimacy can exist independently, so international or state legitimacy does not necessarily mean acceptance by society.

The circulation of power and subaltern agency indicates that a positive hybrid, emancipatory and post-liberal peace cannot rely on only one of these forms of legitimacy, especially if it is to be experienced in everyday terms. There must be a balanced blend, which might be termed 'hybrid legitimacy'.[43] Different forms of legitimacy may coexist and interact, and, indeed, be complementary and compensate for each other's limitations. Legitimacy, defined as local consent and consensus for systems of representative authority, is essential to guarantee the stability and resilience of any socio-political order, from the community to the state and ultimately to the international level. Local legitimacy may also demand wealth allocation and redistribution, as well as support for the community's well-being, order and security.[44] State formation assumes legitimacy arises from power, peacebuilding from liberal norms, and statebuilding from security and neoliberalism. Local voices might root state formation in socio-historical processes of conflict and cooperation, as well as learning from external actors.

The implication is that the dominant Western understanding of the rationality of peace (democracy, human rights, development and a vibrant civil society within a neoliberal state) is only one among many.[45] To deny this is merely to ignore the 'post-colonial burden of history' according to which the West long regarded its subjects as inferior and requiring less sensitivity, and simultaneously refused to accept the limits of its own rationality or to extend its responsibilities fully, instead relying on its 'power'.[46] A post-colonial approach to peace does not imply relativism, but rather pluralism.[47]

Internationals often think that the local resort to the 'traditional' is driven by contests over power and is focused on particularistic norms, interests and identities. Internationals mistake the 'traditional' for the 'backward' when in fact in the contemporary world it mainly indicates difference: indeed, traditional systems are flexible, and in any case the concept of the traditional was an invention of colonial government and research.[48]

The local is the site of a range of agencies aimed at building agreement and consensus for institutions, law, redistribution, identity and education, and providing security and public services. These are positive processes from which legitimacy emerges. This type of legitimacy would normally be a form of socio-political consensus for institutions and laws, and yet statebuilding and peacebuilding tend to import these from outside. The international legitimacy this represents therefore supplants local legitimacy, meaning local agency is sidelined and yet continues in parallel, often disconnected from the state and international frameworks. This is a basic contradiction that requires resolution, if peace, stable states and an 'international community' are to be meaningful, socially, politically, legally and materially.

'Alternative' forms of peace and state represent a hybrid arising from both the clash between, and integration of, elements of the international, the state, and the local, according to different types of power and legitimacy. 'Hidden' resistance to comprehensive and integrated planning attempts to harmonise the international system and homogenise the state have already made sure of hybridity. This has spurred micro-liberation struggles, and the exercise of critical forms of agency for peace, from the local to the transnational. Foucault described this as 'heterotopia',[49] in which fragments of possible worlds and incompatible spaces become related or superimposed. Different voices[50] contest both universal claims and assumptions as to 'natural' power hierarchies, producing a peace register that forms from the local to the global alongside conflict dynamics. The interventionary progression from the liberal values of the 1992 UN document *Agenda for Peace* to the far more interventionist defence of rights under the 'Responsibility to Protect' doctrine from 2001 also happened to coincide with the intervention/invasion/statebuilding agendas of the 2000s.[51] These expressions of power and norms are in tension, but also coexist, with subaltern agency, which has pushed hard for local rights, needs, representation and identity. Any democratic, empathetic and emancipatory approach to peacebuilding and statebuilding would need to take the latter seriously if a fourth-generation approach connecting a peace process to empathy, emancipation and the everyday in the context of hybridity is to emerge.[52]

One and a half billion people have been affected globally by conflict since the end of the Cold War,[53] so peacemaking impacts on a significant percentage (over 20 per cent) of the world's population. Rarely are political or economic elites affected, however. External intervention in 'other' societies raises serious issues about methods, ethics and, of course, global inequality and the idea of transitional justice. Unsurprisingly, the most prominent related discussion of the second decade of the twenty-first century has been about the disconnection between governments and their peoples. This can be extended to the disconnection between the donor and UN system and post-conflict citizens around the world. From the perspective of the recipient – the subject of intervention – it looks like a neocolonial practice aimed at legitimating Western interests. Legitimate forms of state and international authority often do not parallel local sites of legitimate authority, which are thus in tension with one another. If international peacebuilding actors or the neoliberal state cannot provide peace, security, rights and development, or respect local identity, then it is no surprise that local actors begin to think about how to achieve these goals as part of their own peace strategy.

This 'local turn' is part of a recentring of the history of peace.[54] It raises crucial questions: if peace is also defined by the 'powerless', what is the relationship between power and peace, and how might an emancipatory and positive hybrid peace relate to power? The international system's potential for peace (as well as war) is now well understood, but most policymakers and academics are ignorant of, or resistant to the idea of, the local dimensions of peace. This realisation has meant that peace in IR is being 'decolonised';[55] it has become necessary to understand more clearly the encounter between international peacebuilding, statebuilding and development, as well as interests and ideologies, and local forms of politics, identity, history and custom. This is required if legitimacy in local and international contexts is to be developed for any peace system. The local must in this sense be understood as already 'modern', political and agential, and globally integrated in spite of and because of power. This is reflected in a new language entering into the discourse of peace.[56] Regular but disconnected statements – about the beneficial role of social actors, particularly women or elders, and a wide range of organisations – draw on custom and tradition, and seek to modernise them. These patterns are connected to the belated recognition of the social, political, economic, and also cultural and historical, infrastructure of peace, increasingly described by internationals as 'peace architecture'.

Ethical and methodological frameworks are required to constrain Northern experimentation in the stabilisation and modernisation of states and societies elsewhere, and their unintended consequences for so much of the world's population. The notions of 'do no harm' and 'conflict or context sensitivity'[57] are the only limited contributions so far. The continuing use of the hegemonic vernacular of the liberal peace 'programming' in technocrat mode (good governance, SSR/DDR – Security Sector Reform and Disarmament, Demobilisation and Reintegration – the field, capacity-building, intervention, etc.) underlines how limited this improvement has so far been. The recent trend towards accepting 'good enough'[58] outcomes is also indicative of the tension peacebuilding and statebuilding are subject to, locally, in terms of international consensus, and the resources intervention brings to bear. Such processes often provide international support for elite local power structures rather than peace structures. Participatory processes are supposed to provide local subjects of peacebuilding and statebuilding with a place in these processes, but they also indicate the power relations that subjects are involved in: with their own elites, and with international donors and officials.

These developments, together with notions of 'local ownership', indicate a growing realisation that peace, the state, democracy, law, development, rights and needs should be determined locally and contextually. They may be mediated internationally, if a general legitimacy and more precise legality is to be preserved over interests and potentially disruptive top-down experimentation and its unintended consequences (though internationals often claim a 'lack of capacity' when local actors are given ownership).[59] Yet claims about a lack of local capacity is also an excuse for a lack of international resources or will to deal with inequality, and a lack of understanding of local agency. Kofi Annan calls this a kind of neoliberal 'ideological vanity' that takes priority over the needs and sufferings of others.[60] The realisation has now dawned that any peace should be local.

This has implications beyond top-down conceptions of 'conflict sensitivity'. An emancipatory peace, which carries local legitimacy, cannot arise without being anchored in the security practices, political institutions, customs, identity, social characteristics, economic needs and environmental constraints of the space in which it is being made. This may mean going back to the different epistemologies of peace, not to mention ontologies, suggested by the work and heritage of China's Confucius, Iran's Jamal al-Din al-Afghani, India's

Mahatma Gandhi, Pakistan's Muhammad Iqbal and other thinkers from outside the West. They developed indigenous understandings, struggled against Western domination, or sought to learn from Western modernity while preserving local values and culture.[61] All saw the benefits of modernity, in terms of development, gender rights, civil liberties and the rule of law, but all were also wary of the way power was imported through reforms, of leading indirectly to domination, racism, hierarchy following external political interests. They were aware of parallel concepts to political liberalism that were also part of their own cultures. They saw the dangers of a universalism that was not negotiated universally and that effectively acted as a cover for imperialism and capitalism. Some were also interested in the concept of emancipation, in social justice and distributive justice across the international order, while also understanding local contextual dynamics. Though this study does not discuss such non-western political discourses, it is mindful of them.

The missing link in the struggle between the processes of state formation, peacebuilding and statebuilding as sites of order and peace is peace formation. It indicates a potentially positive hybrid peace, driven partly by local, peaceful agencies (though often critical and resistant) that operate in 'hidden' local cultural, social, economic and political spaces, and which are increasingly more visibly at the international level. These represent an assemblage of local, state, transnational, international and transversal, formal and informal 'peace' processes. Peace formation constitutes a widening pool of political subjects as formative of the state, economy, society and the international community. A crucial dilemma is whether peace-formation processes, as seen in many post-conflict situations (and even in the 'Arab Spring') and which often coexist with violent state-formation processes, create parallel structures to the neoliberal state that internationals persist in trying to produce, from Bosnia to Afghanistan.

This raises the further question of what obstacles exist for a positive hybrid peace to emerge, and how they might be overcome.

These processes have been difficult to describe, and the policy and academic literature has struggled to find an appropriate language to capture their variety, not least because they stand as a challenge to many of the policy instruments and concepts that internationals, donors, the UN system and IFIs hold dear. A common description has often been 'grassroots peacebuilding', which is seen as conflict transformation, and often involving 'civil society' (meaning that it is controlled by externally directed NGOs rather than by indigenously formed institutions) and donor-supported. Local practices of peace often engender a struggle against structural and historical forms of violence and inequalities of all sorts, as well as governmentality. They are conducted within a range of social forms, which have an impact on political, economic and security structures, as well as on norms and ideology.[62] These 'local' processes are vital for legitimacy and so for order in general, and cannot be imposed externally.[63] 'Formation' places authority and legitimacy within the social-political and historical frame of its subjects in a specific networked context. It seeks to determine the terms of emancipation. 'Building' activities conversely anchor peace to the norms, knowledge systems and techniques of the hegemon, which seeks to maintain the status quo, and so will give rise to a negative hybrid peace, one often allied with local conflict structures rather than peace formation.

Peace formation arises from within a specific, though networked, socio-political context. However, it learns from many sources, transnational, transversal and international, but is always rooted in the intimate context, in space, time and culture, where it is expected to maintain peace.[64] Democracy assumes local agency should not be blocked.[65] Understanding the smaller-scale and often invisible local processes of peace formation ensures that larger-scale peacebuilding, often aimed at statebuilding, can be significantly improved. This does not mean cataloguing or speaking on behalf of peace-formation agency, but merely seeing it as one of several foundations of a legitimate and emancipatory peace.

'Local agency' should be seen in relation to peacebuilding in a complex way. The local might be seen as transnational, transversal (grassroots to elites), traditional and modern, liberal and non-liberal, separately or simultaneously.[66] It is a recognition of the essential constituent of legitimacy, often confronted by power and its modernising tendencies.[67] The local constitutes the international through networks and relationality, but, in this, some geographical locales are more important than others. Power geometry, which pits local actors against the states and the international, cannot be avoided once the local is taken seriously.[68] As power circulates through direct, structural, governmental and subaltern forms, the local represents fluid identities and movement, rather than static and fixed identities. As Latour has argued, networks imply that the local is always continuously connected, perhaps entangled across many scales, with the international, while remaining 'continuously local'.[69] 'Agency' refers to capacity in a political sense. This is related to discursive agency and social praxis.[70] It is often critical, hence the term 'critical agency', whereby discourses encounter the politics of peace and attempt to shape them.[71] It may extend to forms of resistance, and certainly, from a peace-formation perspective, a political project is at stake. This may involve negotiation with international actors, taking on international norms, operating the liberal state, forming contextual institutions, large-scale and organised political mobilisation, or individual, community and alternative forms of civil-society organisation (in a 'local-local'[72] context).[73] It implies a mediation between its different facets, and also with the international community, so that international statebuilding is modified by the actions of its many recipients in diverse contexts, from Afghanistan to Timor-Leste. This may represent noncompliance (or stagnation), as in Bosnia, or more outright resistance, as in parts of Central America, or a behind-the-scenes peace process within civil society or the local-local, as in Cyprus, Kenya and Sierra Leone. It may also lead to wholesale adoption of international agendas with a twist, as in the 'authoritarian democracies' that have emerged in Namibia, Mozambique and Rwanda, or it might lead to parallel peace processes, as again in Cyprus, where elite-level deadlock is contradicted by a vibrant and long-reconciled intercommunal movement.

This study adopts several methodological approaches, as must any study investigating different ideologies, ontologies and theories of peace. Its starting point is an eirenic perspective, which uses peace as a central viewing point in order to refine our understandings of its potential.[74] This relates to the fact that criticism, the state and peace are all central to international political theory,[75] and so to any progressive or emancipatory project. Yet they are burdened by a legacy of contradictory meanings and contestation. This study is underpinned, first, by a Foucauldian interest in the way in which a genealogy of discourses and social practices – here related to state formation, statebuilding, peacebuilding and peace formation – uncovers the practices and discourses of resistant and critical agency.

Secondly, borrowing from Escobar, it is informed by as close an approximation as possible, given the author's positionality, to an acute anthropological reflexivity vis-à-vis the unintended (or intended) consequences of late-liberal/neoliberal modernity's claims about legitimacy and the liberal peace.[76] A post-colonial engagement with local agency and resistance is also, of course, necessary. Thus, it is also inductive, requires context sensitivity, an action approach, and an acceptance of cultural legitimacy, agency and authority. It also requires a recognition that it is not the author's place to represent any one approach or voice, but merely to reflect on these factors and on authorial positionality simultaneously. Furthermore, care has to be taken in making claims about what can be known about others, and how elites, states and international actors may wish to instrumentalise such knowledge.

This approach allows for some engagement with the voices and agencies of peace in a liberatory, empathetic and emancipatory mould (eirenism), in a local, state, international, normative and critical register. This allows for their comparison and for a dialogue to emerge, which represents the politics of peacebuilding, peace formation and the state more accurately than has hitherto been possible. This means, as with Habermas, that concerns about power, legitimacy and justice need to be foregrounded while simultaneously making claims about critical agency, the subaltern, and networks that form around peace and oppose all forms of violence.[77]

The book draws on a number of case studies with which I have had a long empirical engagement, including Bosnia, Kosovo, Cambodia, Timor-Leste and Cyprus. It also draws on a wide range of other cases, where peace formation and peace infrastructures have emerged, including Afghanistan, Sierra Leone and Colombia. In addition, it explores others where there has been a much more limited empirical engagement, examining the related literature, policy and statistics. I have also consulted a range of UN, donor, agency, IFI and INGO documents, data and personnel where pertinent. An important caveat should be noted: policy documents, while often taken as being statements of the utmost precision, representing a tense balance of political interests among their signatories, are actually often conceptually and theoretically flawed. Numerous policy instruments in this field start from the assumption that the state, international system, law, rights, norms, the social contract and related concepts are all agreed. This is far from the truth. Many of them make mistaken assumptions about these concepts, not realising that there are multiple variations. This makes using policy documentation problematic, because so many empirical and theoretical errors creep into them (and so into their practices).

Chapter 1 explores the dynamics of state formation, mainly drawing on regional-studies literature. It shows how state-formation dynamics arise out of, and are a response to, various tensions in political, social and economic areas, which lead to violence, crime and an uneasy compromise to mitigate these effects between elites and subjects, often over who holds sovereignty, wealth and the means of making war. It connects these debates to discussions of state fragility, failure and collapse, and illustrates how these perpetuate the myth that any peace tends to be negative.

Chapter 2 examines the statebuilding response to these often violent and criminal state-formation dynamics (often also described as failed states). It argues that statebuilding approaches have mainly focused on security and institutional design, within a legal and constitutional setting framed by neoliberalism, in order to mitigate violence and criminality, and to guarantee individual rights and freedoms. However, statebuilding approaches have focused on a securitised understanding of the state in the context of global markets, meaning that rights and needs dimensions have been marginalised: a 'small' state in terms of social justice has been the result, ironically in the very post-conflict contexts where social justice is most needed. Thus, statebuilding creates a negative hybrid peace because it follows the power and interests of state and international elites.

Chapter 3 turns to a discussion of peacebuilding. It argues that peacebuilding has traditionally been seen as a broader activity than statebuilding's engagement with security and state institutions. It engages with the range of norms, civil society and a social contract envisaged by liberalism and the international liberal peace. These external normative frameworks ultimately aim at a positive peace but an institutional and normative mismatch with local contexts tends to promote a negative hybrid peace.

Chapter 4 turns to an examination of peace formation and the local dynamics for, and of, peace that are exactly what external liberal peacebuilding and statebuilding should support, but often do not. Peace formation also parallels state formation in which violence and crime become embedded in state institutions: peace formation is a response to such dynamics and an attempt to develop localised responses according to a specific socio-historical, political, economic, cultural and environmental context. It may lead to formal and informal frameworks for both negative and positive forms of hybrid peace, depending upon how inclusive it is and how far international actors enable it.

Chapter 5 compares the emergence of the international peacebuilding and statebuilding framework with the development of local peace-formation processes, and how they may complement or block each other in the production of more positive forms of hybrid peace.

The Conclusion turns to a discussion of what improvements peace formation may offer for the understanding of peacebuilding and statebuilding in terms of achieving a more positive form of hybrid peace. Furthermore, it engages with the question of what this means for the various practices of intervention.

1

The Legacy of State Formation

'The historical unity of the ruling classes is realised in the State, and their history is essentially the history of States and of groups of States.'[1]

Introduction

The concept of the state has always been flexible, as the word itself suggests (a 'state' among many possible 'states' and forms). The view that it indicates fixity of a sovereign and Westphalian sort following a Weberian perspective, which translates into a dominant, realist concern with power, security and territory, has a vice-like grip over IR and political science more generally. It represents the convergence, arising from nineteenth-century European politics, of a model of bureaucracy, intervention and the control of populations through the state, which would enjoy high concentrations of capital and thus the means of coercion.[2] This model was then exported from the

West to the decolonising world during the course of the twentieth century.[3] It requires strong state structures that can integrate the material and identity dynamics the state represents into a bureaucratic set of political institutions in order to produce viable state governance and a subjugated population, favouring powerful elites.[4] Order and territory may eventually be assured, but this discursive process provides continuity for powerful interests. Populations and their elites use violence in order to form a state in their favour. Much of this discussion revolves around the way conflict and power shape the state, and whether this may eventually lead to a social contract or be shaped by the hegemonic power of elites.

Mainstream state-formation theory thus offers a Hobbesian view of a state of nature in which everyone is at war with each other, delving deep into ontological fear and a related perception of history as driven by primitive violence.[5] The government, acting as a Leviathan, is the only actor that can secure peace, albeit in a negative form, by assuaging violence through a limited social contract. Such arguments have formed the basis for many contemporary analyses of conflict, statebuilding, state fragility, and weak or failed states.[6] State formation theory offers a historical view of the emergence of the modern state, in European political history and philosophy, as well as a view from the American Revolution and Civil War, and the processes that led to the modern states of Japan and Germany before and through World War II.[7] From this basis, a range of databases and indexes have appeared that connect the state with war and peace, such as the Correlates of War dataset, the Failed States Index and the Uppsala Dataset.[8] All of these use the state and its role in violence as an organising framework. Such modes of thought in which the state is both the object and proponent of violence imply that anti-colonial conflicts, separatism, secession and post-colonial civil war – all examples of state formation – are the dominant forms of twentieth-century conflict.[9]

Derived from a strategic and somewhat parsimonious analysis of European history, this rationale has been used to describe the dynamics of conflict all around the world. Yet it represents a reductionist logic, based on the understanding that violence is a biological imperative, is inherent in human society, and is then transferred to the state and international relations, in classic realist fashion. This argument has, along with liberalism, influenced engagement with conflict and development issues, and has supported a link between peace, the state, security and development.[10] A narrative linking localised and naturalised dynamics of violence, power and status with the formation of a state, itself a prototypical member of the liberal-peace architecture, has been widely accepted. The next step in this rationale is to legitimate intervention and an externalised and interventionary statebuilding or peacebuilding process. External and often relatively ignorant engagements with local and contextual dynamics of power have mainly led to the moderation of intervention but not its ending, as Kofi Annan argued when he described American 'high-handed' approaches in Iraq.[11] The elevation of Western rational-legal assumptions about institutions, security, property and power often equates to a form of Orientalism in relation to the state's intended subjects.[12]

This chapter illustrates, through a range of case-study sketches, how the evolution of state-formation arguments through mainstream power modes to less well-known sociological, structural, and anthropological modes provides a basis for understanding why modern statebuilding tends to lead to negative forms of hybrid peace.

General Dynamics of the Debate

Despite the conceptual framing of Westphalian sovereignty for the modern state and indeed because of historical debates about its provenance, there are many terms available to describe different types of state. Communist, socialist, capitalist, democratic, monarchical, constitutional-monarchical, authoritarian, expansionist, totalitarian, bureaucratic, post-colonial, patrimonial, failed, failing, weak and collapsed remain in the lexicon of terms to describe states. The state has been written about ad nauseam in a number of different disciplines and from different methodological perspectives. In IR and political science, it is of particular interest for realist-theoretical approaches, which focus on power and sovereignty. Others versions may be found in sociology (Weber, Tilly), anthropology (Evans-Pritchard, Radcliffe Brown), history and economics (Keynes, Marx, Friedman and many others).

The dominant assumption of state-formation literature is that a state provides security, autonomy, territory and an infrastructure in which conflict is mitigated by either exerting checks and balances on power and redistributing resources, or by merely assuaging power so that inequalities are maintained. State capacity changes over time and may produce a conservative and negative, rather than an emancipatory, form of peace. The state may be the instrument of structural violence or the instrument of its mitigation. According to Marx, the state is a vehicle for predatory elite interests that exploit society, whereas according to liberal theorists it offers the potential of checks and balances by which a civil society and a social contract produce a stable and relatively just order.[13] In the nineteenth century, nationalism, a driver of state formation, was viewed as a positive process from the dominant elite perspective, whereas today most elites and societies hold very negative views about nationalism, even if they assume the state is naturalised.[14]

State-formation arguments are generally associated with the processes by which local actors gain power and eventually create a Weberian state, which falls under their control. States are both the product and the instrument of force.[15] They require autonomy, central to traditional conceptions of sovereignty. Power is centralised, territory is clearly defined, and the state in Westphalian form is driven mainly by a struggle to be confirmed as the power holder. Its objective qualities and capacities focus on security, and its recognition arises from its capacity to make war, domestically or internationally. War-making is the basis of state formation because it leads to the centralisation of political power over a specific territory. Taxation is the basis for the internal expansion of state authority, success in which then leads to an expansion of its security, administrative and political capacities, and the emergence of a strong state.[16] This may spill over into regional ambitions, meaning that state formation is not solely of domestic significance.

The processes of state formation are often given momentum by acute tensions between tradition and modernisation.[17] Yet the state rather than society is the unit of analysis, even if society is deemed to be the source and target of violence. Depending on the perspective adopted, nationalism is seen as a way of mobilising en masse for a common good, or as a threat to social cohesion where identity is a contested factor in the state-formation process. It provides the power necessary for the state to consolidate and expand. This means the state is understood as a historical product of force, patronage and power, rather than mainly of recognition. Alternatively, it provides a range of core functions as recent debates on sovereignty argue (as in modern state contexts).[18] State formation offers a narrative of modernisation and development, authority and power.

Tensions between local actors and elites over a range of historical, material, political, economic, social and territorial factors led to the emergence of violent and criminalised forces of state formation. These were, at least in the European experience, tamed by the modern sovereign state. This gave rise to an order maintained by an uncomfortable mixture of norms, law, expectations, force and institutions organised on a territorial basis. This was a state order based on a balance between force and compromise. From a contemporary perspective, rational-legal standards for statehood are paralleled by historical 'shadow states', where elites use the state for their own ends while partially reforming it to follow international standards.[19] State formation often implies an illiberal social contract where state resources are used to support elites and to bribe citizens, for as long as this is domestically affordable. This is partly because it preserves local patterns of power responsible for state formation itself.[20] In modern terms, this process might be called the securitisation of the state.[21] This dominant version of state formation implies the formation of unstable regional security complexes fed by localised dynamics of power, violence and criminality.

The literature on this dominant version of state formation confirms a Weberian focus on state sovereignty and territoriality, as well as on elites and the violence they mobilise in order to control the state and population, or to attain regional ambitions. Another characteristic, also borrowed from Weber, is the Orientalist tension between traditional, non-Western society, the modernity represented by the Westphalian or liberal state, and a hierarchy that places the rational-legal state structure at the pinnacle of contemporary political development[22] by virtue of its bureaucratic power and core functions. This balances internal power structures in order to provide a legitimate authority structure.

Key State-Formation Debates

State-formation debates have been influenced by the work of Charles Tilly's famous historical and sociologically informed narrative charting the emergence of the modern state. The state is fundamental both to the international system and also to the organisation of domestic political life, maintaining a division between the domestic and international spheres. This assumption is dominant in the revolutionary or evolutionary, indigenous or externally promoted canon of mainstream IR, development, and peace and conflict studies today. It carries the classic narrative of the emergence of a Westphalian form of sovereignty at the domestic level. The struggle to form a state is the basis for domestic power and order, as well as for status in the international system.[23]

The historically oriented literature explored the traditional power systems and socio-historical patterns of politics in Europe in order to show how they formed the state as a natural and inevitable outcome of their contests. This literature later influenced the more policy-oriented, political-science, anthropological, sociological or area-studies debates about the dynamics of a disorderly or orderly progression from a traditional or colonial territory, or a post-conflict environment, to the modern state. Accordingly, the nature of the state depends on the interests of dominant political classes, and their economic and ideational strength determines the level of conflict, the nature of the state, and its durability and responsiveness.[24]

State-formation debates have revolved around four key state dynamics identified in Tilly's work as summarised by Schwarz: the juxtaposition of capitalist accumulation and class conflict, and the contradictions they reproduce; crises in governance resulting from threats to political elites; challenges from the global political economy; and geopolitics.[25] The state-formation process represents the control of elites over society in order to mobilise collective agency so that the state can fulfil basic functions associated with sovereignty, security and some public services deemed necessary to provide a historical continuity of power or justice. The matrix of these functions leads to the particular character of the state, whether predatory, security-oriented or fulfilling a social contract in liberal style. The more one state in a region is security-oriented, the more other states in the region will tend to follow suit.[26] Thus, 'war made the state and the state made war', as Tilly famously argued.[27] This underlies the fact that state formation may have both internal and external dynamics,[28] relating also to war preparation and to rentierism.[29]

An extension of this argument has led to a focus on how in practice state formation requires mobilisation for development, security and the creation of institutions supported by power or consensus, enabling taxation to be raised. This enables the expansion of state power in both domestic and regional settings, making the state the centre of domestic and international discourse and an epistemic hierarchy. The formation of state power turned at some point in the post-colonial era into a simulation of state power, where quasi-states were formed with limited capacity based on an anti-colonial international legitimacy and limited juridical and material capacity.[30] Thus, war-making was not the only means by which a state emerged and maintained itself: it also needed to have economic and social capacities as well, engendering both local and international legitimacy that comes from being representative of local identity and historical narratives, needs and rights, as well as from fitting into the international system. War-making alone might lead to the demise of the state if it cannot fulfil such contextual and redistributive functions.[31]

This implies that state–society relations matter as much as material power. States are said to be the product of social as well as material forces, requiring an assessment of their 'stateness', in which these forces shape their institutions through social movements and non-state actors, as well as the projection of exclusive identities, as in the ethnic democracies of the contemporary Balkans.[32] States may form from either (or both) the top down or the bottom up, depending on whether elite or social forces dominate. Soon, therefore, the debate turned into an investigation of the social processes inherent in state formation, in which power became accountable: a social contract.

In liberal political theory, the state represents a 'Great Arch'[33] that binds rulers and citizens into a mutually dependent relationship. This emerges through historical violence between classes, and the outcome is dependent on their power relations, norms, interests, material capacities, culture and identities. The aim of the Great Arch is to form a solid institutional base through which parties can combat anarchy, revolution and insecurity. In this Great Arch, the state lives through its subjects in a relationship based on rights, law, a social contract and consent, rather than outright power.[34] The liberal political theorists of the Enlightenment, notably Locke, described how this would provide a solution to the internal and external violence that had blighted Europe and undermined what were to become known as human rights.[35] Before the Arch comes into being it must be forged, and this often occurs through violent contestation between different groups. It may well be that attempts to form this contract never come to fruition and that state formation thus describes a never-ending cycle of violence: instead of the state representing an architecture of peace, it merely represents a container for the contestation of power. If state formation is to lead to a Great Arch, a social contract between elites and citizens or subjects must be forged through a form of cultural revolution. In this sense, central and predatory authority is slowly dissolved and pushed out to the furthest reaches of society, interweaving tense relations, either violent or consensual, between governors and the governed (as in the liberal revolution in Mexico in the nineteenth century).[36]

Through this account of the historical formation of European liberal states, what is normally emphasised in the engagement of IR and political science is a long-term historical process in which power is contested and rulers mobilise armies to ensure the flow of revenue required to make a state viable, without necessarily creating such an Arch.[37] Such thinking is underpinned by a sense that state formation is an archaic or retrogressive process that needs to be tamed, and that might, if properly understood and countermanded, be progressively guided from war to peace and democracy. This perspective reflects the attempt in the twentieth century to transfer the European Enlightenment state to the post-colonial and post-socialist worlds.

The state has the advantage of internal legitimacy as well as being the sole recognised political form on the international stage. State formation – however violent – is internally driven, as opposed to being a result of invasion or colonial occupation. The role of external actors is crucial, however. The formation of international organisations in the twentieth century extended the European process of state formation to the rest of the world through decolonisation. Dominant states and former colonial powers guided new states[38] in the hope they would emerge peacefully in acceptable, modernised, later cosmopolitan and, more recently, neoliberal form, while not representing a burden on, or serving as a flashpoint in, the international system. External actors require an understanding of these processes in order to mitigate, intervene in, or influence them in order to build a state commensurate with international standards and interests.

The way in which state formation has been represented as an inevitable outcome of the clash between different interests and groups in society has been influenced by the methodological and epistemic implications of the 'eternal wisdom of realism', later modified to a degree by liberal thinking about the social contract. However, this is a contract formed through violence rather than negotiation, and may infect the international system unless it is tamed by hegemonic powers.

The type of state that emerges from state formation is controversial. Do the forces of violent contestation mean the resulting state is forever weak and about to collapse, or do they lead to the formation of a strong, but not necessarily equitable, state? If a strong state emerges it needs firm control not just of its territory and the means of violence, but also of its place in the global order and economy, in order to maintain a political and economic position that would enable domestic prosperity and stability, and international competitiveness. The race to achieve this may, however, be one of constant and violent setbacks. It may be that a strong state would resemble a neoliberal state, in which resources and security are controlled by a small, elite group who refuse to redistribute equitably. Or it may represent a socialist state where relative equality is used to assuage interest groups. It may represent a social welfare-oriented or social-democratic state, with significant military capacity, but also the necessary political freedoms and laws to promote national cohesion and political and economic dynamism. Thus, conflict can be seen as being about 'development' in a variety of different ways.[39] All of these debates assume that the rational-legal, bureaucratic and sovereign state, projecting power or conforming to cosmopolitan norms, and embedded in the global economy, is the only type of architectural structure available.

Critiques of State Formation

Mainstream state-formation theory's view of local agency as negative and violent represents a 'romanticisation of the local'.[40] State-formation theory provides the basis for the differentiation between 'closed-access societies', which are fragile, underdeveloped, hierarchical, centralised, patrimonial and conflict-prone, and liberal, open-access societies.[41] Such Orientalism justifies the interventionary and disciplinary character of the liberal peace and statebuilding, as well as the pre-eminence of international over local legitimacy (expressed through the right of humanitarian intervention over sovereignty).

What is crucial is Tilly's insight into how 'strong, durable, effective, and responsive to its own population' a state is.[42] Modernisation theorists argue that the consolidation of state power only occurs when security, institutions, ownership, rights, and domestic and international legitimacy have been achieved.[43] State formation also then becomes constitutive of the international system while also being shaped and even tamed by it. Tilly and others were reaching for a less reductionist understanding of state formation, and in doing so began to open up to a range of other possibilities in which structural, social, anthropological, post-colonial and subaltern dynamics influenced the nature of the international system, rather than merely being the subjects of states. Such arguments imply that the state has social, anthropological and redistributive functions: that is, it is an instrument of social justice. What is often missed in political analyses of state formation is that Weber, Tilly and others working in this area were always clear that the state was part of the social world, and could not be instrumentally separated into military, economic or political institutions without taking account of the broader context provided by history, culture and society.

Early on in the debate, Radcliffe Brown saw the state as a fiction, an ideological construct representing a collection of humans who are related in a complex manner.[44] Such an analysis meant that anthropologists focused on social, cultural and historical practices.[45] The state was consequently regarded by some anthropologists as a metaphor for a broad range of relationships at local and global levels. The neatness of its conceptualisation in political science, they argued, actually masked its social, chaotic and imperfect nature.

As the state became the focus for a discussion of institutional development, the capacity of civil-society organisations and their historic struggle for rights and reform became an obvious next concern for scholars. Sociologists, such as Michael Mann in his monumental *Sources of Social Power*,[46] followed a similar path. They offered a sociological and structural perspective in which society and individuals exhibit political agency to address inequality or injustice, thereby also helping to shape the state.

Sociological and anthropological perspectives did not adopt an instrumental or technical view of state formation or indeed of the state itself. Ultimately, such analysis implied an ethnography of the state, by which the state's positionality, characteristics, structures and social forces were interrogated, if only by using the methods of a colonial-style understanding of social context.[47] This critical possibility is an important part of debates about the state today. Tilly pointed out that 'state intervention in everyday life incited popular collective action, often in the form of resistance to the state'.[48]

Thus, a powerful critique has arisen from a long-standing anthropological engagement with the state. Mirroring Tilly's interest in social movements and mobilisation, this has emphasised the need for historical, structural and sociological perspectives. It has had some impact on mainstream discourse. A dominant consensus has been arrived at through the evolution of these debates, that 'complex networks of state and non-state actors can be understood in terms of an emerging shift from "government" to "governance"'. Thus, local and international forces converge on the state, which is why its form and formation are significant for both local and international order.

From this perspective, the state may be seen as a range of institutional and relational practices aiming at coherence, justice and legitimacy, even though they develop in the context of power relations.[49] Influenced by Foucault's work on governmentality, state-formation and statebuilding processes are to be seen as 'integrated into global and historical contexts ... and as cultural processes'.[50] From this perspective, state-formation processes can be seen as the means whereby local actors reappropriate political control from external or elite power for indigenous social groups or networks. This means that states have the potential to be both socially organic and sovereign.[51] They are a product of cultural revolution,[52] a social process related to the political, economic and securitised dynamics of state formation, but also representative of a significant set of agencies, and in particular connected to contextual legitimacy rather than merely an elite compact or international law and norms.

Such social and anthropological conceptions of the formation of the state set into sharp relief the reductionism of mainstream approaches focused on political economy or security, and their bureaucratic and institutional imperatives, which also tend to favour masculine and patronage-based networks of power and control.[53] They also point to the importance of rituals and symbols of statehood,[54] its meanings, norms, assumptions and non-rational elements.[55] They highlight the everyday cultural dynamics and forms of state practices that arise from the interaction of power and agency at multiple levels to produce a state.[56] This reproduces the modern state not solely as a result of rational and bureaucratic knowledge. From this perspective the state is a hybrid international, liberal and local framework, where power is exercised from the local to the international standpoint. Such an analysis of state formation moves away from material interests and an international- or state-level, industrial-scale mobilisation of agency towards everyday dynamics.

The state should be considered as being formed via the intersection of many different group relationships.[57] The production of subjects (citizens) within a state is therefore a much more complex and difficult affair than many elites or internationals imagine, collapsing the distinction between the international system, state and society. Even the concept of civil society is not as clear-cut as it is in IR and state-building or peacebuilding debates, where it has until recently been unthinkable that local agency should be acceptable in anything other than a liberal-civil form. The state is not simply a set of interlocking institutions, but rather a constant performance of power relations and encounters, everyday and social practices, meanings, identities and alterities (that is, acute differences).[58]

This means that the contours of the debates on state formation range from a violent clash of interests resulting in domination to the mitigation of violence and abuse of power through systems designed to provide checks and balances in response to the claims of citizens, and their agency and rights. From the former perspective, the state is an ever-changing arrangement of power relations and resistances,[59] whereas from the latter it is a fixed, liberal architecture that guarantees rights and lends itself to being 'built' through formulae and blueprints. Essential to state formation is the control of the means of violence by a local compromise between elites and subjects within an epistemic context, which has material substance and meaning for the self-determination and autonomy, identity and rights of a given population.

It is notable that Tilly himself engaged with issues of civil society and social mobilisation, commenting somewhat wryly that 'progress' had been abandoned and that the state had taken over the political imagination as shorthand for the relationship between peoples and territories.[60] He appealed for a weakening of the sort of state that was evolving from power-dominated state-formation processes because it was contrary to the requirements for a social peace.[61] What is clear is that the mainstream debates on state formation prioritise both the state and the negative, violent agencies of local elites and populations, while ignoring other, more positive capacities. Individual autonomy is an expression of power-seeking and violence is a natural political tool vital for the formative state. Thus, mainstream state-formation debates offer a logic arriving eventually at a victor's or negative peace, mainly maintained through power-sharing and balance-of-power arrangements within and between states, dictated by a security dilemma and the relative power of various factions. It offers a crude version of conflict management in first-generation, victor's-peace form. All local agency is dominated by violence and its perpetrators. Foucault perhaps best captured the range of dynamics the state-formation literature presents, as well as the inherent possibilities of the state. In an often-quoted statement he argued:

> To pose the problem in terms of the state means to continue posing it in terms of sovereign and sovereignty, that is to say, in terms of law. If one describes all these phenomena of power as dependent on the state apparatus, this means grasping them as essentially repressive: the army as a power of death, police and justice as punitive instances, and so on. I don't want to say that the state isn't important; what I want to say is that relations of power, and hence the analysis that must be made of them, necessarily extend beyond the limits of the state . . . because the state can only operate on the basis of other, already existing power relations. The state is superstructural in relation to a whole series of power networks that invest the body, sexuality, the family, kinship, knowledge, technology, and so forth. . . . [T]his metapower with its prohibitions can only take hold and secure its footing where it is rooted in a whole series of multiple and indefinite power relations that supply the necessary basis for the great negative forms of power.[62]

Structural forms of critique, including Skocpol's, exposed the inequalities that drive state formation.[63] Such revolutionary processes involved the breakdown and reformation of state structures according to class, inequality and grievance, and subsequent resistance, solidarity and mobilisation. As Marxist theorists also argued, the uneven development of states via the dynamics of state formation and its consequences for the international system (or international community) have far-reaching implications for the state's legitimacy.[64]

Furthermore, the history of the states-system is 'post-colonial' rather than merely representing a replication of European history, as state-formation debates normally imply. The post-colonial (rather than subaltern) critique of the modern state is often rather ambivalent in that it both embraces the Westphalian state and simultaneously argues that it is a product of Western power.[65] The formation of the international system is partially predicated on external hegemonic forces that create certain kinds of state, rather than internal forces. Post-colonial theorists add the argument that Weberian, Orientalist characterisations of other societies as traditional, premodern, customary or non-Western perpetuate the hierarchy that places the state as a specific form of polity at the apex of an international system designed to regulate violence and interests, rather than as representing the interests of widely divergent social groups. This leads to a concern about the construction of legitimacy, whether international or local, connected to justice or power.

Scholars in the Western European context have generally emphasised the role of formal institutions, whereas in the Middle East, Africa and Latin America they have uncovered a more complicated picture, blurring the boundary between formal and informal, tradition and modernity. In these contexts politics and institutions are more thoroughly embedded in issues relating to culture, custom and history, often connected to both colonial praxis and resistance, as well as the growing influence of Western modernisation or development principles.[66] Family dynamics, tribes and parallel political structures in so-called 'segmentary societies' which may lead to fragmented states or prevent an industrial-scale mobilisation of economic or political capacity from a formal perspective are often cited as playing a more significant role than Tilly envisaged. They introduce a dimension of both political economy and political culture beyond the assumptions of the Western European historical processes of statebuilding, in an increasingly significant informal terrain and interaction of politics and society.[67]

Starting an analysis of local agency from the premise of mainstream state-formation literatures replays the argument that all local agency and all resulting states rest on inherently violent tendencies. The state's role is to enact prohibitions and exercise productive, rather than progressive, power. Thus, state formation brings about a negative peace at best. Historical, structural, sociological and anthropological approaches attempt to break out of this narrative but they too are constrained by the fact that the state is ultimately representative of power relations. For example, anthropological approaches have often been applied in recent practice to instrumentalise social processes – as with the counterinsurgency (COIN) strategy in Afghanistan,[68] and to romanticise local agency as either primitive or ineffective.

Links with Liberal Peace and Neoliberalism

This is perhaps why much of the literature that has emerged utilising the state-formation approach is aimed at explaining and preventing not just internal violence but also regional escalation. The earlier focus on states, power and interests lends itself to a positivist and realist methodological and theoretical orientation, which goes some way to explaining why so much of the recent generation of statebuilding literature, particularly from the US, is positivist, focused on problem-solving (how to build/fix a state), and adopts the lens of realism. Much of the discussion of state formation from the 1970s until the end of the Cold War focused on the emergence of European states along Westphalian lines. States were contested at the elite level in order to maintain security, power and privileges, access to resources and control of institutions, while also creating or maintaining territorial sovereignty and boundaries, and constructing a regional system of states or a balance of power. Devoid of its sociological, structural or anthropological dimensions, this logic was extended to explain processes of decolonisation, development and ethnic conflict after the end of the Cold War, and later peacekeeping, peacebuilding and statebuilding. This set the scene for the neoliberal statebuilding practices that emerged in the 1990s, under the rubric of liberal peacebuilding, in which states were built as part of an envisaged liberal peace.

Given that mainstream state-formation theory points to the emergence of 'state-makers' who suppress participation and rights, adopting the neoliberal state as the model for external intervention is in itself paradoxical. It exposes the new state to the global economy and has in practice been unable to engage with the rights, representation and transformation needed on the ground to escape embedded structures of power and conflict. Tilly argued that embedding the state in the global economy enhanced social and class divisions on the ground and disguised the importance of elite control of material resources, which are then used to co-opt state institutions.[69] Sovereignty is essential to prevent this process because it provides a level of autonomy from international intervention.[70] But it has not prevented the double rupture that state formation dictates for society: first war may form the state, and secondly external intervention may reconstruct a very different form of state.

Accordingly, this rationale indicates that violent state-formation processes could only be curtailed by the peace, security and development structures that gradually came into being after the Treaty of

Westphalia (1648), and including the UN Charter (1945), the Agenda for Peace (1992), the Responsibility to Protect doctrine (2005). During this period of global institutional and state development, the forces of state formation were gradually brought under control by an emerging international peace architecture and social demands for a just order, as exemplified in the epoch of decolonisation. Much of the post-Cold War period of humanitarian intervention, peacekeeping and peacebuilding can be read as a similar endeavour to control the violence of state-formation processes.

Drawing on state-formation approaches, some key motifs emerged in peacebuilding and statebuilding. Framed by its own disciplinary limitations, Huntington's work suggested that 'civilisational forces' define the state and international order, in turn defining conflict:[71] Rotberg connected weak and failed states[72] to discussions of conflict prevention, regional security and US foreign policy. Thus, emergent states were 'nativised' in an Orientalist fashion in which violence and ignorance drove their formation. Posen's 'ethnic security dilemma' is an excellent example.[73] This premise was used to produce a problem-solving analysis of an ideal state's core functions, and thus their comparative viability. Formation dynamics could now be measured against a modern notion of the state and replicated through statebuilding practices. As Tilly himself explicitly argued, drawing on his observation of European history, states may be built by external intervention in a state-formation process to prevent violence and to influence the nature of the states-system that emerges.[74] The European or Western state thus became an ideal for political order.

State-formation literature is also crucial to the progressive aspects of the contemporary projects of both peacebuilding and statebuilding through its alternative structural, sociological and anthropological strands. A more nuanced and paradoxical view sees the state both as a danger to others and to human rights, and as a potential framework for liberal rights and law. On the one hand, the Tillyian version of the state has what Mann has termed 'infrastructural power', which enables it to exploit civil society.[75] On the other hand, historical and structural dynamics raise the issue of equality, sociological approaches raise the issues of identity, cohesion and a social contract, and more informal processes illustrate the potential of critical, social agency to shape the state as a framework for peace.

Consequently, processes of peacebuilding and statebuilding have been designed to develop a liberal social contract in contrast to the predatory state. Informal processes seek to mitigate or control the state and its discursive framework. The reality is that both infrastructural power and critical agency are at play in state formation. Ultimately, statebuilding and liberal peacebuilding aim to build a framework that runs against the current of both elite power and social critical agency (though the latter is normally a supporter of substantive democracy and human-rights processes). Yet neoliberalism and global capital tend to support elites over social actors, accumulation over solidarity.

Empirical Rationales

The state-formation literature provides an intensely depoliticised, ahistorical and sometimes apocalyptic view of what might happen where predatory, violent and weak states emerge, where past practices of politics, identity and custom fail to prevent war, and where constant collapse threatens and undermines political, social and economic order. An excellent example can be found in Robert Kaplan's analysis of sub-Saharan Africa states, where state formation is seen as a realist process in which the inevitable clash of primitive interests creates local, regional or global disorder.[76] Such assumptions are also commonly made about historical and tribal dynamics in the Middle East,[77] determining the heavily securitised architecture of the putative Palestinian state, as well as in the context of Afghanistan's long civil war, the attempt to undermine the Taliban and the latter's links with terrorist actors.[78] These assumptions were used to justify the statebuilding mission that followed the invasion of Afghanistan in 2001.[79] From this perspective, the various forces of state formation proved too pernicious in their regional and global effects to be allowed to continue.

This logic focuses on power and predation. The sociological and anthropological possibilities of state-formation debates, conversely, are only used instrumentally to expose violent resistance and its networks (as with the COIN strategy approach in Afghanistan). Similarly, instrumental support of civil society or peace movements rarely reaches beyond a superficial approach to NGO-supported peacebuilding, where NGOs become the subcontractors for donor 'programming' aimed at building a liberal state. This avoids the possibility of alternative currents of agency or forms of polity. The sociological and anthropological possibilities are used to expose these dimensions in order to 'neutralise' them, rather than illustrate the possibilities of alternative currents of agency, forms of polity or issues.

Cambodia

In Cambodia, ongoing state-formation analysis has meant the country's problems have been identified as mainly relating to a specific feudal, ideological and predatory elite at the apex of a complex social and kinship network.[80] Despite the impact of colonialism, local conflict dynamics were used to justify liberal peacebuilding through a UN mission after the Paris Peace Agreement in 1991, which was deemed necessary to remove the Khmer Rouge and previous modes of politics. A contest over the nature of the Cambodian state in recent history, running through power relations (both local and Cold War), historical identity and political organisation, ideology and, of course, the regional impact of the Vietnam war, eventually led to the emergence in 1975 of the Khmer Rouge, whose goal was an agrarian and socialist transformation of the state.[81] This in turn led to an invasion by Vietnam in 1978. Social, economic and patronage issues led to a situation where the contestation of power meant state formation and collapse, as well as societal and economic collapse, which all went hand in hand. State-formation arguments allowed many of Cambodia's problems to be identified as local and regional rather than globally influenced. Heritage, identity, and social and political structures (including language) were rejected, and the focus of internationals rested solely on mitigating power via the liberal-peace framework. The Comprehensive Peace Agreement in 1991 was an amalgam of modernisation and development, peacebuilding, transformation and reform practices. It pointed towards the creation of a liberal state[82] with the support of the UN Transitional Authority in Cambodia.[83]

Of course, state formation was a historical contest for power but it was also a social process.[84] Negative anthropological arguments were used to ignore heritage, identity and social structures. This oversight established the basis for the focus of liberal peacebuilding.[85] A Western and Weberian perspective on state control of power veered towards a territorial and interest orientation, missing much of the historical complexity of its social aspects. Thus, state-formation processes were said to depend on a network of patronage and domination rather than on a social contract. State formation historically favoured a neofeudal state presided over by elites who controlled patronage networks.

Certainly, because authoritarianism still dominates politics and institutions, and because a vast cross section of society remains politically and economically marginal to the modern state as well as to the liberal international, politics remain undemocratically contested, poverty is rife, human-rights regimes are weak, development is limited and the free market, despite drawing in foreign investment, still works against the vast bulk of society. From a mainstream state-formation perspective, this indicates that the state has formed to maintain embedded structural violence, and that this is essentially a local process. Conveniently, state-formation analysis provides the basis for statebuilding and peacebuilding as legitimates both on their own terms. Yet conflicts in and around the Cambodian polity have long been heavily influenced by regional and global interests and ideologies. The dominant state-formation debates set the scene for a victor's or negative peace. This warrants an international discourse that is both absolved of responsibility for the historical state of Cambodia and provided with legitimacy for intervention. It implies there are no local practices or institutions that are of value for peacemaking and the modern state.

Timor-Leste

Though Timor-Leste had suffered a colonial history, had declared its independence in 1975 and was promptly invaded by Indonesia, when the UN became involved in peacebuilding and statebuilding there in 1999, it was assumed that self-determination, self-government and statehood had emerged from the contested dynamics of a primitive process of state formation.[86] This perspective pitted local elites and much of Timorese society against the Indonesian state and military (and divided the Timores) – as well as ultimately against the UN. State-formation processes led to contradictory processes of state formation: guerrilla and civil support for, and opposition to, both internal collaborators and the Indonesian occupiers. These tensions were finally brought to an end after the Indonesian government agreed to a referendum on independence, meaning state formation would be replaced with international peacebuilding and statebuilding in 1999. New norms and processes of politics based on liberal law and economy were to be established in the context of a modern, secular state rather than of local and regional contestation of the territory.

State formation did not end at the point of international intervention, however: internationals became only one of several groups that contributed to the process. Sociological, structural and anthropological analysis also revealed how politics were being contested on the grounds of identity, custom and inequality. This is very different from the realist perspective, even though the facts observed are similar. These societal dimensions did not become apparent to international actors until after several new rounds of violence in the mid-2000s. Internationals thought these problems were a function of an incomplete state, incapable of controlling violence, offering rights and attracting investment. Their biased perspective obscured customary cohesion, historical issues and inequalities relating to colonisation and identity as political forces. Thus, there emerged a general consensus that the externalised attempt to build both peace and the state had been unsuited to contextual conditions, which were driven by more than a simple contest over power.[87] Rather than the new state representing an end to a solely negative process of state formation, it actually represents its continuation.[88] It has only been because local actors took it upon themselves to address inequality and bring in customary processes to ground the state in local culture and legitimacy that matters eventually appear to have improved. This points to the value of the sociological and anthropological dimensions of state-formation theory as bottom-up counterpoints to the negative perspectives of peace that state-formation theories imply.

Bosnia-Herzegovina and Kosovo

Several states in the former Yugoslavia in the period 1990–99, including Bosnia-Herzegovina and Kosovo, have often been analysed through state formation's power perspectives. From this perspective, the collapse of a state that guaranteed social property and rights led its constituent peoples towards a focus on exclusive identities, which was exploited by ethno-nationalist politicians.[89] The US-brokered Dayton Agreement in 1995 brought to an end the war between the various Serb, Croatian and Bosniac disputants in Bosnia-Herzegovina, establishing an ethnically organised state chaperoned by the international community through the Office of the High Representative. In Kosovo, the NATO intervention in 1999 was designed to prevent Serb forces from repeating their violent tactics in Bosnia-Herzegovina, this time directed at the long-oppressed Kosovo Albanian community. In both cases, the ethnic framing of international analysis and the resulting institutional frameworks rested on a primordial view of power and identity, in which the state becomes a vehicle for deep political contests and a negative peace framework at best.[90] This led to the emergence of ethnic democracies in the Balkans. The choice for the role of the state was between sharing power between ethnic groups by mitigating their state-formation impulses, and giving in to them and allowing new nation-states to emerge from the violence.

In the case of Bosnia-Herzegovina, identity, religion, security, military force, territory and civil society were all swept along in a state-formation project driven by the idea of a 'Greater Serbia'. Such contestation has continued in 'negative peacetime', indicating the ways in which indigenous processes of state formation are conducted not only through violence but also through structural forms of violence. Indeed, it is no surprise that Dayton is now seen less as a peace settlement and more as a ceasefire, commensurate with state-formation processes' power dynamics.[91] The process of state formation has also transferred itself from a state that few of its participants want after Dayton to the Republika Srpska, the other political entity that constitutes Bosnia-Herzegovina, along with the Federation of Bosnia and Herzegovina. In general, Bosnia-Herzegovina appears from a top-down perspective to be becoming more, not less, ethnically polarised,[92] providing a warning about how assumptions regarding state formation drive internationals into adopting the very particularistic and ethnicised binaries they claim to be seeking to transform. At the same time they may have missed signs of local legitimacy and capacity to manage conflict. The state continues to rest on elite politics (which are often predatory) rather than building a local social contract, democratisation and reconciliation, or reconstructing the regional pluralism that existed before the war.[93] In practice, state-formation debates have been used to legitimate the construction of a neoliberal state with no regard for pre-war structures and the hard-won agreements they rested upon.

Debates about state formation in Kosovo rest on ethnic mobilisation and violent resistance to Serb control in recent times, drawing their sustenance from historical identity factors embedded in a 'shadow state' that paralleled formal government in the 1980s.[94] The NATO and UN strategy tried to shift the process from state formation to liberal peacebuilding whereby sovereignty was not necessarily a key aim; instead, norms and law were the focus in a framework that kept alive the hope of reintegration into Serbia. However, local actors aiming at the creation of a Kosovo Albanian state had been engaged in their own state-formation process, both through violence and by moving more subtly into the open via a creeping administrative occupation of the core functions necessary for governance. Though these were controlled by internationals after 1999, a long-term goal had been independence for local actors, harnessing what were often neopatrimonial dynamics to create the institutions necessary for the state. Eventually, this led to the cooptation of international peacebuilding, such that it was guided towards the self-determination cause of the Kosovo Albanians.[95] The state in Kosovo has hence become implicated in the ethnic, sovereign and territorial dynamics of inclusion and exclusion, cooperation and rejection, and there is limited space for pluralism in between these positions despite concerted local and international efforts. State formation appears to provoke conflict, at the expense of international and local peacebuilding movements, from a top-down perspective. In both Kosovo and Bosnia-Herzegovina, the neoliberal state itself has formed around sovereign exclusivity where a more pluralist framework is necessary.

Conclusion

What has emerged from mainstream state-formation analysis is a focus on the state as mainly aimed at security and the mitigation of power struggles through direct and structural forms of power, meaning a victor's peace at best is possible. As the examples above show, the states that have formed from a mixture of local and international involvement tend towards a negative form of peace purely on the basis of an internal struggle for power and resources. However, the focus on power tends to obscure more positive aspects of state formation. From this perspective, state formation represents an extension of early twentieth-century colonial-style analyses of local politics.

To summarise, state-formation debates have moved through three stages: a mainstream and top-down, externally driven debate focused on power and clashing interests at an elite level; a turn towards bringing in social and structural forces in a more liberal sense (representing the formation of a Great Arch) and leading to the formation of institutions that balance elite and social power; and a sociological and anthropological turn, offering contextual, bottom-up, post-colonial and subaltern insights relating to questions of inequality and justice as well as agency. The latter two stages offer a more sophisticated understanding of how a society develops its own legitimate peacemaking mechanisms, leading to a contractual state with a negotiated identity, while the mainstream power approach rests on a Northern blueprint for the modern, neoliberal state. The tension between these various understandings of the formation of the state is illustrative of the potential for either a negative or positive form of peace to emerge.

The first and second stages illustrate clearly how statebuilding and peacebuilding may be a response to state formation, because they concur on the probability of a mainly negative peace. They show how statebuilding extends the link between external intervention and local dynamics of conflict, in which elites retain control of power with greater or lesser respect for the rights of citizens. Such realist and liberal approaches to state formation have also been influential in inadvertently describing the process of the formation of a post-colonial international system whereby the state has become naturalised over the interests, rights and needs of subaltern subjects. The social and anthropological dynamics of state formation have been partly drawn on in more critical approaches that suggest that both positive and negative forms of peace are possible. State formation is also driven, at least in part, by subaltern resistance both to violence and to state intervention in everyday life.[96] Historically, of course, it has been common for elites to bargain with restive populations, often in a heavy-handed manner.[97]

The sociological, anthropological and structural, as well as the broader historical, dimensions of state-formation debates have yet to make a significant impact. Yet these imply an engagement with the everyday dynamics of life within a post-colonial, post-liberal and probably post-Westphalian understanding of the state in question.[98] They indicate how the emergence of the modern state carries forward a historical perspective of identity, rights, needs, justice and alterity in both the state and international system, which cannot alone be resolved by power or by externally designed institutions. An understanding of how any society produces compromises, institutions, justice and legitimacy would be a next step. This would suggest that there are alternative types of polity to any mainstream state-formation architecture or its statebuilding counterparts.

State-formation debates that focus on violence tend to reflect the Hobbesian, problem-solving and positivist bias of the day, and have led to the formation of theory and policy designed to create states that can respond to such forces. The legacy of state-formation debates in this mode is paradoxical: the state ameliorates itself via a struggle between domestic and international agencies. Internal struggles to produce nation-states in which specific elites harness the state's resources for their own interests (often expressed via regional or imperial ambitions) have normally led to national states emerging through complex configurations of power.[99] These are not well suited to development settings, identity and cultural differences, or alternative epistemologies; rather, they are suited mainly to maintaining the continuities of injustice and power. In sum, state-formation debates have undermined the possibility that peacebuilding and statebuilding approaches may aim at developing a positive, emancipatory peace.

On the other hand, the social/anthropological and structural turn in state-formation debates raises issues such as human security, identity, inequality, local ownership and a social compact.[100] These are connected to subaltern frameworks of power and to contextual forms of agency. They challenge the teleology of violence that may lead to a sovereign state, instead acknowledging the historical and socio-political compromises associated with internal struggles for justice. They highlight the influence of local agency in mitigating the conditions of everyday life, along with the consequences of elite power struggles, inequality and difference. Positive, and probably hybrid, understandings of peace and the state may be drawn from such views.[101]

II

Statebuilding: Failed by Design

'Reason would drive [states] to give up their savage lawless freedom, to accommodate themselves to public coercive laws, and thus to form an ever-growing State of Nations, such as would at last embrace all the Nations of the Earth. But as the Nations, according to their ideas of international Right, will not have such a positive rational system, and consequently reject in fact what is right in theory, it cannot be realised in this pure form. Hence, instead of the positive idea of a Universal Republic – if all is not to be lost – we shall have as result only the negative surrogate of a Federation of the States averting war, subsisting in an external union, and always extending itself over the world.'[1]

'The government is best which governs least.'[2]

Introduction

In 2011, a UNDP report stated that one-quarter of the world's population still live in 'fragile states', and so placed 'statebuilding' at the forefront of international relations. Statebuilding represents an attempt to make the whole world subject to an ideal, modern political order, in which a strong state provides law, order and accountability to its citizens.[3] Even so, historically there have been many different types of state-polity, ranging from federations and confederations to condominiums and protectorates, and various ways of organising territory and democracy. In modernity, however, states are expected to conform to a set of common standards while enabling self-rule, autonomy and self-determination for their subjects. Theoretically, the ideal state can be exported through intervention and global governance, and neatly organised around populations living in different territories. Such assumptions have been supported by the fact that most of the political projects of the last century and more, from nationalism to industrialisation, decolonisation and national liberation, have centred on the state. Many of them have been premised on the liberal idea that the state can provide security and public services, thus balancing negative and positive versions of peace.

The state – and in particular the liberal/neoliberal state – is the only framework that theoretically hedges against all threats in the international system in a Hobbesian world, and so it is understandable that this is the model that is constantly adopted. It implies a dominant, impersonal, rational, centralised and unified authority, control of the means of violence, and management of inequality and stratification. It requires a legitimate authority structure that can wield military and disciplinary power, and that has the flexibility to respond to changing demands for progress as well as to external pressures. It avoids the creation of rents. A successful state implies a positive form of peace, and statebuilding indicates how one can be built and maintained through intervention.[4] Yet it is also a political and legal architecture imbued with the epistemic power and bias of the global North. Furthermore, territorial sovereignty is a curiously archaic political framework for a world in which many networks promote fluidity and contingency, rather than fixity and predictability. Such qualities are contradictory, pointing to a negative peace as the focus of statebuilding.

'Negative sovereignty' indicates that a state reflects external perceptions of legitimacy; 'positive sovereignty' indicates that it also offers public goods to its citizens.[5] State architecture establishes hegemony through the rules, power, hierarchy and nature of legitimate authority. This occurs simultaneously with its promise of autonomy, self-determination, development, representation and rights. Statebuilding extends this paradox into new geographic spaces of instability, attesting to how far the state is seen as the source and solution to conflict, representing a panacea inextricably linked to monopoly over the means of violence and the coordination of development.[6] Statebuilding extends historical power forwards with its various contradictions: justice, rights, progressivism and liberalism, as well as injustice, political and economic interests, territorialism, nationalism and recidivism. It is a reflection of the Hobbesian state of nature, the social contract enforced by the Leviathan and the property rights that Locke refers to as a fundamental aspect of nature.[7]

According to the UN system, the IFIs and donors, the state is the crucial actor when it comes to the broader agenda of peace as well as to security.[8] Statebuilding is an extension of twentieth-century decolonisation and the much-maligned 'structural adjustment' projects by which market democracy replaced socialism in the 1990s.[9] Statebuilding's genealogy can also be traced back to the nation-building experiments in the US after its Civil War, and in Germany, Japan and much of Western Europe after World War II. To policymakers, statebuilding has represented an alternative to the traditional power-driven patterns of politics in Europe and its former colonies, enabling them to oversee an orderly progression from a traditional or colonial system to the modern states-system. Ensuing states should be sovereign, unified, secure, liberal, rights-observing with a strong rule of law, and industrialised, and should provide a minimum of public services and welfare if the market cannot do so.[10]

This chapter examines, through a critical lens and a range of case sketches, how statebuilding approaches have emerged as an antidote to mainstream state-formation approaches. This implies that a positive peace is their aim. But, in view of the empirical evidence, this chapter argues that statebuilding has actually produced a negative hybrid peace.

The Rationale of Statebuilding Theory

Statebuilding is focused on establishing a state monopoly over the means of violence, and a shift away from the authoritarian (strong) states that were so widespread in the Cold War era, which were the outcome of unmitigated state-formation processes. Statebuilding's focus has been strongly influenced by security issues, though it is also assumed that the state should have competency in the areas of rule of law, taxation, development, the environment and public services. These are the core functions of states as defined by the IMF and World Bank. However, the state is primarily seen as an essential vehicle for security and development, through which aid and reform can be better coordinated, so that 'good enough' governance is achieved.[11] For the US and UK in particular, security, property rights, basic services and public finances are most important.

Statebuilding has emerged as a way around the consent problem of intervention. The state is the vehicle for the diffusion of norms of territorial sovereignty, individualist norms and property rights supported by Western conceptions of law, and international rules for conduct between states.[12] Statebuilding also overcomes accusations of racial, material and normative bias towards a specifically Western and Northern set of interests by claiming to deal only with the desirable structure of the state in a scientific way. It was designed to produce a 'light footprint' – as in Afghanistan after 2004 – that would not be objectionable to international or local partners, especially after the controversy over intervention in Kosovo in 1999. However, it was rapidly confronted, both in Iraq and Afghanistan, with the fact that such a deep form of intervention could never be conducted lightly.[13]

Statebuilding is also concerned with the 'soft security' issues of local peace and human security, because these are thought to be contingent on stable markets, institutions and regional security. A liberal-social contract is deemed the solution, ideally. Indicative of this broader ambition for the state, the Millennium Development Goals indicated that poverty reduction and public services were important state functions,[14] meaning governance is seen as a tool to provide for its citizens, leading to stronger states (but not 'strong states', which implies authoritarianism). Thus, statebuilding and 'good governance' have a close relationship. The US Agency for International Development (USAID) has argued that governance should be addressed in order to increase the local legitimacy of government, with enhanced security, democracy promotion, reform of institutions and development as its targets.[15] Thus, legitimate construction of local authority and state–society relations – that is, local knowledge and support – has been recognised as significant for statebuilding at an institutional level, though political will to support this approach remains uncertain.[16]

However, statebuilding reflects the neoliberal preference for a smaller state architecture, anchored by, and in, liberal democracy and human rights, the global economy and global governance. Markets are crucial in providing access to resources and opportunities, even though neoliberal ideology partly undermines the developmental and democratising approach that statebuilding proposes.[17] This meant that the end of the Cold War saw many totalitarian or authoritarian states replaced by weak states that could not maintain order or provide services.[18] However, a positive peace would imply that a state met the needs of its citizens and would connect with 'cultural borders',[19] achieving an 'organic' form of social contract. On the other hand, an externally constructed nation-state would not be organic and would fail to understand the claims or identity of its citizens. A state that would achieve a positive peace would be a pluralist 'national state', which would also therefore tend to be a hybrid.

Statebuilding draws on the security and sociological dimensions of mainstream state-formation theory. In general, statebuilding has ignored its structural or anthropological dimensions, which see the state as a 'field of power' in which a wide variety of formal and informal agencies operate.[20] It has failed to capture the associative dimensions of historical social and community-level frameworks. Instead, it indicates a securitised, privatised, contractual praxis: governance occurs through the state, led by international actors, to produce a limited, conservative form of peace. In these terms, peace rests upon an externally designed social contract. Civil society should comply with this contract rather than be constitutive of it. Thus, modern statebuilding creates a distant, technocratic and bureaucratic institutional framework, rather than a living, social entity. Because it is organised around the need to respond to the various negative dynamics of state formation, human rights and civil society are a rhetorically important flourish but are of lesser concern.

Since the 1970s, Lesser Developed States (LDCs) have provoked a variety of social, economic and security concerns for development actors and donors. Contemporary statebuilding is a natural extension of this logic of an emerging connection between development and security. The World Bank and IMF have focused on economic development, though they have often been accused of weakening the social capacity of the state and the welfare of the population through favouring growth over equality.[21]

A more critical genealogy of statebuilding can also reach back much further into colonial history in its 'imperial' phase: colonialism adopted a civilising mission of tutelage to promote the eventual self-sufficiency of colonial territories, if not their independence, as well as to open up those territories for profit. The creation of a civil service, police force and military, as well as a public infrastructure, was part of this process. Later, under pressure for self-rule, the creation of institutions often mirrored liberal institutions of the time, adding another layer to this process, which was roughly parallel with the emergence of colonial anthropology, the distant forerunner of the modernisation and development debates that are now unconsciously built into statebuilding praxis, via the connections of the Academy with the emergent institutions and interventionary practices of the twentieth century.[22]

These dynamics have influenced recent conceptions of peace from a statebuilding perspective. Building the state is crucial to domestic and international understandings of positive peace, following the 'iron' law that liberal-democratic states and free markets tend to be more peaceful.[23] This guides a 'good governance' agenda, with a particular vision of a neoliberal state integrated into the international community as an outcome. The state should be strong in security and territorial terms, but governance should be subtle and small-scale, leaving the market to shape the nature of interactions between citizens within the liberal human-rights and property-law framework, enshrined in the constitution of any state that has endogenously shaped itself. Such states should mirror developed states in the global North ideally (Denmark is an oft-cited exemplar), be secure, with a strong rule of law, rights and democratic system, a free and fair media, and an active civil society which implements constitutional safeguards on power. States should also provide effective minority rights and frameworks for pluralism.[24]

As Tilly has argued, the state can be characterised in different ways: (i) high-capacity but undemocratic, where security is a dominant issue and function of the state and there is little public debate; (ii) low-capacity and undemocratic, where force is dominant; (iii) high-capacity and democratic, where force and participation combine to form legitimate politics; and (iv) low-capacity and democratic, where insecurity and participation are both high.[25] The aim of the statebuilding process is to produce the third version, where integration between interpersonal, formal and informal networks of trust (kinship, identity, religion, labour) is high, where inequalities related to gender, race, ethnicity, religion, class or caste are low, and where power is relatively decentralised.[26] The state still needs to be able to maintain order, however, meaning decentralisation and the adoption of localised patterns of power must be balanced against elite and regional interests.

In reality, statebuilding has had to wrestle with the fact that its attempt to order the world has been met with widely varying types and capacities of agency. The issue is whether the state incorporates its subjects or vice versa.[27] Statebuilding proposes a 'high' standard of 'stateness' in institutional, economic and normative terms as an objective that many post-colonial, developing and post-conflict polities may or may not follow. Many do not have the resources to do so, or to compete in the global marketplace. Consequently, statebuilding is based upon a relatively weak local and international consensus.[28] The UN, UNDP, World Bank, EU, a range of international NGOs and key supporting bilateral donors, many of which have local (normally meaning 'national') partners, follow this line.

Statebuilding in Cambodia, Bosnia, Kosovo, Timor-Leste, the Solomon Islands and others has produced weak institutions. It has failed via development or governance strategies to engagement with the material needs issues related to rights, and has failed to create citizenship whereby the state was legitimated locally, and not just internationally.[29] This has created empty states and a virtual peace. Human development indexes have barely improved from the inception of the mission or intervention while the Gini index on inequality has often increased, meaning that prosperity is mainly felt at elite levels (though security benefits all). Apart from statistical evidence,[30] qualitative evidence from politicians, bureaucrats, international personnel, local leaders and a range of NGOs overwhelmingly points to a dissatisfaction with all of these missions and both their objectives and their current status. On the other hand, security has often improved, both at a national and an everyday level. These patterns are also replicated for other missions, most recently in the context of Afghanistan, but they span a wide range of international involvements in post-conflict sites.

Rwanda is often taken to be a good example of a desirable statebuilding outcome. Though its human-rights record and military adventures across its western border with the Democratic Republic of Congo are often criticised, it is seen as a state that is democratic and focused on providing a peace dividend, developing a vibrant economy, and offering public services, education and health in an accountable manner.[31] However, Rwanda illustrates that statebuilding's normative dimension is secondary to its security, political and economic architecture. In practice, the formal state often remains weak and incapable, is hijacked by previous state-formation elites or becomes endogenously donor-driven. As external actors have been unwilling to take complete control of post-conflict states without consent (as in Timor-Leste after the withdrawal of Indonesian forces in 1999), they tend to be propped up by a mixture of external support allied with dominant and often problematic elites. In other words, the reality is not a positive peace, but instead a negative form of hybrid peace. After the interventionary quagmires of the 2000s in Afghanistan and Iraq, an even more jaundiced version of state-building – a diluted, 'good enough' version – has emerged.[32] Again, Rwanda, with its mix of an authoritarian and liberal state, is often used as an example, on the basis that it offers hope that a stable present might lead to future reforms. This represents an uneasy compromise between mainstream state-formation approaches and statebuilding in order to stabilise existing inequalities.[33] At best, this is a negative hybrid peace in which the root causes of conflict have not been addressed, though the institutional framework of the state exists and is mainly of benefit to elites or existing power structures.

Core Functions, Efficiency and Measurability

One powerful interpretation of state-formation wars is that they are 'development in reverse' in domestic and regional terms. The state is either a vehicle to protect elite interests often related to the so-called 'resource curse'[34] or it engages in transnational crime or supports terrorism abroad. In general terms, this is then taken to necessitate a range of external interventions to bring about security, democratisation, marketisation and the rule of law. Significant development is often required for the latter functions to emerge, which also necessitates intervention in forms that facilitate their development relatively quickly in order to provide a range of political, economic, civil and security 'peace dividends'. For these purposes an international architecture of development, peacebuilding, statebuilding and security actors is harnessed, making the rebuilding of the state the basis for a bureaucratic understanding of statebuilding since the late 1990s.[35]

This state's core functions range from the minimal function of security and law and order to the 'activist' functions associated with legitimate institutions, public services, welfare and social support.[36] The World Bank supports the concept of the territorially sovereign but globalised state, even if it does not support a centralised version.[37] Its 1997 report talks about the importance of dealing with poverty, marginalisation, the vulnerable, decentralisation, unemployment and public services in an equitable manner for ordinary citizens, so that state and people are closely connected.[38] However, statebuilding is managed by external administrators;[39] democracy is a secondary consideration until the state is stabilised. The state is therefore a piece of bureaucratic architecture rather than a social configuration, though the statebuilding paradigm that the UN supports means that the state has domestic requirements, not merely international responsibilities.[40] Statebuilding is an externally driven modernisation process that focuses mainly on international forms of legitimacy and adopts the principles of advanced (or late) capitalism and neoliberalism.

The OECD has argued that statebuilding rests on three pillars: core functions of state structures; legitimacy and accountability; and the market.[41] In particular, it argues that statebuilding generally requires that external support of all kinds is channelled through state structures in order to support their development.[42] The state is responsible for security and justice, for revenue creation and collection, for providing basic services and for creating jobs, and the better these tasks are achieved, the more legitimacy the state would receive from its citizens as well as from the international community. A civil society is essential for a liberal social contract to come into being, though it is expected to be NGO-led, individualistic and compliant with liberal-peace norms. The state would focus on a 'foundation of law and property rights' but should also be aware of the need to protect the marginalised. It should be decentralised, competitive and meritocratic.[43] Statebuilding itself would emanate from the international, passed down through systems of global governance to the state, the diplomat, the programme officer and the official working at both state and local levels.[44]

Thus, states have three sets of functions that should be thought about in the context of statebuilding: minimal, intermediate and activist.[45] These range from a basic security and rights approach to greater intervention in terms of redistribution: as the state becomes more activist, it becomes more involved in the markets and develops a more vibrant civil society.

Taxation is one of the core areas of state competence that illustrates some of the dilemmas of the bureaucratic statebuilding discourse. Taxation is a political activity aimed at establishing an authority that is indicative of the viability of the state. However, individual property rights imply a commitment to capitalism that may not often be clear in specific contexts or may be under dispute: for example, in the statebuilding project in Nepal after the end of the Maoist insurgency there. The ability to collect tax and to spend it is politically contested. To deny this contest is indicative of a negative peace. This contest provides a state with its identity as either a neoliberal state, focused on amassing sufficient capital for basic infrastructure, or a social democracy focused on raising capital for a broad range of services and welfare and infrastructure measures that equalise citizens. Taxation also provides the state with powerful instruments to catalogue and control its populations, which many of them, used to perceiving the state as predatory, may resist. A centralised state may make competition more severe, though it may also have greater potential to mobilise for key priorities than a decentralised state.

Statebuilding is often based on a peace agreement establishing liberal-peace parameters for the emergent polity, as in Cambodia after the end of the Cold War, and it also fits into the older 'modernisation paradigm' whereby the economy, society and institutions were to be improved according to external models of progress (a literature long discredited).[46] More recently, statebuilding has been deployed where there has been no peace agreement, as in Afghanistan. The broader the consensus, the more positive the peace that may emerge, but also the more hybridity may challenge the bureaucratic rationale of statebuilding.

Authority in, and legitimacy of, the state is contested for diverse reasons: partly because of the collapse of socialism, which removed legitimacy for equality in material terms; the role of the state in the Asian crisis in the 1990s and the authoritarian states that emerged with decolonisation; the crisis of the welfare state and procedural democracy since then; alternative historical processes or regional dynamics of state formation; and the phenomenon of state collapse and fragility and the humanitarian crises this has engendered.[47] Not least, there is a major tension between the bureaucratic logic of the tension between 'rules and discretion' which illustrates the difficulties of formal statebuilding in situations where more informal political processes are common. This is contrary to the more 'scientific' expectations of external actors such as the World Bank (and related indexes on social capital, corruption, public-service quality, institutional capacity, budgets, etc.).[48] The World Bank can only deal directly with states (which it often describes as 'clients') and has in any case to make sure its resources are deployed profitably through a type of arbitrage on interest paid for the cheap money it lends out for development purposes.[49] Thus, the tension between the 'measurable' and 'buildable' state and the social, cultural and political dynamics of the population it houses is a major problem for statebuilding practices. It creates a gap from which hybridity emerges, in positive or negative form.

Statebuilding is faced with the historical weakness of states to promote positive peace either through centralised planning or a light-touch 'night-watchman state': 'a minimalist state would do no harm, but neither could it do much good'.[50] However, it is a crucial institutional part of global governance.[51]

Indexes and Intervention

The next step in the development of the rationale of statebuilding is to see the viability of states as measurable. This can be used to produce a hierarchy of states, the lowest in that hierarchy bring those that receive the capacity-building attention of other hegemonic states, donors and agencies for reasons of support, reform and, of course, regional security. This logic produces a hierarchy in which key states such as the UK and US are natural exemplars of a positive peace achieved through the establishment of a neoliberal form of state. Statebuilding endeavours to replicate these exemplars through coercion, capital, external legitimacy and leadership, as with statebuilding in Afghanistan during the 2000s.[52]

State weakness in the areas of security, crime and terrorism, measured against a liberal-peace and neoliberal-state format, is seen as a threat to international peace and security, as the events of the 2000s showed, especially in relation to states such as Afghanistan, Somalia, North Korea and Pakistan.[53] Conflict-affected states, as a 2008 US Department of Defense document made clear, are seen as a threat to the regional and international systems.[54] Such states are measured against ideal standards and qualities that can be indexed, compared and related to practices of intervention. These rationales have spawned a range of indexes, which assess various factors of state fragility, mainly underpinned by a mixture of Weberian, bureaucratic, liberal and neoliberal understandings of the state. These are often focused on territorial notions of sovereignty and core functions related to security, democratic political authority and law, as well as basic understandings of the rights and services required to maintain minimal legitimacy and to trade freely. However, they do not show any understanding of how the state emerges from society, instead seeing it as a bureaucratic and functional framework.[55] Rotberg argues that states fail when they can no longer provide 'positive political goods' in relation to these; they then lose the support of their citizens.[56] Such states are contested by warring factions and support criminality, and violence often spills across open borders,[57] as in Angola, Burundi, Sudan and many others at various points in the last twenty years. When legitimacy collapses, Weberian understandings of the weaknesses of states set against such measurements can also be seen as providing a justification for statebuilding interventions.[58] Clientelist, corrupt, patrimonial states invite such interventions, as do various understandings of why states may be weak (because they are post-colonial, neopatrimonial, resource-cursed, clientelistic, shadow states, denying human rights, engaged in ethnic cleansing, and other reasons). States are seen as failing, collapsed or predatory, neither meeting cosmopolitan standards nor providing for local, regional or global security or access to global markets and resources.

The World Bank conceptualises state fragility as resting on 'indicators of state effectiveness', including governance performance, the rule of law, governance effectiveness, corruption and human rights.[59] State fragility represents a continuum from the ideal through a variety of limitations until complete collapse is reached (such as in Somalia from 1991 to 2004). Various state-fragility indexes also reinforce externalised perspectives of what the core functions of a post-conflict state should be.[60] State fragility is the inverse of specific, often ideological forms of statehood. Though state authority and capacity as well as its relationship with society are part of this construct,[61] these approaches work on the fallacy that all states are the same and their strengths should lie in the same areas; likewise, that the liberal peace is unproblematic, as are neoliberal states, external trusteeship is necessary, and that the global North had no role in the conflict-affected state's collapse.[62]

Such a rationale drives the analysis of any conflict towards local pathologies and completely negates any broader considerations rooted in historical processes, including colonialism, global inequality, powerful strategic interests, displacement, immigration, settlement and other external forces that may have been exerted on the local population. Statebuilding is thus heavily reductionist, relying on a very narrow process to counter state-formation dynamics, just enough to maintain a semblance of order and progress. Its rationality leads to a negative hybrid peace.

The Rationale of Statebuilding

The practice of statebuilding illustrates the epistemologically centred way the West thinks about security and politics, in that what is considered 'good practice' emanates from a conceptually clear (though probably highly inaccurate) understanding of the development of the ideal state itself. It requires certain 'habits of mind'.[63] Individualism is one of these, in social settings often obviously motivated by community or group rights. Individualism is necessary for property rights, often contrary to customary or shared understandings of resources, especially in subsistence settings. Civil society is often equated with externally driven NGOs, which are normally new arrivals in a post-conflict environment and are not representative of local legitimacy or voices.[64] Security provides the rationality of the state in the first instance.

Formalism over informalism (or public over private, official over unofficial) is another deep-seated bias of statebuilding. It is often unquestionably based on a set of Anglo-Saxon legal norms, which immediately come into tension with local norms (which are often drawn from multiple influences).[65] Statebuilding requires a hierarchy in which security, good governance, development, public services and a safety net are ranged in roughly this order, running from the Washington consensus[66] to its aftermath in which priorities are selected.[67] Statebuilding assumes that local elites often reject reform in order to maintain their own power base, and that localised social and customary practices are pre-modern and therefore ought to be removed or altered. It is shorn of its historical and social context, re-established as a procedural infrastructure representing best practice and good governance via an ideological preference for a neoliberal form of state. Such modernisation legitimates itself by claiming a monopoly on representation, rights and prosperity, with any other alternatives being regarded as backward, inefficient or unjust.

Even so, the modernised state's own evolution has been varied, moving from the notion of national reconstruction after World War II, to the idea of a liberal state in the 1990s, to the neoliberal and small state of the latter part of that decade, to the realisation that small states may be equally problematic since they cannot provide security, welfare or rights. Yet there remains a general endorsement of the conceptual approach related to statebuilding and the neoliberal state over historical context. Trouillot describes this as a silencing of the past – a 'provincial universalism'.[68]

The form of state that has emerged as the focus of statebuilding is problematic from a local-scale (as opposed to elite- or international-scale) and ethical perspective, because it generally cannot engage with short-term and pressing issues, and its institutions, security and rights frameworks depend on external support. Statebuilding creates quasi-liberal states without full sovereignty.[69] This means that they are propped up by the UN in development, security, SSR/DDR and democratisation terms; the UN also provides legitimacy in the absence of local forms of recognition (at least from the UN's perspective). Donors and IFIs support this and provide resources and tutelage. Troop-contributing states provide the means for immediate and longer-term security. International markets offer opportunities for investment and economic development. Civil society is supported to a limited degree by actors most visible to the international gaze and is seen to be separate from the state, rather than constituting it. What emerges from this is a neoliberal democracy, with an embryonic civil society and a limited capacity to engage in global markets and thus dependent on internationals for basic provisions, and unable to provide public services and so again dependent on external forms of authority. The post-conflict state is held together by a material and ideological alliance between international personnel and local elites.

Statebuilding's neoliberal democracies are weak states by design. They would fail without international support, and they reflect a compromise between international and elite interests and identities, rather than those of its general population. Citizenship tends to be polarised around elite preferences, which depend for support on alliances with a range of international actors. In the architecture of a state thus failed by design, what is crucial is the capacity, ideology and professional interests of internationals and how elites mimic them, rather than public services and citizenship, a social contract or legitimacy. For this reason, the statebuilding process represents international and elite interests, lacks a social contract and so becomes authoritarian or even neocolonial in the view from beneath. Any claims of creating a positive peace dissolve into what at best is a negative hybrid peace.

This has the unintended consequence of playing into the hands of local elites: a weak civil society, property- and boundary-focused security, and a weak state give them security and control of the neoliberal state and its assets. It justifies elite control of power, enables them to maintain a legitimate place in the market, and undermines representation and rights. Trickle-down justifies their economic positions, international contacts provide them with legitimacy, and the neoliberal nature of the state allows them to share as little wealth as possible. Yet the forces of both nationalism and sovereignty allows them access to the industrial agency that the modern state represents in military and economic terms. Furthermore, the international concern with efficiency and coordination, as well as its liberal bias, allows them to argue that their own citizens are not yet ready for autonomy and to re-establish authoritarian patterns of governance. Inadvertently, internationals support the emergence of authoritarian or majoritarian, unrepresentative and unequal states (mirroring and exaggerating the dynamics now becoming apparent in many established liberal democracies). Statebuilding processes provide a range of processes and opportunities for elites to maintain their power, both at the international and national levels, as well as maintaining Westphalian notions of territorial sovereignty long thought to be outdated.

Thus, there are major differences between the neoliberal conception of the state produced by external actors, and the possibly historically, culturally, customarily and ideologically oriented polities that might emerge in local contexts. Because of the focus on the state-formation dynamics of power and security, the neoliberal version seems most appropriate according to the ideological bias of statebuilders working for major donors. Such models dominate the world's statebuilding processes, from Timor-Leste to the Balkans, but have not so far been effective in creating a positive hybrid peace.

The Local and Society

Statebuilding attempts to address local communities of different normative and value systems but it focuses on state architecture rather than direct links with those communities. Though it has effectively emerged out of the modernisation pains of European societies, and the latter's increasing need for governance to regulate wars, statebuilding has erred on the bureaucratic and technical side rather than supporting the associative and cooperative frameworks any community would entail. The local and society tend to be secondary in this process. UN agencies, such as the UNDP or the Peacebuilding Commission, engage with local communities to some degree since it is in their mandate, but such contacts are more difficult for the World Bank, which expects to work with the state and its government.[70] Internationals have tried to engage with the legitimacy of a range of informal and formal local actors, but in turn this requires that internationals have a detailed understanding of local-scale and informal political processes, which they often do not have. 'Field' missions may do better at this, but often their view of the local is limited and knowledge is also lost in transmission back to headquarters in New York or Washington.[71] This means that statebuilding is handicapped in terms of its local legitimacy.

The resultant states are not aimed at fulfilling the needs of their inhabitants, confirming their socio-historical identity or protecting their modes of interaction and organisation. Instead they respond to the ideological, security and economic objectives of dominant international and regional actors, as determined by the realist 'war makes the state' tradition of state-formation theory. Because the structural, sociological and anthropological traditions of state formation have been ignored, many post-conflict states are not constructed on the basis of local needs or identities at all.[72] Rather, they operate on the basis of maintaining a disciplinary distance between local and elite or international actors.[73] This has led to statebuilding becoming an inversion of liberal notions of the autonomy of the political subject and of the state.[74] This can be clearly seen in the role of the Office of the High Representative in Bosnia, which has the final say in domestic law and politics, or in the UN and its early 'standards before status' programme in Kosovo, and in the UN proclaiming sovereignty in Timor-Leste before independence was declared in 2002.

International actors such as the World Bank are aware of the problem of the local versus the international, the need for local legitimacy and ownership, not to mention consent. Yet there tends to be no engagement with the problem that their modernising strategies effectively dismantle what local capacity there is while the liberal state and its replacement political and economic processes are built. The World Bank may be now becoming aware of the issue of communally owned property in post-socialist or communally oriented societies, for example, but most post-conflict sites also host major developers using communal land for extractive projects with full international consent.

Statebuilding lacks an understanding of local alterity: of other ways of life; other constructions of rights; other understandings of the role of the state; different balances between society, the economy and institutions; other ideologies; contextual and environmental constraints. It appears in short to be a neocolonial project, replicating the Anglo-American version of the state and Western values as if they were indeed universally regarded as progressive. It is easy to see how such a process may give rise to a negative hybrid peace.

Jekyll or Hyde? What Is Statebuilding Creating?

The process of statebuilding has raised the question: what kind of hybrid polities or states are actually forming as a result?[75] The international perspective of a model state is driven by the Jekyll (good) and Hyde (evil)[76] nature of statebuilding and state formation. Statebuilding aims at producing a neoliberal state and a positive peace (meaning Jekyll from the perspective of its backers) in order to block the indigenous forces of state formation (Hyde). Yet if a positive peace necessarily has to draw on both local and international forms of legitimacy, it must also necessarily be hybrid. This means that international and local views of the 'good' or 'bad' state are more ambiguous, and a positive hybrid peace may have to be more closely aligned with contextual forms of legitimacy. Yet internationals have been reluctant to accept that their models may be compromised, at least until statebuilding's more recent refocusing on a 'good enough' model of state. The following empirical sketches assess the degree to which the 'failed statebuilding' design has led to a negative or positive form of hybrid peace, in a range of contemporary statebuilding examples.

Cambodia: Early Signs of Tension

One of the earliest post-Cold War democratisation missions, in Cambodia, is now one of the longest-running attempts to create a neoliberal state. There are many problematic dynamics at play here, some of which show continuities with the past, while others are a result of external strategies. Though Cambodia now has the framework of a liberal or, more precisely, neoliberal state, it also houses a predatory elite, with the population suffering from acute poverty and weak provision of democracy, human rights, resources and law.

Neoliberal reforms have also produced a predatory business environment rather than delivering employment.[77] A liberal social contract has not been achieved even though the original UN Transitional Authority in Cambodia (UNTAC) mandate aimed at the replication of the liberal state as a condition for material assistance. The Cambodian case illustrates the neoliberal statebuilding process's weaknesses, the limits of its capacity, the opportunities that it presents for predatory elites and the lack of capacity of internationals in such development (and non-Western) contexts.

The linear evolution from state weakness to state strength can have contradictory effects. Cambodia has had reasonably successful elections and has established a working government, but not in the manner international actors either expected or wanted. These undemocratic processes, and actors, have supported an authoritarian, not to mention corrupt, elite, and the democratic opposition has had to spend periods in exile. An active civil society is developing as a response, though again mainly in spaces and styles determined by internationals and the NGO community they sponsor.

A hybrid form of state exists which incorporates the components of the liberal and neoliberal peace at a level perhaps not appreciated by international actors but very strongly modified by its local context, social and power configurations, and cultural norms. However, an authoritarian dimension of governance dominates the state that has emerged. Ultimately, the focus has been on building the state rather than a contextualised social contract or citizenship. It might even be said that such a situation is in the interests of statebuilders, because rather than demanding an ethical dimension of rights and representation, as well as redistribution, the state emerges from a technocratic contest over statebuilding. Clearly, however, the state has been locally modified by both local power structures and a range of international and locally supported reform processes. The inability of the state to have a material impact on the lives of most of its citizens has undermined its local legitimacy, though at the same time it is being adapted. At best, however, a negative hybrid peace has developed. For internationals, the state is somewhere between Jekyll and Hyde: a forerunner of the 'good enough' model that was to emerge later in the context of Afghanistan. Cambodian statebuilding has significantly improved security, but it has not so far succeeded in offering social justice or gaining local legitimacy and instead has ended up supporting an authoritarian-tinged democracy.

Palestine: A State for Whom?

Developments in the occupied Palestinian territories, and the putative Palestinian state as referred to via the two-state solution framework, were perhaps an early hint of the extreme form of the statebuilding paradigm that would emerge in Iraq. Here the façade of the formal state has less to do with the preferences of international institutions or key donors such as the US or EU, and more to do with the state as a vehicle for regional order. Broader and local questions of justice and rights are secondary to this. Turner has described this as an outcome of donor collusion with the Israeli state over a peace that is effectively a thinly veiled occupation or act of neocolonialism (and perhaps even a way of preventing a 'viable' Palestinian state from emerging).[78] Here statebuilding is most obviously aimed at a negative peace from an international perspective. From a local perspective, a negative hybrid peace might be the outcome.

The state that is emerging is constrained and almost completely under the control of Israel.[79] It has no autonomy. Against the wishes of most Palestinians, it is also a heavily neoliberalised state in which many Palestinian governance and social practices are being transformed. Even though many internationals have said Palestine is ready for statehood[80] and donors have continued to fund the state-building project, the two-state solution is blocked by deadlock between the two sides over the issue of settlements. Israel's almost permanent state of emergency and its 'stratified citizenship' with respect to the status of various Palestinian groups constitute a colonial practice that maintains the State of Israel and prevents unity among Palestinians,[81] shaping a 'failed by design' statebuilding process.

The charade of statebuilding exaggerates the (extremely constrained) autonomy and limited role of the state, particularly in terms of providing resources, public services and even, in this case, security. The Palestinian state appears to internationals in a 'Hyde' persona even though it might be more accurately characterised as an extension of the Israeli security apparatus; and the attempt to connect it with global markets has failed. Its sovereignty is contingent,[82] and its elites and populations are purposefully fragmented so that they have to rely on reduced local resources and capacities.

If there is a lesson to be learned about statebuilding from this case, it has to do with pacification, self-sufficiency and a fragmented agency that does not conform to the liberal notion of statehood. This approach to statebuilding has only limited concern with international norms, or the rationalities of administration, law or local legitimacy. Though statebuilders preach inclusive states, they practise exclusive statebuilding almost as if the aim were to produce a nineteenth-century European nationalist state. Statebuilding has been unconcerned with what Palestinians want in material, everyday terms, is not based on consent and has attempted to undermine their own national liberation movement (with only limited success, however).[83] It is indicative of the way statebuilding is being used to produce very limited, quasi-sovereign, materially helpless states, which mainly contribute to regional stability by supporting the existing hierarchy, often by reproducing small ethno-national units. This form of statebuilding creates both a negative peace at the regional level and a negative hybrid peace internally. It looks much more like Hyde than Jekyll.

Ethnic Polarisation through Statebuilding in Bosnia-Herzegovina and Kosovo

The collapse of Yugoslavia was related to the failing balances of its political system and the weakness of its mixed economy, which had been instrumental in sharing sovereignty and providing social and economic protection to maintain order.[84] In another example of the limitations of statebuilding, Bosnia-Herzegovina appears to have been becoming more, not less, ethnically polarised since Dayton, with increasing undercurrents of separatist political agendas. The state and the statebuilding process have been a vehicle for retrogressive ethnic polarisation not seen in the decades before the war in the 1990s. The government is perceived by internationals to be weak and constantly deadlocked. Local politicians have deferred difficult decisions to internationals because they are unwilling to make any concessions on their positions. The Serb entity (Republika Srpska) has continued its separatist agendas, while Croat parties threaten to do the same. As a result, Bosnia-Herzegovina is dependent on the UN, Organization for Security and Co-operation in Europe (OSCE), NATO and the EU.[85] There has been a growing tendency on the part of local actors to opt out of the liberal peacebuilding process. The root causes of the conflict remain unresolved, and there is a fragile socio-economic and security environment. The usual mix of power-seeking rather than sharing, nationalism, predatory elites, poverty and cultural obstacles prevails over the liberal project. The resources of the state have tended to be exploited by nationalist politicians to consolidate their power rather than to reconcile communities or deal with everyday problems.

Ultimately, the Dayton Agreement of 1995 has maintained some aspects of the conflict it sought to bring to an end because it was driven by a mainstream state-formation understanding of a power struggle between ethnic groups. Its framework mitigated this power struggle but also maintained it, and the model of state it has supplied – the neoliberal one – has been unable to induce pluralism in either identity or material terms. Indeed, statebuilding has dismantled many of the protections that stabilised the pre-war society. Statebuilding has at best promoted a negative hybrid peace, though, given the trusteeship role of the Office of the High Representative, it is doubtful that internationals were keen on allowing for much hybridity at all. At best, a mainstream state-formation perspective means that statebuilding has been based upon a stereotype of populist ethnic identity and its supposed territorialism.

In the case of Kosovo, the state has been framed by ethnic separatism rather than pluralism, and even civil society is relatively segregated.[86] Political elites have become adept at mobilising peaceful and violent resistance, as well as the utilisation of neopatrimonial clan networks, which have ultimately coopted formal institutions; in this case local agency sees the state as its vehicle. A quasi-state, in which parallel structures and informal systems compete in distributing resources, perpetuates ethnic inequalities. It does so while providing administration and liberal politics. Other issues, including those relating to self-determination, are assuaged. This is a negative version of a hybrid peace, in which the limitations of international intervention and statebuilding combine with local attempts to build a viable state and prevent a continuation of historical Serb domination of the Kosovo Albanian community. For example, though the state has accrued international recognition and adopted many liberal norms as well as neoliberalism, women exercise only limited property rights.

Some critics have claimed that Kosovo represents a 'hybrid political-criminal' enterprise, which undermines the international statebuilding mission.[87] Even so, it has a very high degree of local legitimacy among Kosovo Albanians. The state's widespread international recognition also suggests significant legitimacy. What can be agreed upon is that its form, function and purpose are quite different from what was imagined during the heyday of the UN's Interim Administration Mission in Kosovo (UNMIK). The declaration of statehood in 2008, with strong support from the US, UK and other states, became the goal of the Kosovo Albanian community during the 'standards before status' period, leading to the knock-on effect of further secession becoming the potential goal of the Serb community's political strategy. Yet this dynamic contravenes the basic pluralist and power-sharing expectations inherent in the liberal state, while the usual problems relating to international trusteeship, ethnicised politics and high unemployment remain. The latter issues were deemed comparatively insignificant in the face of what had become a race for sovereignty and recognition. Statebuilding in Kosovo has essentially become a race for power and statehood and has resulted in the marginalisation of other internal identity groups and their agendas.[88] Kosovo Albanian officials and actors took the state-in-waiting they were handed inadvertently by internationals and used it to develop their own claims for sovereignty. Though this process has led to a negative hybrid peace, if an agreement can be made with the Serb community, and if issues related to social justice – in particular, employment – can be mitigated, a more positive form of hybrid peace is possible.

Liberal politics in the region rest upon the defence rather than the reform of mutually exclusive identities and institutions within which 'liberalism' is acted out in connection with international, rather than local, actors. Internationals have ignored local identity (except as an ethnic category), religions, pre-existing ideology (that is, socialism) and the historical forces that have shaped the polity as well as the relationship between society and the state.

Custom and a Hybrid State in Timor-Leste

In Timor-Leste it was clear that self-determination, self-government and statehood were widely desired long before independence. Even under Indonesian occupation, a high degree of decentralised governance was present.[89] A smooth progression towards statehood appeared to be confirmed for the new state of Timor-Leste in May 2002. As soon became clear, however, building the infrastructure of a state was not enough to contain violence related to basic problems with respect to political competition, the control of institutions such as the army and police, and unemployment and poverty. The local had been excluded from the statebuilding project, meaning it lacked legitimacy – especially with the growing monopoly of power by one key political party (the Revolutionary Front for an Independent East Timor – FRETILIN) which formed the government from independence until 2007. Of course, these factors undermined the social contract that the liberal state is supposed to be based upon, in a context where protest, resistance and violence have often been resorted to for very specific liberation goals.

It was belatedly recognised by the UN after the violence of early 2006 that the 'underlying causes' of the crisis were 'political and institutional',[90] and it soon transpired that this problem referred not to problems of institutional effectiveness, but to the character, role and objectives of those institutions. In essence, this was a recognition that the state was failed by design, and that it needed to play a more active role within the historical, structural and social context in which it was based. Two near-collapses of the state soon after independence illustrated that a negative hybrid peace was not just a problem in the intellectual terms provided by aspirations for social justice, but that its unsustainability had concrete consequences for human life.

Political and institutional reform failed to address actual underlying causes such as poverty, deprivation and long-term unemployment, as well as identity issues or the actual connection of the state to the epistemology of the local, or to the world-view of Timorese communities. The new state has had minimal impact on everyday life, and though it has reduced violence, it has not eradicated it. After the violence of 2006, in which the state nearly collapsed, President Ramos-Horta requested that the UN return and provide a more long-term approach to peace and development, but not via a new trusteeship.[91] A more contextualised approach was required. In the context of the more cooperative approach that has been taken with internationals since, any stability can be attributed as much to the more traditional patterns of social power and support systems that exist at the local level as it can be to the state itself. Indeed, the state has had to reshape itself to connect more with local problems, especially material ones, local identities and custom. The state is 'yet to come', according to much of the population.[92] The various international actors have also had to work within hybrid frameworks to a greater extent than they are perhaps comfortable with. All of these changes to the project of statebuilding can be encapsulated by the recent election of a new president who is far more interested in the potential for an indigenous form of state, locally determined (including through language), while also internationally embedded.[93] A more positive form of hybrid peace is now possible if identity and needs issues can be addressed in the broader regional and international context.

Conflicting Foundations for the State in Afghanistan

Afghanistan is one of the most developed examples of contemporary neoliberal statebuilding, where the process is aimed at 'constructing sovereignty for security'.[94] This has provided the space needed for donors to move in and build institutions, according to a 'robust' mandate (meaning coercive external capacity). UN legitimacy has been important in improving domestic legitimacy. Aid has been channelled through the government to support the development of the state's capacities while trying to avoid dependency and patronage structures,[95] and it has been used by internationals to 'buy loyalties' and local compliance with external policies.[96] The 'light footprint' approach that marked the early part of the statebuilding process indicated that a 'good enough', negative peace was expected by internationals, even if a hybrid version was not.

The fact that the Taliban were excluded from the peace process is now widely understood to have been a mistake (as is the reluctance to engage with the 'creeping invasion from Pakistan').[97] This meant that statebuilding was exclusionary, with little attempt to bring about a reconciliation. Most of the population have had little contact with the statebuilding process, though they may have had more contact with its military components. As such, the state continues to be regarded as predatory, and foreign intervention as self-interested.[98]

Indeed, there is little local legitimacy for the emerging Afghan state, and little sense of ownership or sustainability. It is dependent on foreign capital and knowledge, it is authoritarian, lacks a broad reach, and is therefore not very representative.[99] Statebuilding did not engage with the existing order based upon patron–client relations and eldership, other than to try to disrupt them.[100] In response, a shadow state has emerged which is controlled by informal power structures and networks, representing a partial and superficial liberal-peace and neoliberal-state reform process.[101] The police and army are externally dependent, people are confused about competing Islamic and international, liberal and utilitarian, criteria for legitimacy, there is a lack of a social contract and the state cannot provide basic public services.[102] The latter situation has arisen partly because it does not have the means in terms of tax revenues but also because the neoliberal model of statebuilding does not envisage the state providing such services. Furthermore, the failure to establish the rule of law means that while pre-existing dispute mechanisms are the basis of much of peaceful politics, the centralisation of state power around a presidential system has unfortunately supported neopatrimonialism.[103]

An international control-versus-local ownership dynamic has emerged in which various parts of the state have been captured by different local and international networks. Historical sources of legitimacy for the state (Islam and nationalism) have not resolved their contradictions in this process of externalised statebuilding, especially relating to the place of Islamic law and the inclusion of the Taliban in any emerging polity. Yet, in opposition to the neoliberal model of statebuilding, Islamic political thought has long recognised the role of the state in contributing to public welfare as well as to security.[104] Thus, while the state itself has legitimacy among the people, its political framework and government are more problematic. Government and its institutions are used corruptly, meaning any attempt to extend the government into society risks rejection or insurgency,[105] partly because of the failure of the state and the international community to engage with the realities of everyday life.

Yet many people do aspire to a modern state, just as some aspire to a theocracy. Resolving this tension was partly the aim of the Quick

Impact Projects, as well as state institutions such as the Provincial Councils. The statebuilding project and its opposite numbers – local power holders and seekers – are locked in an escalating spiral of violence, to which decentralised and local governance seems a possible answer. Contradictorily, centralisation is also required if a viable modern state is to come into existence. This paradox means that statebuilding produces additional local tensions rather than resolving old ones.

A myriad of unofficial agreements have attempted to mitigate such gaps. These give a viable façade to statebuilding,[106] creating a virtual peace, while local dysfunctional dynamics feed the conflict and internationals continue to construct their unsuitable blueprint state. Much of what has been positive in terms of stabilisation has arisen at the local and social level rather than through the state. Yet internationals have sought to build a 'good state' and regard local involvement as corrupting its purpose, risking the formation of a state that is 'Hyde' in nature. Certainly, there are ongoing hybrid forms of politics in this encounter between intervention and state formation, but it would be charitable to describe this as approximating to a situation of negative hybrid peace.

Conclusion

What emerges from statebuilding's focus on the hardware of the neoliberal state as a response to processes of state formation is a negative and often hybrid peace. Thus, the statebuilding frameworks that have emerged from Cambodia to Afghanistan aim at a negative peace, by virtue of their assumption that state formation is a violence process, but they also represent the development of a hybrid political order. The domestic and the international are blurred, with strategic interests, power and structure interact. This mirrors the 'mediated state' argument of Menkhaus,[107] where state and non-state authorities encounter each other over matters of security, governance, development, welfare, rights and identity. Krasner's 'shared sovereignty' concepts of local ownership and participation likewise began to emerge in a post-liberal critique of statebuilding.[108] Hybrid forms of state and peace may offer space for civil society and local-local actors to mobilise, but they may also mask the continuation of old inequalities and hierarchies.[109] However, the state appears to be stranded between international prescriptions, elite domination, and local preferences and needs. Furthermore, where improvements occur, it is often in the context of capital city-states, focused mainly on the capital, having little impact beyond key urban centres.

From the subject's perspective, from Kosovo to Timor-Leste, it is their lack of autonomy from elites and internationals that prevents them from designing their own state; imposing a design that is *a priori* 'failed', dominated by external power, has become problematic. A negative hybrid peace has normally been the result because of a mismatch in identity, institutions, law, norms and material requirements. This has caused a change in the approach of the main statebuilding actors. Attention has turned to social context, informal authority and practices, local ownership, 'institutions taking root', connecting governance with peace and a social contract or compact, and being recognised as legitimate in local contexts.[110] There is also a growing realisation that inequality and the domination of capital flows and material resources by a fixed elite is not conducive to democracy, law, development or justice.[111] This shows an attempt to move towards a more locally legitimate and 'resilient' version, which also recognises custom, tradition and locally legitimate forms of authority, and merges them into a modern state that is legitimate, durable and resilient. This represents a step forward, but it still deploys the somewhat neocolonial language of equating the international with modernity, power and norms, and the local with tradition, custom and informality. State–society relations have made an appearance in World Bank literature as a necessary component of a legitimate and just state and model of development – but, of course, due to its bias towards states on a political level and markets on an intellectual level, states and globalisation are still its starting point.[112] However, community-based programmes for security and service delivery are a step forward as long as these are planned locally. The experience of community policing in many post-conflict examples, or programmes such the Afghanistan National Solidarity programme, suggests progress, though dilemmas associated with a desire for state control and a simultaneous lack of capacity continue. The increasing use of job-creation programmes and the emergence of women's organisations in places such as Burundi, Sierra Leone and Liberia are also positive developments.

Nevertheless, power relations dictate how the internationally supported state tries to amalgamate with local organisations, as with the Community Development Councils in Afghanistan, the local development councils initiated by the UNDP in Cambodia and the decentralised government in Rwanda. What passes for decentralisation, however, is often little more than a way for internationals and the state to try to govern the local.[113] What is more, many internationals see the challenge as being to make 'domestic expectations fit with the needs and realities of assistance on the ground'.[114] The idea that communities will accept their relative deprivation in national and international terms is indicative of the weakness of the statebuilding paradigm, which is effectively an attempt to mitigate but embed global and national hierarchies, thus minimising the need to change the international status quo, while pushing for local reforms. The recourse to local agency signifies from this perspective 'self-help' rather than assistance with an emancipatory peace. The focus on the state creates significant internal competition over who controls the state, how and in whose interest, despite international norms. It also blocks cross-border and internal pluralism. This is why the UNDP, for example, has returned to a discussion of the liberal social contract as essential for the legitimacy of the state.[115] Even though it talks of a context-sensitive approach, the state it envisages is somewhere between a social democracy focused on a narrow range of public services, law, rights and governance, and a neoliberal state where an efficient, small state enables self-help or 'resilience'.[116] Of course, the alternative, Western state model also has weaknesses: social democracies dependent on capitalism are vulnerable to external shocks that may undermine their ability to mitigate internal tensions, as capitalism's recent crises have shown. It also requires an enlightened 'vanguard' group that is able to implement such a policy (something the donor community might be expected to undertake).

There is little acknowledgement that the state itself may not be perceived positively in local contexts or be part of an 'imagined community'. Context-sensitivity, resilience and engaging with the marginalised remain within the framework of a liberal polity. Policymakers have tried to respond, from the early attempt of the IMF and World Bank to bring in the concepts of 'local ownership' and 'participation', which have since been modified to 'national ownership', or to OECD-DAC attempts to engage with context as the starting point for statebuilding. This turn to ownership heralded an increasing concern that most interventionary practices did not engage with local sources of legitimacy or carry political will and capacity. It rested on a quantitative approach to evaluation (that is, in terms of a range of indicators, from productivity, GNP and per-capita income to life expectancy) and therefore missed out on the complex social and political factors that create a sense of order and stability. A broader understanding of the 'practices of the state',[117] denoting the diversity of actors, processes and relationships according to ranges of power, norms, codes and identities, would be a better approach. This is something that Hamid Karzai has argued in the context of Afghanistan, where 'liberation' turned to domination and a lack of respect for local practices and identities.[118] He developed his 'big tent' strategy to try to be inclusive of difficult actors such as the Taliban and a range of factions in the state itself. However, this attempt at creating a state inclusive of powerful actors has led to its cooptation by warlords and a continuing Taliban rebellion, underlining the weaknesses of statebuilding as an elite practice that is supposed to trickle down. Karzai argues that liberal democracy can be achieved only if it respects local identity, religion, tradition and society.[119] The social contract is therefore really an endorsement of international agencies' ideal state on paper and 'good enough' outcome in practice, rather than offering any sense of the state's contingent nature, and the way it emerges from a mixture of interests, authority, legitimacy, and roots in historical and social institutions.[120] As opposed to the replication of Northern models with their Jekyll and Hyde tension, local political processes need to take a prior role so that the state is based on accommodation rather than governmentality and direct or structural forms of power.

Statebuilding ironically seeks to create 'open-access societies' and in doing so endeavours to exclude the local, historical architectures of the state so that underdevelopment, hiearchy, centralised power, patrimonialism and conflict-proneness are replaced.[121] Legitimacy is provided by the framework for liberty in political and economic life, as well as the security, institutions and law, that the state creates. Economic liberty is supposed to provide individuals with the freedom to support themselves materially, providing their legal human rights with substance. Yet statebuilding also relies on traditional elites because it tries to exercise governmentality over local structural power holders. These tend to occupy the state, using it for their own purposes. Internationals overlook the subaltern power that may be wielded when society loses faith in institutions, the state or the capacity of internationals to connect with them.

The failure of such statebuilding approaches often arises because the 'imported state' is top-down and externalised, fails to penetrate local society, and meets communitarian forms of resistance. Such 'trusteeship' states are incompatible with democracy and pluralist understandings of rights, and indeed tend not to develop any significant capacity under international tutelage, as shown by the cases of Afghanistan and Iraq.[122] Furthermore, '[f]ar from weakening the political elite, neoliberalism guarantees its safety against the aftershocks the state and its personnel would feel from economic collapse'[123] caused by structural adjustment-style policies. Indeed, these states only have any substance when viewed from their exterior, meaning local agency has to formulate itself around essential tasks, despite the state rather than through it, even when it comes to confronting structural or governmental power.[124] Local populations bear the brunt of statebuilding's failings. They often begin to point to their need to deal with such problems and, through local and extra-state associative networks, develop new modes of political participation. This points to the need to reduce the gap between the state and its subjects, so the state is representative of a consensus among the population. Yet it also points to the dilemma posed by the neoliberal state that has emerged from the attempt to merge power-driven understandings of state formation and liberal approaches to statebuilding. It cannot make representation or human rights concrete because it has limited material redistributive functions, and so reverts to territorial sovereignty as a default setting, making it at best a political anachronism relating to elite power rather than society and legitimacy.

A situation can emerge like that in Sierra Leone, where the military and police have been reformed, government has been decentralised, elections have been successfully held, but living conditions for ordinary people are unchanged.[125] As in Liberia, many state institutions are controlled by external actors, producing a 'disorderly order' under trusteeship.[126] This confirms the flawed logic that local legitimacy is not required for any intervention or subsequent state or peacebuilding mission. Local agency is only allowed to be autonomous after it has been constrained by external governmentality embedded in the new state. Statebuilding represents an extension of a conservative version of the liberal peace,[127] lacking emancipatory content and capability. 'Good enough' outcomes are achieved when internationals feel regional security and basic domestic rights are secured.

This means that the state is all but meaningless to its citizens, except perhaps as a national symbol, a system of governance based upon mainly alien forms of rights and law, and a way of organising institutions, markets and security that may or may not affect them. The issue is whether the state incorporates its subjects or vice versa, as a positive hybrid version would imply.[128] People's experience of citizenship in a modern state is very limited, far more so than their everyday experience of custom and law, local institutions and informal modes of governance. Increasingly, policymakers recognise the need for redistribution to even out serious inequality, but this is normally not the function of taxation. Internationals have become concerned with the way aid may undermine the government's capacity and ownership, so have recently focused on budgetary support for the formal state by channelling aid through the government. This is supposed to prevent parallel institutions from emerging and undermining the state's legitimacy,[129] but given that the latter refers to external legitimacy, a negative hybrid peace tends to ensue. Indeed, it might also be argued that parallel institutions are required to maintain state legitimacy from a local perspective, enabling a more positive version of a hybrid peace.

Statebuilding has become focused on security, institutional design and bureaucratic matters, which is hardly going to satisfy post-conflict societies, which require contextual legitimacy and material capacity. The state is supposed to represent its society's ontological position, to maintain order for it as well as being a source of order.[130] The state is widely distrusted from this perspective, and is seen as being dominated by elite or conservative interests, or by those of global power.[131]

Thus, many emergent 'states' are failed by design. They have varying combinations of declarative and constitutive qualities: none meets the ideals of either tradition of sovereignty but is reinventing politics through a mixture of agencies. So far, statebuilding has produced few high-capacity but undemocratic states, some low-capacity and undemocratic states, no high-capacity and democratic states, and many low-capacity and democratic states, where insecurity and participation are both high.[132] Normally, they all have full recognition, though in some cases, such as Kosovo, this is not the case. From the perspective of inhabitants, statebuilding reinforces their subject status, exposing them to continuities of elite power, external trusteeship-style forms of authority and the forces of globalisation. Subject status, as Thoreau noted long ago, means that the 'right of revolution of all men' has not been placated and the state coming into being is not legitimate. The state being built is now an international assemblage,[133] a performance of state construction, which has little to do with its subjects' particularities. Statebuilding is often contradictorily both Jekyll and Hyde when viewed from beneath or outside; more often it follows accumulated historical interests and an international system formed in favour of its hegemons. Patterns of exclusion from the local to the global indicate at best that a negative hybrid peace is emerging. As internationals recognise such unintended consequences of their intervention, their attention turns to how to exit without embarrassment, as with the long-planned departure from Afghanistan.

III

Liberal Peacebuilding

'[B]y stimulating the importation of Western models into societies in the South, it [statebuilding] reveals its own inadequacy; by inciting peripheral societies to adapt, it raises hope of innovation that may very well be false; by rushing the process of world unification, it encourages the rebirth and affirmation of individual characteristics; by endowing the international order with a centre of power more structured than ever, it tends to intensify conflict. By seeking to bring historical development to an end, it suddenly launches History in varied and contradictory directions.'[1]

Introduction

STATE FORMATION FOCUSES on violent indigenous processes that lead to the creation of a state that represents powerful interests often influenced by regional factors. Statebuilding mainly offers a modernisation-oriented response to these dynamics in the context of the construction of the neoliberal state via externalised strategies of intervention and conditionality. Thus, problems with local autonomy and local legitimacy soon arise. State formation represents liberal peace as being constantly threatened by local conflicts, statebuilding plays a disciplinary role in countering them via the development of a neoliberal state, and peacebuilding provides a liberal normative framework in which the individual is positioned as a citizen with a range of rights and protections. If conflict is driven by a series of asymmetries from the local to the global, then state formation exploits those same asymmetries by exercising direct and structural power. Statebuilding and peacebuilding mitigate conflict through mainly governmental power. Peacebuilding represents a broader normative framework in which statebuilding is nested in an attempt to advance both state and international legitimacy, and justice.

The liberal-peace project developed from the theories of the Abbé de St-Pierre, Kant, Penn and others, and from the early campaigns against slavery and for social welfare, enfranchisement and disarmament. It has moved from theory into practice, exemplified in a number of democratic revolutions, national and transnational campaigns on key liberal issues: the development of a liberal social contract and liberal state institutions, civil society and the redistribution of wealth, individualism and political autonomy. It eventually became an ideal held by key Western states (specifically the US and UK) built into constitutional arrangements, domestic law, and embryonic forms of international law and organisation, taken by some optimists to be early signs of world government or world federation. Liberal peacebuilding, as it has come to be known, aims at a positive peace by virtue of universal norms guiding representation and rights. Its universal claims indicate that hybrid forms of peace are probably undesirable.

In the light of the discussions in the previous chapters about the way state-formation theory has influenced statebuilding in a range of cases from Cambodia to Afghanistan, this chapter briefly explores the tension between liberal peacebuilding's attempt to offer a positive peace and its encounters with its recipients. It argues, referring to a range of critical themes and empirical examples, that these have indeed tended to lead to a hybrid form emerging (because of subtle resistance), often also of a negative type.

The Development of Peacebuilding

To deal with the potential lack of local-scale consent, and therefore socio-political legitimacy for external intervention, peacebuilding was originally theorised in the peace-research literature as a grassroots, bottom-up process in which a local consensus led to a positive peace (in liberal terms, but also within a social-justice framework).[2] As the concept evolved, it came to represent a convergence between the agendas of peace research, conflict resolution, conflict management approaches, and development and liberalisation debates.[3] Peacebuilding is a reflection of Rousseau's more positive understanding of a social contract in which society is interdependent, as opposed to Hobbes's negative version in which it is based upon little more than fear.[4] Peacebuilding is, however, strongly influenced by the 'dominant ideology' of the West. It reflects an attempt to represent the 'peoples' the UN Charter originally spoke of in the new world order that emerged after the end of the Cold War. Significantly, it has responded to accusations of racial and normative bias towards a specifically Western and Northern set of preferences by claiming to be universal in a normative sense. Its claim to represent the peoples of the world and their rights and needs, rather than the interests of the state, is an important part of this attempt to capture legitimacy.

In practice, through the UN system it has also had to bring together conflicting political interests in the UN Security Council, which has often led to mandates too broad to implement, too narrow to address the conflict properly or too vague to guide a mission. However, a convergence of norms and interests after the end of the Cold War – a peacebuilding consensus – culminated in the post-Cold War liberal peacebuilding project. This was a response to post-Cold War conflicts, many of which revolved around collapsed or fragile states (meaning any non-liberal state that was subject to conflict). It required the development of more ambitious forms of peacekeeping, which evolved rapidly from multidimensional peacekeeping (via integrated missions) to peacebuilding and now statebuilding. At first, it relied on the consent of local actors, and later, on occasion, without local consent. As a result, the demands on the UN and its supporting actors multiplied and diversified enormously during this period.[5]

Liberal-peacebuilding policy debates focus on security, confidence-building, peace dividends and national capacity[6] as an organising framework, structured by the UN Department of Peacekeeping Operations (UNDPKO), Department of Political Affairs, the UN Development Programme UNDP and the UN Peacebuilding Commission.[7] The peace architecture that has emerged with liberal peacebuilding includes human rights, development, reconstruction, gender, humanitarian assistance, international organisations (IOs), agencies, IFIs, NGOs and non-state actors. A broad definition of peacebuilding has been adopted, mirroring the conceptual pressure the concept of human security has provided in the UN system over the last twenty years. It is supported by various funds such as the World Bank State and Peacebuilding Fund, the UNDP Crisis Prevention and Recovery Trust Fund and the European Commission Instrument for Stability. While needs and identity are generally seen as secondary, democracy and human rights are central to peacebuilding (as they were in Cambodia or El Salvador in the early 1990s), as are the state, civil society and local ownership.

Nevertheless, the state is the entry point for any donor or UN peacebuilding activity. Liberal peacebuilding has rarely focused on the formation of political entities other than states, though it has many supporters who focus on its internationalist and normative side (the international organisation of peace, security, development, human rights, democracy and a rule of law). However, it needs a state to support these normative frameworks in the absence of regional or global actors capable of maintaining such regimes. Peacebuilding thus cannot address local dynamics without equating the local with the national.[8] There is a general fear of undermining the authority of the state given that it remains a basic institutional building block of the international system.[9] Yet, to a certain extent, liberal peacebuilding also contradicts autonomy, political self-determination and difference in the interests of a common peace. In the UN system, the term 'peacebuilding' is generally preferred because there are concerns that statebuilding (and the associated state-fragility or state-failure discourses) is widely perceived to be an attempt to override the norms of sovereignty and non-intervention (as the recent cases of Afghanistan and Iraq would suggest).[10] 'New donors', Brazil, Russia, India, China, and South Africa (the BRICS, and more specifically, India, Brazil, and South Africa – IBSA) and post-colonial states are also sensitive about this danger.

In keeping with its international-development frameworks, peacebuilding has become dependent on universal blueprints – effectively, standard operating procedures. It often has little access to the knowledge required to build peace in the political, social, cultural and economic context of non-Western and developing communities in the global South. Enclosing the liberal peace in the contemporary neoliberal and small-state model has exacerbated such problems, meaning the state has been the site of marketised politics and institutions, reflecting the power dimensions of state-formation arguments rather than the emancipatory goals of peace. Social and anthropological state-formation debates have influenced the development of peacebuilding, however, and there has been some recognition that social forms of democracy have historically been more suited to post-conflict environments (as long as an external actor is capable of supporting it financially, as with the US's Marshall Plan strategy after World War II). Peacebuilding has generally been more sensitive to difference, in theory at least, than statebuilding.

It rests upon a northern consensus about the liberal peace (mainly in the eyes of the West but followed by many others) and has gradually linked peace processes with a somewhat contradictory search for a progressive form of politics and a neoliberal state. This evolution was a relatively quick process, starting with the role of the UN, in particular in Cambodia, Namibia and El Salvador, around the end of the Cold War and soon after, and rapidly developed via international trusteeships in Bosnia, Kosovo, Sierra Leone and Timor-Leste into a statebuilding project. It later provided part of the justification for the UK and US invasion of Iraq and Afghanistan.[11] It grapples in classical liberal fashion with the idea that interventionism is sometimes necessary to uphold the conceptual integrity of liberalism and international law. One of the newer UN instruments – the Responsibility to Protect Doctrine – developed to maintain the discourse of human rights versus sovereignty in this manner. This approach has meant that energies and resources were focused on building the shell of the liberal state, into which it was hoped local politics, society and economics would move wholesale. Liberal peacebuilding has become more all-encompassing and sophisticated, and also more 'donor-driven', initially more confident of its own legitimacy and less concerned about local partners' particularities and now far less confident.

Legitimacy is a crucial concept in a more normative way for peacebuilding than it is for statebuilding, where it is understood juridically. For peacebuilding, it emerges from international liberal principles, accepted rules, custom, conventions and associated standards as commonly understood by citizens as a socio-historical legacy in a Western context.[12] Authority is understood as both local (in Weberian terms, traditional, charismatic and legal) and wide-ranging, but international authority in the expansive range of areas that liberal peacebuilding covers (legal, normative and technical) is taken to be pre-eminent.

Liberal peacebuilding has been applied in a wide array of contexts: Eastern Slavonia, Timor-Leste, Kosovo, Bosnia, Cambodia, Liberia, Afghanistan and many others. Its universal international political and normative framework is taken to command automatic and a priori consent at local, state and international levels, marginalising tricky questions about sovereignty, autonomy, the right of non-intervention, and the need for local political actors and institutions to create social, economic and political systems that reflect their history, society and specific needs. Even so, it aims to transform local political structures into a democratic and human rights oriented framework (framed by notions of good governance)[13] with a legal and enforcement capacity, which is both internationally and locally legitimate. Authority is vested in global liberal governance, international law and norms that in a top-down manner guide state governments in their relationships with neighbours and their own citizens.

Such thinking connects to a range of debates whereby modernisation theory has been replaced with a developmental approach based on liberal and democratic state parameters.[14] In El Salvador, early on in this experiment in 1992, for instance, it was recognised that human development, poverty reduction and addressing the root causes of conflict were crucial to peace.[15] Nevertheless, these in turn were secondary to security and the creation of state institutions. This balance has been captured in a range of policy documents and associated doctrines, including the UN secretary-general's report *Aftermath of Conflict*.[16]

Liberal peacebuilding has achieved some progress in practice, including demilitarisation and a decline of violence in both interstate and domestic environments, and the delivery of emergency humanitarian assistance. There is widespread acceptance of democracy, human rights, gender equality and the need for development in a state framework, though there is limited acceptance of international authority over the state. Institutional and government capacity has been supported or developed, elections have been held, civil society has been supported and popular participation enhanced, technical assistance provided, along with financial resources and political support for liberal institution-building, and justice systems have developed. Some progress in development has also been achieved, though this has often been in a patchwork manner, limited to areas in and around the capitals: this relates to the emergence of post-conflict city-states. These improvements may well provide the basis for long-term economic, political and social improvement.[17] The question is whether the liberal peace that this approach offers would be seen as emancipatory by its recipients, or whether it is more likely to lead to a negative or positive hybrid form.

What Type of Peace Does Liberal Peacebuilding Produce?

Liberal peacebuilding has, over the twenty years since it first began to emerge (for example, in the Guatemalan peace process),[18] gathered around it a vast number of international personnel and resources, as well as institutional expertise, in more than thirty peace operations.[19] It is an exercise in a significant amount of governmental power. Its encounter with conflict-affected societies has not been straightforward, however. So far its record has been mixed: it has often resulted in authoritarian regimes despite the best of intentions.[20]

Many tensions have arisen because liberal peacebuilding is inconsistent in its design, its support of the state and its relationship with local counterparts, and it is insufficiently well supported by international actors. Deficiencies have arisen, according to some assessments, because local actors are given too much say and thus insert their illiberalism into the process of peacebuilding (often by capturing the newly installed democratic process).[21] Alternatively, they are given too little say, thus undermining the legitimacy of the peace. Legitimate authority, power, norms and customs, both local and international, vie with each other in any conflict-affected environment.

Many of the concepts utilised and developed as a result challenge dominant frameworks of IR. Structural violence and the notions of negative and positive peace[22] illustrate the deficiency of realism and liberalism in understanding the extent of violence and its indirect impacts. The notion that transnational networks make up much of international relations, and that within this context security was based upon interdependence and 'humans',[23] has challenged key concepts such as the hierarchical balance of power, which reordered states as the key actors in IR. The Burtonian presentation of a set of basic socio-biological human needs[24] as navigation points for policy gave agency to individuals and implied that a general peace was not idealistic, and, as Azar added,[25] would rest upon the satisfaction of the needs of individuals in their social context. This provided an important avenue through which peace could be defined in terms of an absence of structural violence and a win-win situation for all concerned actors.[26] Peacebuilding, as originally understood as a grassroots activity, implied a hybrid form of peace, in that local and liberal values would merge.[27] However, it was heavily imbued with an underlying assumption that a liberal peace should be its goal, this being part of emerging thinking about human needs, human security and human rights, and democratisation thinking, along with a concern with social justice. Consequently, liberal peacebuilding later appeared to point towards a positive peace (but definitely not a hybrid peace) because it was mainly a top-down process, resting, therefore, on external norms, values and expertise.[28]

The positive aspects of this approach represent the most advanced Western and global consensus on peace. It has had some success in reducing violence and building compliance with liberal norms and institutions, and is derived from very significant expressions of collective human social agency (though principally understood from a Western, individualist and rational perspective). This agency is aimed at liberating the individual from slavery, poverty, discrimination and inequality, and situating his or her inalienable rights in the guaranteed legal, political and economic context of a state and international system designed to make these eternal and concrete. It has an emancipatory intent reflective of human agency. It harnesses the crucial and much-needed capacity of the UN, keeps alive dreams of liberal internationalism, and offers post-conflict citizens democracy, human rights, law and markets. Yet there have been few outright successes to speak of. Of course, this depends on how success is defined. If success is interpreted as not relapsing into violence, then the data shows that about half the states remain stable five years after the end of a conflict.[29] If it depends on providing citizens with a significant prospect of better lives in a progressive political framework, however, the picture is much worse.

Consequently, peacebuilding is torn between two versions of liberalism. The conservative version focuses on the state as the vehicle of security and regulation, underpinned by territorial sovereignty.[30] El Salvador provides one of the earliest examples of this approach: in

1992, the liberal-peace framework served as the basis for its peace agreement, called locally a 'negotiated revolution', which the UN and World Bank subsequently helped implement. By the 2000s, El Salvador was being cited in US policy circles as a statebuilding model for Iraq.[31] However, the Peace Accords and the subsequent peace-building process did not touch upon structural, social or economic issues, and, more recently, neoliberal policies have undermined any broader peace dividend (beyond the immediate improvement in security) for the general population. Inequality has actually worsened since the peace agreements, though poverty has generally been reduced.[32]

Such failings are set into relief by a second version of liberalism, which offers a more socially oriented and critical perspective of peacebuilding as an emancipatory and empathetic activity, more concerned with a sophisticated order of justice and equity in an everyday societal context (although this approach is still centred around Northern epistemology).[33] This more expansive version of peacebuilding represents a multilevel approach, attempting to incorporate the local, state and regional aspects. It has also become multidimensional, bringing together a wide range of actors who are able to deal with a broad range of conflict issues and dynamics.

This approach has influenced the (albeit restricted) development of the UN Peacebuilding Commission (PBC), which came about partly as a result of pressure from non-aligned countries. Though it offers a meta-narrative about how conflict may be sustainably ended (aimed at an inclusive, integrated and comprehensive approach),[34] it follows the more emancipatory version of peacebuilding and of peace – as can be seen in its mandates in Burundi, Sierra Leone, Guinea-Bissau and Liberia, among others.[35] The PBC's Peacebuilding Fund, and Peacebuilding Support Office integrate and coordinate these processes.[36]

In essence, these two versions of liberal peacebuilding indicate that it has become unstable, shifting between state security, markets and sovereignty, and liberal notions of emancipation, with grassroots and bottom-up processes. Peacebuilding is ultimately a transformative activity that seeks to keep domestic authority and legitimacy in line with international authority and legitimacy.[37] This represents a significant tension between conservative and more extensive versions of peace, which is also reflected in the growing roles of the EU, emerging donors, the G7+ and other actors. Though they generally follow the liberal peacebuilding consensus, they also advocate subtle (or sometimes more radical) improvements or more significant changes in direction.[38]

The peacekeeping operations in Namibia, Cambodia, Angola, Mozambique and El Salvador seemed to offer the hope that the peace engendered by UN intervention could go beyond patrolling ceasefires and would instead contribute to the democratisation of failing and failed states by applying different levels of external transitional administration. Both conservative and broader versions were part of global governance, which now became the new imaginary of a positive peace in the minds of policymakers, political scientists, IR and development scholars, and peace and conflict researchers. Peacebuilding still mainly focused on top-down, elite-led, official processes. These debates and praxes offered what was seen to be the most sophisticated methodology for peace, which could now be created through the scientific application of liberal and rational-legal knowledge systems. In fact, it formed a new governmentality, propagated by the UN and IFIs, states, donors and NGOs, as part of the new global governance. Without incorporating citizens in conflict-affected societies, however, this could not be said to be a positive peace. Thus, though liberal peacebuilding aims at a positive form of peace, hybrid political orders and at best negative forms of hybrid peace have developed.

Critiquing Liberal Peacebuilding

Liberal peacebuilding's key problem has been the juxtaposition of its normative and cosmopolitan goals with its inability to recognise difference and redistribute a peace dividend at the grassroots level. Power and the peace dividend has instead generally stayed in the hands of elites. Any improvements in development for the general population are set into harsh relief by escalating inequality, which is perhaps the result of the liberal-peace model being heavily influenced by neoliberal versions of capitalism.[39] This is perplexing because the body of UN documents – agency and secretary-general reports, as well as General Assembly resolutions since World War II – suggest peacebuilding should also represent the culmination of an emancipatory process. It is envisaged as supporting local rights and agency, rather than pre-existing power structures or hierarchies.[40]

Ultimately, broader and narrower versions of peacebuilding understand peace, the state, the international community and conflict-affected citizens as liberal, neoliberal or soon-to-be-liberal actors. From this perspective there is no room for hybridity in terms of norms or rights, which carries deleterious implications for law, institutions and material needs. This sheds doubt upon the peaceful and democratic claims that are being made, if conflict-affected citizens are not to be fully represented, have their needs responded to, identity respected and rights enabled, either by the international community or indeed by the state.

Yet an important aspect of the liberal peace is the argument that conflict cannot really be 'resolved' unless the concerns of civil society are met and, furthermore, that there cannot be a liberal peace unless there is a vibrant civil society. It is generally accepted that peacebuilding approaches should be particularly sensitive to civil-society actors' expectations and needs.[41] Yet civil society is conceptualised according to a legal, rights and economic rationality, where society conforms to the liberal peace, rather than as a space of political contestation over the role and nature of the state or against hegemony. This mirrors the different understandings of civil society of Hobbes, Rousseau, Adam Smith, Gramsci and Marx.[42] It reflects a Western and often culturalist bias against how societies organise legitimate authority structures outside the global North, which means any positive peace offered by liberal peacebuilding may exclude its real subjects in conflict-affected societies. This is a contradiction for liberal peacebuilding because the balance between legitimate authority and authoritarianism depends on civil society's relationship with the state and power. This means that peacebuilding – a multidimensional and multilevel process including a wide range of actors[43] – must respond broadly to political, social, economic and developmental tasks in varied contexts. Without this, external guidance in, or control of, almost every aspect of state and society means liberal peacebuilding will face a legitimacy deficit and a lack of local knowledge and accountability. It may therefore revert to a problematic mixture of consensual and punitive strategies.

Thus, liberal peacebuilding raises questions about the nature of the universal peace it implies. The reform of governance is highly interventionary, has a rational and mechanical problem-solving character, and is constructed procedurally by those in possession of such specialised bureaucratic knowledge as is deemed necessary to be passed on for its creation. It appears at times to be insensitive, to be an extension of paternalist neocolonialism, deferring autonomy and rejecting local norms as well as socio-historical political structures and institutions. Liberal peacebuilding ignores politics and meaning for its subjects.

These problems are amplified by liberal peacebuilding's alliance with neoliberalism. It is mainly in the realm of international political economy that more critical positions emerge about missed opportunities for development and a peace dividend. This is related to a hidden global and state class structure, the extraction of natural resources from the global South and the inability of weak economies to protect themselves or compete with other states.[44] Managed economic integration into the global economy with strong state support is the lesson of the history of post-war reconstruction; it is a lesson that contradicts the ideological neoliberalism that mars most statebuilding and peacebuilding projects. Peacebuilding is not simply supported by 'invisible hands', austerity or structural-adjustment regimes.[45] Indeed, development tends to disrupt pre-existing economic patterns and fails to replace them with anything more suitable or 'indigenously' resonant, as in arguments about Cambodia and in other cases,[46] which has ramifications for legitimacy. The liberal-peace framework has been aimed at reforming or creating neoliberal democracies open for international trade rather than social democracies created to reconcile and support their citizens' welfare. This reiterates global inequality and doubly marginalises post-conflict economies. Structural adjustment-style processes have long been under scrutiny in terms of their contribution to peace. Post-conflict citizens are deprived of crucial welfare support to make their rights a reality, and are exposed to the efficiencies of international markets, dominated by long-established producers.

This shift towards a neoliberal form of peace contradicts the fact that many donors are themselves social democracies (as with the Scandinavian donors, Germany and the UK to some extent) and maintain a strong welfare component in their own states, or have used protectionist measures to stabilise their own polities and competitive advantages in an earlier epoch (as with both the US and the UK). Most theories appear to agree that poverty, relative deprivation and inequality are causal factors in, or at least encourage, conflict.[47] This contradicts the lessons of the historic Marshall Plan and the development of the EU, to name two very significant examples. 'Neoliberal peace', it has to be concluded, is overly idealistic about the capacity of markets to make peace, but it is a cheaper option than the Marshall Plan model, which nevertheless led to social democracies emerging in the European peace process after 1947. In the longer term, however, neoliberal influence over peacebuilding may be more costly: it misunderstands the way that market systems in post-conflict situations allow those versed in their practice and circumvention to undermine rather than support democracy, human rights and the rule of law. Furthermore, control of material resources enables the subversion of representative political systems, which in conflict-affected societies are already weak. Many conflict states today are marred by predatory elites and unsustainable, extractive and exploitative economic practices (often supported by multinational corporations), as well as environmental problems. This is particularly problematic because most post-conflict states rely for their citizens' survival (often 80 per cent of them or more, as in Cambodia)[48] on subsistence strategies and customary landownership, both of which are undermined by marketisation. This once again has the contradictory effect of reinforcing local and global inequality.

For such reasons it is inevitable that disputants and citizens in conflict-affected societies will attempt to renegotiate this process according to their own interests, culture and frameworks. In other words, the positive peace according to cosmopolitan values that liberal peacebuilding claims to create appears as a negative peace to its recipients unless it also incorporates their views, needs and rights. It should not be surprising, therefore, that out of eighteen UN attempts at democratisation since the end of the Cold War, thirteen suffered some form of authoritarian regime within fifteen years.[49]

This underlines the wider implications of peacebuilding beyond any simplistic assumptions that the holding of free and fair elections means that positive peace is automatically self-sustaining.[50] More critical positions point to the need to consider what a positive hybrid outcome would be. This would include issues related to history, society and identity, as well as material issues. The role of IFIs has driven economic structural-adjustment and development projects through neoliberal strategies that have failed to provide the economic opportunities and welfare that would be expected within a liberal state. The relationship between peacebuilding and justice and the problems of establishing post-conflict social justice have often been undermined by such factors. This problem revolves around the definition of justice itself and the argument either that justice needs to be incorporated into any self-sustaining peace, or that social justice may have to be secondary in the short to medium term to the creation of negative peace. Justice has often remained subservient to stability and a limited notion of peace because so many individuals and organisations in conflict environments are implicated in violence, corruption or crimes against humanity.[51] In effect, from the perspective of its subjects in conflict-affected societies, liberal peacebuilding has been turned into a system of illiberal governance rather than a process of reconciliation.

Even worse, at a state level, and encouraged by statebuilding approaches, elections and elites are dominated by, or produce, hegemony and resource control while attempting to curry international favour. Rights, transparency and redistribution are avoided by elites. They amass control of the resources of the state, territory and labour, as well as cement their position in global capitalism. Democratic checks and balances are undermined and civil society is marginalised or controlled while public services are undermined, and justice is avoided in order to direct the peace dividend towards elites and away from citizens.[52]

From such critical perspectives, liberal peacebuilding has failed to come to terms with the lived experiences of individuals and their everyday needs vis-à-vis their welfare, culture or traditions.[53] There has emerged a monumental gap between the expectations of peacebuilding and what it has actually delivered in practice. There are several common complaints: that there are not enough resources available for its vast scale; that there is a lack of coordination and too much duplication among the agents of intervention; that the peacebuilding process is mainly owned by international actors rather than by its recipients; that the issues that face a conflict society in cultural and welfare terms are ignored; and that peacebuilding is mainly driven by neoliberal marketisation and development agendas. Liberal peacebuilding is also criticised on the grounds of being inefficient, wasteful and ill-coordinated, unable to mobilise sufficient force to stop violence completely. It is sometimes forced to compromise with local warlords, to compromise customs that include gender inequality or rigid racial, class, identity or religious hierarchies. From a local perspective, it has been perceived as neocolonial and coercive; in focusing on conditionality as its main method of inducing compliance, it ignores the culture and needs of post-conflict states, it reiterates global and local inequality, with national elites easily able to hijack the process, and it is generally unaccountable to citizens.[54]

Privately, many policymakers and bureaucrats agree with this analysis, and the UN, World Bank, and many donors and NGOs have constantly adjusted their approaches to engage with such critiques. Discussions of 'local ownership' and 'participation', for example, in the UN and World Bank are indicative of a concern that peacebuilding and statebuilding are more or less irrelevant to some or many post-conflict citizens' everyday lives.[55] Indeed, the latter have developed their own way of coping, far from the governance and reform in their capital cities, and irrespective of concepts of statebuilding in alien international fora. It has also become clear that democratisation itself may be an inherently violent process, as the recent violence in Iraq and Afghanistan attests. Democratization may also lead to stalemate because of ethnic nationalism, as the situation from the Dayton Accords from 1995 until today suggests in the context of Bosnia-Herzegovina. In the latter's Brčko district, even positive stories about peacebuilding are often not all they seem when examined closely: there is a consensus that there has as yet been no reconciliation in Bosnia-Herzegovina.[56] The continuation of the 'two schools under one roof' system of ethnic division in educational establishments and the constitutional momentum towards separation rather than cooperation indicate that a social peace has not been achieved and indeed may have been hindered by the ideology and philosophy carried through liberal peacebuilding.

Liberal peacebuilding is top-down, defers local autonomy and self-determination, and demands compliance with international norms and policy frameworks. Elites and citizens from El Salvador and Kosovo to Timor-Leste have demonstrated their disapproval of such approaches. They have sometimes done so overtly, through demonstrations and even violence, as in Kosovo and Timor-Leste in 2004 and 2006, but more often they have done so behind the scenes, being careful not to undermine the peace efforts but rather wanting to influence their direction, as in parts of Central America, Rwanda and Namibia, where the liberal-peace consensus of the donors has simultaneously been adopted but also modified. Public adoption has camouflaged private resistance: local everyday resistance, hidden and obvious, has arisen within the span of resistance agendas.[57] Sometimes, this is very understandable: in the Palestinian case it appears that the role of donors, from the EU to the UN, however well meant, has been exploited by the Israeli state to subsidise the cost of the occupation of Palestine. Turner calls this an 'assemblage of colonial and imperial practices', in which peacebuilding has been influenced by, or even driven by, counterinsurgency, both in local contexts as well as in the more general terms of maintaining the current order.[58] This strategy is evident in calculations regarding who should be empowered or coerced by external actors. Hidden tensions have caused a post-colonial critique of these 'peace projects' to become very relevant, both in the way internationals respond to emergent problems and in the way in which a wide range of local actors position themselves vis-à-vis such interventions to make the most of their existing and embryonic capacities.

The experimental nature of liberal peacebuilding also raises uncomfortable normative and ethical issues, not to mention very serious methodological problems, in that they represent experiments on 'human subjects' with an undetermined outcome, which may include costs and other forms of unintended results. Thus, critical agendas are much needed, especially in the light of the need for legitimacy, local ownership and the assuagement of local expectations, especially in acknowledging the importance of the everyday lives of the millions caught up in these experiments.

As Suhrke argues, using the example of Afghanistan and contrary to the thrust of the mainstream literature, less international intervention may be better than more in avoiding supporting rentier states, their international dependencies and limited local legitimacy.[59] Ordinary Afghans have been disillusioned and disempowered by international intervention.[60] Suhrke is clear that a significant local component and driving force may be found in local capacities for political, economic, social, military and institutional organisation, whether customary or hybrid. Such arguments, pointing to international exclusion of the very subjects they are supposed to be saving, are now common, as in Kosovo, where a 'local' perspective points to the importance of local ownership in building legitimacy and avoiding local resistance. The UNDP has also recognised this need to connect with informal and hybrid processes.[61]

Such criticisms about the limitations of liberal peacebuilding indicate that at a minimum a significant revision is required to find a renewed balance between local legitimacy and its associated authority structures, and external interests, norms and institutions. This move away from a 'New York consensus' (for which, read the now-defunct Washington consensus) is unlikely to produce a new single blueprint, as critical literatures on peacebuilding have long held. If 'deep local knowledge' and multidisciplinarity are to have any real point other than engendering more efficient biopolitical forms of intervention, they should be used to assist in achieving local, autonomous agencies (as far as these are possible) that lead to a resonant form of peace with a positive impact on everyday life. A social contract between internationals and statebuilding 'subjects' is also required: one that those subjects accept. Peacebuilding should not be a Western enterprise to reconstruct the post-colonial and post-Cold War world and to push it into an industrialised modernity. In practice, liberal peacebuilding is close to being a failed endeavour. These versions of peacebuilding have fallen into the same trap that liberal imperialism fell into around a hundred years ago – full of good intentions but unable to respect difference or improve the wide range of conditions that cause conflict, both in material and rights terms. States without peace and states without reconciliation have been built, and peacebuilding without peace has come into being, reflecting an underlying goal of counterinsurgency aimed at maintaining a relatively iniquitous order.[62]

The new conditions for emancipation and liberation have not been achieved by liberal peacebuilding. It has not created citizenship or a social contract, though it has often reprieved individuals and communities from the worst excesses of overt forms of violence.

Many donors, policymakers, development workers and NGO personnel would claim an emancipatory peace as the goal and objective of the projects they have designed. This emancipatory peace, in the liberal imagination, involves a territorial state, security, democracy, rights, prosperity and civil society, all bound up in a cosmopolitan international society. From a local perspective, however, it may involve further, far more complex, calculations relating to social justice, equality, custom, history, society, religion and identity. The lack of consensus in local settings means that internationally imposed peace frameworks have not always been resonant with their subjects, do not always have their consent, do not create social contracts and citizenship, and are often forms of experimentation with unknown consequences. They are not considered fully legitimate or reciprocal, and have become distant even from the civil, constitutional and institutional agendas for peace that emerged out of the Enlightenment, and more specifically from the historical experiences of the twentieth century. In this way, liberal peacebuilding relies on problematic methodological approaches, depending effectively on subtle coercion, and the ethical frameworks used to guide its construction are in no way commensurate with the ethics by which Western citizens and institutions interact in their own contexts. Experiments where human life is affected in unpredictable ways that are not accepted a priori by the subject are very problematic: they were a sign of colonialism in the past, and are often taken as such by their subjects today. Interventionary practices, even for peace and development, operate as if the local context were an ethical and methodological free zone. They are at liberty to exercise the authority they derive from international norms, law and practices. They are not constrained by local contextual needs, culture or practices, because these are regarded as being of a lower order of development, and as dysfunctional because they may have led to conflict in the first place. Western knowledge systems about peace confirm that this process is based on international, not local, legitimacy (some would say hegemony). The everyday lives of individuals and communities are disregarded. According to the perspectives voiced time and time again by the subjects of these interventions in locations around the world, there is certainly a 'Eurocentric' attitude from Western donors and international institutions to development and post-conflict states and subjects. It is almost as if the echoes of colonial superiority cannot be helped – the relevant actors have learned on the job in internationalised spaces rather than through local consultation.

Thus, though neocolonialism, trusteeship and expediency are not the intent of peacebuilding, many post-conflict subjects of the UN and World Bank, donors and INGOs, in Bosnia or Timor-Leste, for example, might see aspects of it as an affront to their identity, culture and history, and perhaps more importantly to their right to self-determination. The lack of direct engagement with everyday needs in post-conflict situations, especially over the longer term, merely confirms these deficiencies to post-conflict citizens. Defying self-determination places internationals in a weak position, as the process leading up to the unilateral declaration of independence of Kosovo indicated in 2008.

The liberal-peace project is ontologically incoherent. It offers several different states of being: a state-centric world dominated by sovereign constitutional democracies, a world dominated by institutions and markets, and a world in which human rights and self-determination are valued. The only way in which this peace system can be coherent is if it is taken to be hierarchical and regulative, led by hegemons who set political and economic priorities, and this provides the framework in which human rights and self-determination can be observed. Democracy provides the political system in which this process is made representative. The trouble is that the individual is subservient to the structure and system, or is ignored by their biases. Where the gaze of the guardians of the liberal panopticon cannot reach,[63] abuses may follow, often committed by those elites who control the various systems that make up the liberal peace. Effectively, this means that the individual, who is relatively powerless, is required to perform liberal-peace acts such as voting, paying taxes, engaging in the free market and exercising rights in order to keep the international gaze satisfied, but is not to expect that this performance carries any material weight. The assumptions that go with the liberal peace are contested across the world, in Islamic settings or those of other religions, in authoritarian states, in tribal and clan settings, and in societies where traditional and cultural practices do not fit with the Western conception of human rights and democracy. At a very basic level, muted by the preponderance of the liberal international system and global economy, the very ontology and related epistemology of the liberal peace are being disputed by local communities. This is not necessarily on an ideological basis, but quite often because of the system's inefficiencies, its distant directors and executors, its cultural and ideological biases, and its failures to provide sufficient resources to support the everyday lives of post-conflict communities.

Liberal peacebuilding restructures power relations with the aim of creating a peace that maintains the current historical order. Citizens must become liberal and must also contend with a continuation of a range of economic inequalities even if other asymmetries are mitigated. This peace is prone to elite hijack. It is strongly contested by actors who want to determine their own peace or want social justice. This has been taken by some to indicate a hybrid model of governance emerging as a new form of 'peace as governance'.[64] The Loya Jirga in Afghanistan is often cited as an example, as are the parliaments and chiefs in Timor-Leste, the Solomon Islands and Liberia, and various transitional justice approaches in Sierra Leone, Mozambique and Rwanda. Such local processes can contribute to liberal peacebuilding by bringing it legitimacy, access and greater efficiency.

Nevertheless, this may not be the case as any such hybridity may be either representative of local cooptation into the liberal-peace system (colonialism redux) or more balanced towards locally representative traditions (which might be quite democratic, even if not in a formal sense).[65] However, in sum, critiques of liberal peacebuilding from a number of perspectives point to the externally envisioned positive peace it proposes often resulting in a negative form of hybrid peace in situ.

Liberal Peacebuilding Responds

Liberal peacebuilding has tried to respond to the reality of its limitations in practice, as well as to the broad academic critique it has received.[66] Peacebuilding documents have indicated that national (rather than local) ownership and contextual specificity are necessary for peacebuilding, particularly because of its increasingly trusteeship orientation.[67] However, even this is a problematic move in that the delegation of authority and legitimacy to the national level creates similar hierarchical dynamics according to competing forms of authority in the local context (state, ideological, military, bureaucratic, identity, religious, customary, etc.). Another response has been a focus on 'early' employment generation and economic vitalisation, as well as the creation of transitional safety nets.[68] Before and during the current neoliberal era, the UN (even during the 'war on terror') was focused on the broader micro- and macro-level conditions for a sustainable peace outside its state-centric fora. Indeed, there is a 'silent discourse' of some significant critical capacity hidden within the UN system that steers its agency work towards sustainability, equality, empathy and contextual sensitivity (that is, a fourth generation of peace).[69] The work of the UNDP and PBC hints at this contextual potential, though countercurrents have emerged from their attempts to develop an 'integrated approach', as in Burundi.[70] A fuller contextual engagement has been dependent on the various UN bodies being willing to give the PBC control and on the host government giving consent, as with Guinea.[71] So the shift towards integration and efficiency is counterbalanced by pressure from below for legitimacy and accountability, recognition, humility and empathy. The UN also has the capacity to learn in an empathetic manner from its experiences and the subjects of its previous missions, though such potential improvements are heavily counterbalanced by the darker sides of UN politics: state-centric interests at the higher political level, bureaucracy (including status and contract-renewal obsessions, corruption and the incompetence of some employees) and its lack of resources.

Further attempts to refine peacebuilding instruments have emerged recently, notably in the World Bank Development Report of 2011, which talks of a 'social compact', the Busan Partnership Agreement on development cooperation and on a 'New Deal for Engagement in Fragile States', and a UNDP report linking governance, peacebuilding and the establishment of a social contract. These reforms occurred in the context of what was estimated in 2011 to be a $129bn global official aid budget, with perhaps another $50bn in private aid (and another $20–30bn given by China, as well as an unknown amount by donors from the Gulf States). The 'International Dialogue on Peacebuilding and Statebuilding', including the G7+, donors and multilateral agencies, agreed in particular on five main principles to guide its signatories, who undertook to 'align international donor interests with those of fragile countries'.[72] The principles included: local ownership (for which read national ownership owing to the fact that most such agreements are negotiated with states as predominant actors) over institution-building and anti-corruption measures; donor alignment to support these processes through recipients' budgets (that is, at state level); harmonisation and coordination to avoid duplication of efforts; and accountability of donors to recipients and vice versa via civil-society engagement. 'Security, justice and legitimate politics' has become the rallying cry of this 'new deal' version of donor–recipient relations, which also informs peacebuilding praxis and expands upon the old Millennium Development Goals (MDG) model. The OECD-DAC has been tasked with monitoring the achievement of such objectives. Peacebuilding and statebuilding, now differentiated, at least in recent UNDP documentation, are seen to be intermediary approaches by which the MDGs (and their 2015 replacements) might be achieved.[73]

To illustrate the reach of this version of the liberal peacebuilding project, the UNDP alone has offices in over a hundred countries with a direct mandate to support civil-society institutions, citizen participation, the development of democracy, law and state accountability, and to achieve the MDGs. In 2008–09, $3.5bn was spent across ten 'fragile' contexts, which represented one-sixth of available UNDP resources.[74] Within this modern formulation of a classic Lockean liberal social contract, the UNDP has also worked on democratising local governance at the subnational level in order to improve its conflict-prevention capacities and to promote cross-group cooperation and trust. At this level it has encountered different forms of political, economic and social engagement (as it has at the state level) but its response has remained one of advocating liberal reforms.[75] In other words, liberal peacebuilding's encounter with alterity has had limited effect. However, the UNDP has embraced 'hybrid delivery mechanisms' in its attempt to support a social contract, and one that does not depend on single templates for governance. Context must in this new formulation shape governance.[76] Furthermore, drawing on the lessons of its long experience in the field, it has started to support local forms of peacemaking agency and their relationship with the state and the international architecture of peacebuilding. Ultimately, the UNDP approach is still aimed at governmental authority as the root of stability (running the risk of this becoming centralised and predatory unless citizens can be quickly empowered).[77] As with the OECD-DAC approach in general, it is assumed that it is safe to hand a reforming state the responsibility and authority to 'mediate citizen–state' relations, even if the state has historically been seen as predatory.[78] Businesses, local NGOs, and religious and tribal, kin and clan networks and organisations, as well as what the UNDP mysteriously describes as 'self-help' organisations, are also to be drafted in to this process to assist in 'service delivery' through the state.[79]

It is possible that the drafters of international documents, within the UNDP or the World Bank, when they increasingly call for more local input into justice, institutions and service delivery, are not fully aware that this may not take place through systems envisaged by internationals, but instead through local systems, often customary, traditional or neopatrimonial. Internationals may not agree with the way these work, or the order they propagate, which is why the peacebuilding discourse is still an externalised one. From this perspective, legitimacy arises according to international standards. Yet local 'resilience', as the agency and politics of populations in conflict-affected states are now being called, indicates pressure for improvements to the externalised 'positive peace' envisaged by intervention: cases such as Somalia or Somaliland illustrate that institutions may come into being and survive informally at the community level, and even higher, without a viable or liberal state.

Conclusion

Liberal peacebuilding is now being thought of by its proponents in the liberal international community as providing a 'best fit' or being 'good enough' – but not as ideal. This may be more 'realistic', but it is hardly a respectful way of describing locally evolving peace processes. Though 'living' peacebuilding practices evolve over time, they still tend to be underpinned by state interests and perspectives while also showing some adaptation in order to begin to address some of the problems that have emerged. Engaging with the social in the context of a compact or contract, accepting the need for legitimacy (though it is unclear whether this is taken to be general, local or international), people's security (or human security), justice (but not social justice), economic development and 'fair services', as well as the return of civil society and gender equality, are positive steps. These new policies seem to denote a more socially oriented state and a more contextual peace, potentially a positive hybrid peace (also reflecting the increasing complexities of donor relations, where recipients have access to a diverse range of donors). The role of personnel from post-conflict zones or the global South should also not be underestimated. 'System accountability' is improving[80] to a limited degree, but more localised forms of accountability would probably place issues such as local and global inequality on the peacebuilding agenda (which most internationals are wary of engaging with). Redistributive components of local, state and international peacebuilding would be an inevitable outcome, especially if peacebuilding is democratised.

The UN now engages with 'critical peacebuilding tasks'[81] and the international community's version of liberal peacebuilding tends not to reach beyond the state, elites, markets and institutions. Thus, the positive peace proposed often ends up being translated into a negative hybrid peace. Multilateralism has tended to remain at the state level, providing a brake on state interests, but also subtly promoting them over the 'people's' interests and needs. Liberal peacebuilding is ultimately very significantly constrained by dominant international preferences. This cocktail of constraints, as well as the tendency of liberal peacebuilding to work from an ideological basis suitable mainly for advanced capitalist and stable states, derails its capacity for making peace. It also carries a subtly neocolonial undertone of trusteeship. The emerging wider range of cooperation partners, including non-traditional donors, may offer some perspective on these problems. Suggestions to overcome such limitations and biases include restoring the centrality of ECOSOC to the UN system, introducing ombudspeople, and bringing the IMF, World Trade Organization (WTO) and World Bank under the control of the General Assembly.[82] However, while liberal peacebuilding seeks to create 'open-access societies',[83] elite structural and governmental power often displaces local, historical architectures of peace and order with a modernisation (and extraction) project that often seems to run contrary to a positive peace. These deficiencies would be amplified if a positive hybrid peace were its goal.

IV

The Dynamics of Peace Formation

Introduction

LOCALISED PRACTICES OF peace formation are complex, often dialogic, expressions of critical agency aimed at ending cycles of state formation, often where more formal peace processes have entrenched them. International- and national-level peace agreements, peace processes and progressive reforms have little meaning unless they can be contextualised across an array of identity, institutional, legal and material platforms. Using local, subaltern agency, they may also modify the state and create transnational networks connecting with a range of internationals. They offer the possibility of a positive form of hybrid peace. This potential is now widely noted in the academic[1] and policy[2] literature on conflict, peace, development and the state as a logical response to the liberal-peace and statebuilding experiment of the last twenty years. Repeated calls for more civil-society participation[3] and more 'local ownership'[4] have been made by international actors such as the UN, World Bank, IMF, EU, and a range of donors and local recipients alike. A long-standing concern that Lederach and many others have identified is to incorporate grassroots and local actors into peace processes to lessen their dependence on elite-level negotiations.[5] This means taking their subjective views of a positive and emancipatory peace seriously. In an increasing number of post-conflict countries, from Afghanistan to Kenya and Nepal, informal and formal local peace committees and other institutional frameworks have provided everyday support, linked up with international networks and have been drawn into the state.[6] They have a physical infrastructure, which often provides opportunities for meetings, negotiation, mediation and the dissemination of information. In Kenya, this process began with a meeting between a group of women in a remote marketplace.[7] These frameworks develop independently in local contexts or with international support, sometimes in the form of an official peace ministry, and peace process.

What has emerged is neither strictly a liberal nor a local form of peace, but a complex assemblage of related but also separate associations, formal and informal actors and networks, shaped by political contestation involving a range of local and international actors.[8] In a more radical vein, it is also important to note that peace formation offers the possibility of connecting a peace process with a progressive form of politics, perhaps outside the state framework or the norms of liberal peace.

There were hints of peace formation in the early peacebuilding frameworks, which were also connected with the idea of a deeper culture of peace.[9] In the El Salvador programme on establishing a culture of peace, it was recognised in 1992 that human development, poverty reduction and addressing root causes meant engaging with peace as a cultural space, in which historical processes form institutions, law, identity and rights. By 1995, similar programmes were under way in Mozambique, Burundi and the Philippines.[10] This had 'deep culture' implications, relating to social values, assumptions, and historical perspectives and structures,[11] from which the dynamics of social 'resilience' would later be identified. Both modern and traditional, a culture of peace was envisaged in everyday terms, eventually becoming part of a national culture (a predictable conclusion from any intergovernmental organisation). It aimed at respect for difference, solidarity and social justice in general, without taking the path of homogenisation and aimed to establish a wide range of venues and spaces of dialogue in which rights, representation and justice might be engaged with. These should be sustainable and embedded in social dynamics (identity, associations and networks, communities, education, health and political decision-making, for example). It was thought that Political dialogue and processes of change and development, driven by grassroots actors, would eventually coalesce into institutions and a form of polity that might be called a state (but that might not conform to the 'modern' state that international actors imagine is best).

This chapter examines the dynamics and implications of peace formation for a positive hybrid peace and for the state using a range of key examples, cases and themes. It also discusses the pros and cons of emerging local 'peace infrastructures'.

Actors and Dynamics

A key dimension of peace formation, and perhaps the least visible to an external view, relates to how people and social groups, not involved directly in the state or with NGOs and other organisations, maintain and develop peace and stability in their everyday lives. Much of this activity depends on subsistence strategies designed to maintain family life far away from urban centres, tarmac roads and state services. These strategies may mitigate political, security, material and environmental constraints, as well as making the most of any opportunities that arise via the state or external donors. They preserve identities and the integrity of everyday life, and some impact on the shape of the state and the policies of internationals, if only very indirectly, because they are a source of local legitimacy.

Solidarity, participation and empathy are a basis for such agency and the networks it creates.[12] It may be severely constrained by state or external exercises of direct or governmental power, but it still finds a certain traction both as a critical function and as a social practice. It reaches far into society with a legitimacy that is deep, resting on long-standing networks of peace-focused actors with their own distinctive perspectives. Its legitimacy depends to a certain degree on its not having direct or governmental power. Conflict brings its potential to the surface, even if peace formation is also disguised to escape sanction. It is often nationally and transnationally linked, sometimes in informal ways, thus having an impact on the political process, institutions and external actors.

Peace formers often establish networks and organisations that are autonomous from the state and international, while maintaining good relations with them. Networking is a crucial part of this type of agency: across the contours of society, across geographic scales, in the region and among a range of international actors, private and state donors, IOs, IFIs and INGOs.[13] Sometimes this is crafted by individuals from outside the specific country who have a long-standing social and political engagement with it. It may also arise as local organisations and individuals learn how to position themselves vis-à-vis state-formation forces (in order to neutralise them) and external actors (in order to coopt them).[14] These organisations' or networks' solidarity is connected to their immediate social and political context, rather than to a donor programme or a state elite, and extends outwards. However, individuals who operate in the peace-formation space are – or soon become – adept at negotiating at multiple levels. They often operate a form of subsistence peacebuilding, developing functions that generate some income (such as report writing, election monitoring, handicrafts, translation and consultancy, or more basic subsistence functions).[15]

Unsurprisingly, women's groups are often at the forefront, from Liberia to Bangladesh and Brazil, in association with development processes.[16] Such agency is often aimed at providing community and public services – health, education and basic needs – in an everyday setting in the absence of state or international engagement. Engaging with the informal, hidden and marginal capacities for peace involves a far broader historical, social and political understanding, and range of skills. It transcends traditional, patriarchal or neopatrimonial politics, and modern 'problem-solving' approaches to peacebuilding through state reform. Yet 'bottom-up' peace-formation agencies are rarely enabled by international actors, who are concerned not to contradict the liberal peacebuilding or neoliberal statebuilding consensus. Peace-formation processes may operate in relation to local understandings of politics and institutions, welfare and economics, social and customary resonance and identity, law and security, also framed by external praxes of intervention. Theses are non-violent processes, representing resistance and critical agency. This is not to romanticise the local, of course.[17] It is, as Latour has argued, a way of 'reconnecting the social' to dominant, Northern, rational-legal and economic concepts of peace, norms and the state, constructing a more resonant and supportive polity.[18]

In Guatemala, El Salvador, South Africa and Northern Ireland, civil-society actors, NGOs and local leaders were paramount in the peace process, as was their support by international donors and/or the UN system.[19] In Palestine, the expectation is that such agency does not merely shape the statebuilding project or insert alternative identities and norms into the peace process, but that it represents mobilisation for statehood itself. In many countries, from Colombia to Timor-Leste, Ghana and Nepal, peace formation has become institutionalised and is part of, or will become part of, formal government.

Functions that are crucial to such processes include alternative media venues for reporting and monitoring elections, human rights, the political process, community work, educational support, supporting cultures of peace, gender issues, as well as DDR, documenting war crimes, and dealing with trauma, dialogue and reconciliation.[20] In a broader sense, they aim at social, legal and humanitarian justice, political, institutional and economic order, autonomy and self-determination. None of these functions can be carried without local participation and support, and, perhaps more importantly, local consent and legitimacy, whether these are fragmented across many different groups or united in a common script of self-determination. These functions possibly illustrate the most obvious dynamics of peace formation, but they are mainly internationally scripted, providing opportunities and space for local actors and processes to connect with them only if hybrid forms of peace or self-determination are broadly acceptable in the face of regional or international interests. Peace formation also has an indigenous and locally based character, which may connect with these or may maintain its autonomy. Thus, it is doubtful that international networks of NGOs, such as the Global Partnership for the Prevention of Armed Conflict, the European Platform for Conflict Prevention and Transformation, and the European Peacebuilding Liaison Office, are able to connect with such deeper levels of peace formation because as yet they tend to operate on the official level (though this is also necessary).

Peace formation requires a move beyond the traditional concepts of civil society or international NGOs, donors, diplomats and officials facilitating a peace process, agreement or liberalisation. The well-documented cases of organisations such as International Alert, the Carter Center and the Community of Sant'Egidio, or the 'back channels' formed by governments such as Norway in Sri Lanka or the Middle East, or between the UK government and various actors in Northern Ireland, illustrate only a visible part of peace-formation agency.[21] Indeed, the trend of most international engagement with conflict-affected societies has been towards service delivery and monitoring government performance, rather than solidarity with local populations in an emancipatory framework of peace.[22] Internationals of all types tend to form relationships with like-minded institutions, and may even form local institutions or NGOs themselves if they cannot find local partners.[23]

Peace formation does not represent such 'tamed social movements'[24] but builds on the local, transnational and transversal solidarities that concepts of civil society and NGO include or INGO actors assume correctly – when they notice them, that is – represent a crucial form of political agency for peace. It relates to what are often free-standing, rather than externally prompted, peace actors in local-local contexts. In this space, alternative discourses and debates as well as their propagation, critical discourses, monitoring, transparency, advocacy promotion, and social, economic and political support, all emerge. Nevertheless, they may be hidden from view by a limited external understanding of context, or because peace-formation activity places its proponents in danger or at risk of sanction. Peace formation is clearly aimed at building a positive and hybrid form of peace, incorporating contextual frameworks of meaning and aiming for an emancipatory peace. Indeed, it may well be that peace formation is more advanced in such areas of engagement other than the liberal peacebuilding or neoliberal statebuilding frameworks, because peace-formation dynamics are much closer both to conflict and to the problems that undermine the possibilities for progressive politics to emerge.

Autonomous local agency is significant for peacebuilding, statebuilding, development and even for areas related to security. As in Palestine, 'resistance' to conflict systems resting on power, injustice and occupation may be seen as a route to peace via a national-liberation and alternative state-formation process. Even where collective political action remains implausible owing to internal divisions or external strategies of divide-and-rule, there is strong evidence that peace formation develops,[25] producing strategies of mitigation and assistance. Often such approaches are in tension with those that internationals would like to occur. The capacity to mitigate is related to conflict-affected societies' livelihoods and security, and operates in informal spheres, related to community-based networks and priorities. These strategies may not be sufficient to make a stable peace in cases of embedded or extreme violence, but they offer a direction that may be followed and a basis upon which internationals may assist legitimately. To do so, internationals need to be able to engage and understand such dynamics and capacities, rather than attempting to absolve themselves of responsibility via reference to superficial concepts, ontologically rooted in Western epistemology, of 'resilience', 'conditionality' or 'local ownership'. These three concepts imply a failure of international actors to accept difference and 'equaliberty' as a necessary basis for an emancipatory peace, or the inevitability of a hybrid peace in negative or positive form.

Navigating between state-formation dynamics and the managerial hand of internationals is a tricky task that needs both local and international cooperation and sensitivity. In some cases, because of powerful opposition it appears impossible. It requires bridging and translation skills, bringing together local and international initiatives and opportunities. As such capacities become larger-scale, it is probable that peace formation needs to be formalised. As a consequence of peace formation, understandings of rights, law, security and institutions are being expanded to include contextual dynamics: socio-economic needs as rights, customary law, human (now also called citizen or peoples') security, and informal institutions. The implication is that these should have equal standing with external approaches, which should be decentralised (as with the state). Peace formation also expands to learn from, or engage in, debate with external approaches.

This is the case with the Centre for Exchange and Solidarity (CES) in El Salvador, run by an expatriate American with mostly local staff, offering a range of services from language training to consultancy, handicrafts and election monitoring. Their director has excellent local and international contacts, the latter being mainly with small charities and donors. She is of the opinion that local organisations had either followed the line of major donors such as USAID or lacked the capacity to self-organise transnationally, which is why people like her have an important role, especially if they aim at a grassroots position rather than connecting mainly with elites and externals.[26] This organisation wants to be part of local society, does not want to be seen as supporting a 'fancy' international lifestyle, pays its staff fair wages (that is, not the local minimum wage for local staff or inflated Western rates for internationals), and thus, its director argues, has been more stable in the long term and has had more social impact. Similar arguments have been made about another organisation in Costa Rica working on inequality and trafficking issues in the poor districts of San José.[27]

In Cyprus, the intercommunal movement is mainly run by local personnel, though it owes much historically to external support for meetings that have brought people together across the island's dividing line during the last few decades. They have, with minimal resources and much opposition from mainstream politicians and ethno-nationalists across both Greek and Turkish Cypriot societies, formed a wide range of cooperative networks. They have reconciled over issues from history and identity to rights, justice and professional training, and clearly offer the prospect of a positive hybrid form of peace. The movement probably began with a few chance meetings between individuals interested in peace. It has long been marginal to, and marginalised by, both local politics and the internationals' vision of a peace process. Such agency, networks and organisations have replicated across the world in the last twenty-five years or so. They are legally based in their host country and sometimes receive funding from the state and from international donors, and find ways of being autonomous while receiving support.

Peace formation may also be shaped by localised and customary organisations, as with the Traditional Council in Liberia or the Peace and Reconciliation Ministry in the Solomon Islands.[28] Often the role of such organisations is simply to give initial support and create networks for local projects, or to translate international or local initiatives so that they are more easily understood by subjects or, indeed, donors. In the case of the CES in El Salvador, the director has argued that longer-term support is often needed for local projects because they are at a significant disadvantage in competing with the forces of state formation and with global capitalism. The latter is exacerbated by the fact that, at the statebuilding level, internationals and donors put pressure on the state to follow a neoliberal design.[29] The lack of a welfare system means women and children are disadvantaged in particular, though the activity of local peace actors often brings such issues to the fore.

The absence of the state in conflict-affected societies often forces communities and individuals to decide whether to engage with peace-formation dynamics or state-formation processes. The peace-formation group focuses on a particular type of peace and how it might be achieved. Such self-organisation often focuses on consensus, legitimacy and building inclusive networks (including 'hawks' and 'doves'), in order to support social-justice, human-rights and human-security agendas, but in the context of local social, historical and identity variations, it is influenced by religion and historical norms. It should be repeated that women are often at the forefront of such networks and their 'resilience'. Peace formation may be driven by an aspiration for external norms of human rights, for democracy, access to public services and material improvement. It also may be rooted in historical institutions, norms, laws and processes that have been used to respond to conflict, offer mediation, promote dialogue, settle material disputes, and organise the distribution of power and resources.

Implications for the State and the International System

The relationship – and balance – between the international systems associated with the liberal peace and the neoliberal state, and local socio-political systems for managing and resolving conflict, is rapidly becoming one of the biggest issues in conflict-affected societies and the international community alike. For example, the Australian-led statebuilding Regional Assistance Mission to Solomon Islands (RAMSI) has tried to engage with local knowledge and local capacities by building partnerships. This process recognises that local knowledge involves both agency and legitimacy. However, what local knowledge entails is perceived through international filters, although it does involve a recognition that an everyday form of peace holds internationals accountable to local subjects.[30] Indeed, it often appears that local legitimacy does not coincide with the state or international community. This can be observed from Kosovo to Timor-Leste, even if heavily contested in each local context.

Localised tensions, even including issues such as class, caste or gender inequality (as particularly in Afghanistan), are more likely to be resolved in context through a consensual process rather than solely by international- or state-led prescription. It has a stronger chance of dealing with difference because it is locally grounded and, together with international support, has a better chance of establishing a social compact between citizens and state. What is more, as has been realised in the Balkans, society offers and maintains 'patchwork' systems of formal and informal support. This occurs through families, kin, charities and community allegiances that connect informal networks to formal networks of association or cooperation.[31] The peaceful state represents a scaling-up of these social capacities, if it is to be locally legitimate. However, such processes also need international support, enablement and facilitation, whereby alliances with a range of local actors are mutually constituted, converge and become complementary. Peace formation needs to connect to international legitimacy and to state-level legitimacy: it should be formative of both. The narrowing of the gap between them demands a mediation and negotiation process at multiple levels, which mitigates power asymmetry and is indicative of a social contract as well as an international–social and international–state contract. This is a process that carries forward the potential for a positive hybrid form of peace.

The result of international–local cooperative strategies should not be in trusteeship form or, as in Kosovo, where a dominant group has taken over the institutions of state at the risk of marginalising other minorities, including Serbs, or as in Afghanistan, where an embryonic city-state has been limited to the capital and has failed to make headway in negotiating with the Taliban. In these cases, local knowledge has often been ignored, local capacities have not been identified and supported, local limitations have also been ignored, and partnerships have been selected on the basis of external interests or power rather than with the aim of achieving a positive and emancipatory peace.

Local government is often viewed by international actors as a way of capturing peace formation within the formal sphere of the state, and providing for both participation and ownership.[32] This may often be a crucial linkage between social constructions of peace, institutions, power, law, rights and needs, and the state, denoting the evolution of a localised form of citizenship. Thus, decentralisation of the state's control of institutions and power is seen to be a way of placing agency deeper into society through the process of 'subsidiarity'. This has become the focus of statebuilding and peacebuilding in Nepal, Timor-Leste, Liberia and Sierra Leone, where it has been assumed that the externally built rather than locally formed state offers legitimacy to society rather than the other way around, as peace formation suggests. The state is expected to distribute resources, meet needs and, most importantly through local government, directly come into contact with its citizens, giving them a voice. In this vision, the formal takes over from the informal, and the international rather than local takes over the state, in order to address international perceptions of a conflict's causes as well as power relations. This may merely replicate state-level patterns of exclusion unless peace-formation processes direct state policy. In this way, social or local legitimacy for the state may be amassed, allowing for a recognition of the social, historical, cultural and traditional processes of maintaining order and making peace. These have an institutional, rights, needs and identity dimension.

Without peace formation, hybrid forms of peace will tend towards the negative. Most controversially, a negative hybrid peace may be reflected in the attempt to develop a liberal peace in Afghanistan, which requires all sorts of difficult compromises with tribal groups and their historical practices, including the Taliban and various warlords (also involving significant reform on their behalf).[33] Whether this can be termed 'peace' at all is open to debate, but it certainly represents a political rather than a violent process towards a hybrid form. Perhaps more positive forms of hybrid peace are emerging in unexpected locations, however. In Somalia, despite the collapsed nature of the state, local communities have organised themselves to maintain a semblance of stability and order.[34] In Cambodia, a vibrant civil society, particularly in the realms of human rights, has kept pressure on the relatively authoritarian democracy that has emerged since the early 1990s peacekeeping mission.[35] Community-level governance (communes – *sangkat*s – and committees) have been important for promoting local participation in, and consensus about, public services and local governance.[36] In Bosnia-Herzegovina, the conditions of a weak state have been alleviated by local communities' attempts at mitigating them. In Timor-Leste, as in Sierra Leone, Ghana, Kenya, Nepal, Liberia, Mozambique, Guatemala and the Solomon Islands, international and local cooperation are producing a specifically contextual version of peace, to varying degrees incorporating local or customary practices into the modern state via local peace actors and organisations.[37] In general, such examples may represent a slow and often arduous movement beyond the liberal peace towards what might be called a post-liberal peace,[38] where international norms and institutions interact with different, contextual and localised polities, reaching together for a positive hybrid form.

Examples of Peace Formation

Peace formation is varied, mainly emerging from bottom-up networks. Some are related to history, culture and identity. Many post-conflict civil societies are often described as weak, dependent upon fickle donor priorities and funds, and driven by their policies, as has been argued in the cases of Namibia and Mozambique recently.[39] As in many other locations, international characterisations of local peace dynamics are infantilising. But local organisations often continue to engage in human rights, development, education or training work, often within a subsistence context (meaning that they do not receive donor or international support).[40] Sometimes, as in Bosnia-Herzegovina, they operate in a private social and cultural-political register of tactical resistance to state failure or international conditionality, rather than in formal political and public spaces.[41] When such organisations decide to work in this manner, even without significant donor support they find that they are able to survive and develop their own approaches because of the hidden reach of their local networks. Furthermore, this illustrates the crucial importance of including a wider range of issues, associations and networks than the narrow one envisaged by donors' understandings of civil society. For example, in Mozambique, one NGO is using traditional musical instruments to teach people about pluralism, peace and coexistence. Another organisation, initiated by a religious network, has developed a small arms decommissioning project, which has earned worldwide fame.[42] In Bosnia-Herzegovena cultural organisations have created a space for debate about the state as well as for critiques of local politics and international strategies.[43] Similarly, in the case of Guatemala, the majority community of Mayan people has developed numerous ways of preserving its culture and identity, and has increasingly become more successful in finding spaces in which it can survive and coexist with the modern state. It has presented its culture and cosmology in national and international fora,[44] in an encounter between very different cosmologies (local 'indigenous' versus European rational-legal).

Formal conflict-resolution workshops also form a site for peace formation. In the 1990s, workshops run in Cyprus by mainly American or European scholars provided an important platform for social reconciliation to develop. Yet locally they were often perceived to be patronising, and indicated a lack of international awareness and sensitivity about the conflict. Only a small group of people became involved. In these meetings, people interested in peace could meet across the green line that had divided Greek and Turkish Cypriots since 1974 or even earlier. They valued the contact with their 'enemies' and the ability to debate, but they also felt that the workshops, in their efforts to find a mutual accommodation, sometimes glossed over the difficult political and justice issues they faced.[45] On the other hand, the academics who ran them were often frustrated by what they saw as local partners' tendencies not to engage in the way they wanted, and yet to appear to be dependent on them for any contact with the other side.

Despite these difficulties, local participants were able to use these processes to build a peace constituency that did not necessarily lead to agreement but had the potential to help peaceful coexistence to emerge. The workshops enabled local participants to build contacts and networks or relationships that transcended the conflict (though not at all in the way workshop directors expected). It is notable that in the very latest formal attempts to develop a peace process, even the island's two governments and political leaders have recognised the significance of such civil-society movements.

Participants have renegotiated locally exclusive forms of identity as well as challenged prescriptions from external donors. They have also taken the opportunity to work for broader social and political reform.[46] They have drawn on hidden historical practices of pluralism[47] and a range of local and international networks in order to form a hybrid positive peace process, which is perhaps more worthy of the name 'peace process' than the decades-long high-level talks have been. Peace formation represents a complex assemblage that bridges a range of ethno-national, state, informal and international divisions; it has often opposed political elites because it has questioned the nature of the state.

Peace formation, however, has not been effective in influencing the high-level negotiations in Cyprus directly. As two of the island's former leaders argued in 2013 at a public debate on the peace process at the Home of Cooperation, intercommunal work needs the support of the political leadership to make an impact,[48] because the political leadership effectively exercises direct and governmental power. But the political leadership has historically been unable to compromise or engage with the substance of the peace that the intercommunal movement has developed because of its obsession with nationalism and sovereignty. In the absence of support from leaders, peace formation continues to play an important role in Cyprus in terms of mapping out the social, cultural political, economic and material aspects of a solution, but it has not been able to influence the statist peace process at the high level.[49]

Civil-society activism is another site of peace formation. In Sri Lanka, despite the very difficult circumstances for any peace process to take place during the 2000s, certain local organisations navigated around the constraints imposed by separatist violence, nationalist and elitist government, and ethnic and religious chauvinism, with a skill that internationals, such as mediators, donors and the UN, were unable to emulate.[50] While the latter have been undermined by rapacious and paranoid state-level politics, local organisations such as the National Peace Council and others – particularly in the areas of human rights and peacebuilding – have managed to maintain their roles of advocacy and accountability despite difficult and changing local conditions. They have managed with a mixture of international support and their own capacity and knowledge. Some local civil-society members argue that they have taught the international community about the country, its society, history, politics and culture; and about the conditions in which the government operates and how politics develops. In particular, they have disseminated the idea that peace is historically based on the accommodation of great differences in politics and identity, and that majoritarianism has never worked in the long term. Donors have tended to misunderstand such subtlety and diplomacy as ineffectiveness; some expect local actors to take a strong stand against the government (previously, against the Liberation Tigers of Tamil Eelam – LTTE), but this would clearly be counterproductive (not to mention dangerous). Such local capacity raises several issues: how does it maintain itself without significant sanction from nationalists or a pro-war/pro-discrimination lobby? How does it engage with donors without accepting conditionality? In uncovering such capacities, how do internationals make sure that peace-formation actors are not exploited or exposed to risks? Peace-formation actors have aimed to produce a positive hybrid peace in an environment often dominated by mainstream state-formation processes and subject to the direct power of the state.

Statebuilding and peacebuilding offer another peace-formation site. After the wars and during the late 1990s and early 2000s, international actors in both Kosovo and Bosnia-Herzegovina were frustrated with their local counterparts' obstructive tendencies, particularly where these demanded social, cultural, economic, reform or identity changes. The result in Bosnia-Herzegovina was deadlock over the reform of the state, while in Kosovo it brought into being a contested state.[51] In Bosnia-Herzegovina, a number of civil-society organisations, involved in human-rights and transitional-justice matters, and cultural projects, emerged on the ground in an attempt to speed up progress. In Kosovo, a range of organisations had undertaken such work during the Serbian period, and after the war, in 1999, they emerged from the shadows to take control of the state to some degree. While problematic, both denote a potential hybrid form of peace and state emerging via a range of local agencies, some of which contest interests but many of which are also working towards a more positive form of engagement, involving an improved social, economic and political order. Though they have tended to be ignored by internationals, they are present and active,[52] and perhaps constitute a better guide for peacemaking. They are rooted in historical and everyday processes of conflict resolution, reconciliation and related informal networks, which have evolved to support security, and social and political reform.[53]

In Timor-Leste, since the UN peacekeeping operation and especially since the recurrence of violence in 2006, local actors have been crucial in building a hybrid peace that has social, cultural, economic and political dimensions. Internationals initially produced a negative hybrid peace, often bypassing the state and working directly with the customary sector because of its capacity and legitimacy.[54] More recently, the government has tried to engage with more localised potential. Two of the most visible examples have been the return to the landscape of 'sacred houses' as a result of more informal agency, the creation of a social welfare system, and a range of public services via the state.[55] These phenomena have involved a deviation from the liberal-peace and neoliberal-state frameworks. They illustrate the way in which needs and historical identity tend to be highlighted by peace-formation agency. Sacred houses are centres of family and social life, where many issues of local politics and economic support are decided, and also where celebrations and ceremonies take place that bind communities, including conflict-resolution ceremonies. Their re-emergence is indicative of a deeper stabilisation after the failure of international approaches. Income from the Timor Gap oil and gas reserves, combined with a sense in government that a peace dividend needs to be distributed more directly by the state, is enabling the state to gain more relevance in people's daily lives.[56] The government has now made it its policy to incorporate such dynamics – local, socio-historical expressions of identity, peace processes and institutions – into the state.[57] This process has also led to a greater level of decentralisation, involving the establishment of local assemblies and related support programmes,[58] and introducing democratic reforms for local government drawn from the customary system. Decentralisation has devolved a wide range of social and political activities to these levels.[59]

In the Solomon Islands, similar dynamics can also be seen to be at work, though they have been less effective owing to a lack of local resources at the state level. However, RAMSI, the Australian-led statebuilding mission there, has increasingly recognised their importance, as well as the contradictions between the liberal state and capitalist economy, and customary practices, law and institutions. Work is under way to accommodate these two different political frameworks in order to respond to the problems that caused the conflict, relating to predatory elites, exclusive identities and land issues.[60] This may ultimately lead to a new constitutional framework.

Many of the examples above combine Western, secular and individualistic understandings of liberal civil society with local patterns of identity and social organisation, which is communal rather than individualistic, and which operates over generations rather than in the short term. They often oscillate between a negative and positive hybrid peace. The formation of local civil society organisations (CSOs) and NGOs, drawing on contextual and international networks, is often the vehicle for this blend's visibility in any peace process. NGOs fill the breach when the state, government or international actors are not able to gain access or establish their programmes. Though externally funded civil-society actors often do not connect well with local issues because they are externally driven by donor preferences and substitute for a weak state,[61] many local NGOs manage to develop local peace-formation processes while simultaneously engaging with international donors. These NGOs may try to maintain their autonomy and identity in a specific community, and focus on needs as well as rights, but they are able to engage nationally with the state and transnationally with a range of internationals, where it is necessary to assert their agency. For example, in the context of Haiti – as in many other locations around the world – the local roots of such organisations have made them more accountable. They offer solidarity, transfer knowledge to internationals, and receive a range of resources in return, often through a very diverse network of local and international actors.[62] Noticeably, they rarely separate political representation, human rights, economic needs and the role of the state.

Local Infrastructures for Peace

UN, EU and donor efforts to engage in support for local infrastructures for peace represent an institutional turn towards peace-formation approaches and their inherently contextual legitimacy.[63] Creating a parallel system of local and international legitimacy for any polity emerging from violence through a peace process offers significant possibilities for convergence, as compared to the previous 'mono-cultural' liberal-peace system.

Where local agencies have emerged and demonstrated a stake in the peace process and in the nature of the state, local and international actors have often attempted to formalise them into governmental institutions.[64] A rational-legal trend is inevitable in a world divided into states and moderated by international organisations, law (that is, governmental power), and the interests of direct and structural power. This is another example of hybridity emerging, and one with the potential to become positive. The adoption of the rationalities of governance via such an 'architecture' in view of the fact that most communities gain their law and justice, representation, and welfare from localised, customarily or religiously oriented institutions and processes may serve to enable both forms of governance to converge.

Peace-formation agency eventually appears to seek an outlet in the formal institutions of the state through peace-formation processes that shift from the hidden to the informal to the formal. Peace infrastructures connect formal with informal sectors – local, state and often international – through inclusive systems of dialogue.[65] They deal with local violence, political contests, peace agreements and questions of state reform, even if their impact is limited.[66] They have the potential to transform local, state and international patterns of exclusion, bridging informal peace formation with formal politics and the state. They are inclusive even if their members do not agree, are often able to provide early warnings about conflict, and offer an important dimension of legitimate authority and social cohesion.[67] Thus, the emergence of local peace infrastructures may perhaps eventually lead to the creation of peace commissions or even a government ministry,[68] as in Nicaragua in the late 1980s and South Africa in the early 1990s.[69]

This process has been recognised in policy fora. The UNDP's programme in support of local 'peace architectures' links grassroots organisations and local peace councils and committees with local and national governmental institutions.[70] Localised social and political architecture, together with identity, has been linked with the rationalities of the state and global governance. Despite very unequal power relations, such networks are dynamic, locally owned, formal or informal, and contextual. UNDP supports these developments in cases where they are absent, creating new structures for peace and involving the key stakeholders in society.[71]

This programme is aimed at a broad range of issues, creating widely inclusive solutions, connecting local with external peacemakers and reforming domestic governance. It involves identifying, and to some extent promoting, local peace councils and bringing them into the more formal structures of the emerging post-conflict state, but without undermining the informal and subtle legitimacy these structures maintain. Peace is therefore based on bottom-up processes with international support. Because they are locally derived they are also very cost-effective. Such claims appear to be borne out in many post-conflict environments, which suggests that locally driven versions of hybridity are more effective in leading to legitimate institutions and authority from local governance to state level.

The recently established Ministry for Peace and Reconciliation in the Solomon Islands and similar bodies in Timor-Leste and Nepal have endeavoured to bring society and the state closer together in terms of their relations, but also in how one reflects the other. In Timor-Leste and the Solomon Islands, this emerging infrastructure appears to represent a genuine attempt to localise the state, whereas in Nepal the Peace Ministry has effectively been hijacked on behalf of elite interests rather than representing society within the state.[72] In Ghana, local peace councils of elders and activists are becoming integrated into formal decentralised government and a National Peace Council; this involves mediating conflict at different levels using local tools, while also involving the state and international community.[73] South Sudan has established a Ministry for Peace aimed at a comprehensive implementation of the recent peace agreement in a very troubled environment, as well as using traditional methods designed to increase the breadth of stakeholders in the peace process, improve the participation of civil society and communities, and enable a broad reconciliation. The Ministry works – at least potentially – through the government, in partnership with cultural institutions, religious organisations, and youth and women's groups.[74] In Bosnia-Herzegovina, a range of women's groups have acted as peace 'formers' in a similar way to those in Burundi: they have opened up local discussions of peace and have also developed a good relationship with local government and state-level actors.[75] However, as they do not wield structural or direct power, their ability to stop violence is limited to influencing those actors who wield force.

Even so, in Somaliland in the early 1990s, localised peace agreements led by local elders utilising customary law eventually resulted in a constitutional structure that included elected party representatives as well as a clan-oriented upper house. This grew out of widespread but localised peace conferences and discussions across Somaliland driven by grassroots as well as business, clan and political leaders. The absence of outside support, given the non-recognition of Somaliland, meant peace had to be local if it was to emerge at all.[76] Similar patterns have occurred across Somalia, where subaltern peace-formation processes have maintained some order where the state and international community have failed.[77]

Similar dynamics can also be seen in other parts of Africa. After the Lome Peace Accord in Sierra Leone, a Commission for the Consolidation of Peace was established along with national Commissions for Democracy, Human Rights and others.[78] The UN Peacebuilding Commission also helped to coordinate these. A parliamentary group also containing civil-society members has additionally been established, working on a 'national peace infrastructure' that has included a range of fora, including a women's forum.[79]

In Kenya, following the post-election violence of 2007, an Open Forum was created and a Citizen's Agenda for Peace was developed by individuals who gathered from all sectors of society in the weeks immediately after the conflict broke out. This activity was partly based on a peace movement started by a group of women in 1993. A National Policy on Peacebuilding and Conflict Management emerged in 2009, and Peace Committees in all districts were set up in accordance with the National Accord and Reconciliation Act of 2008.[80] This process drew in a number of ministries and levels of government and the media, and was also connected to the high-level peace process. Crucially, it was driven and legitimated in civil society and at the grassroots.[81]

In Afghanistan, it was recognised early on, via the Loya Jirga and lower-level political frameworks, that peace had to be locally driven, at least to a degree. Karzai developed his 'big tent' strategy to try to be inclusive of difficult actors such as the Taliban and a range of factions, in order to respect local identity, religion, tradition and society. But this attempt at creating a state inclusive of both powerful and weak actors has led to its cooptation by state formation actors, often intent on power through violence. Even so, Afghan leaders have been aware since the 1990s of Western conflict-resolution approaches as well as their own tradition of tribal mechanisms for dispute resolution via councils of traditional elders. The Jirga model for debate has been established at local and districts levels through peace councils and democratically elected Community Development Councils. These are part of the National Solidarity Programme run by the Ministry of Rural Rehabilitation and Development. Their activities include welfare support for families, local governance and job creation. They are widespread across the country, numbering some 22,000.[82] Many are versed in Western understandings of peacebuilding and the role of the state, as well as conflict resolution within society, but they are also founded on localised praxes of peace and development.[83] Despite these encouraging signs, it is also very probable that external engagement with these processes – directing statebuilding, peacebuilding and development via a 'functionalist anthropology' similar to colonial anthropology – is more concerned with coopting them into an ill-fitting liberal peace and neoliberal state than in encouraging local reconciliation in whatever political, social and economic framework may be contextually required.[84] Yet, time and time again, there are reports that what has actually occurred is the influencing of the state-building and peacebuilding process by local actors, often local elites, but also by the processes of peace formation. A range of state-formation and peace-formation actors have infiltrated and taken over the state: they have 'captured the intervention' for reasons of both power and peace.[85] Sometimes these processes appear to represent continuity with previous power structures, perpetuating their exclusionary characteristics, but they also often push hard for a more progressive form of state and politics. Similarly, in Kosovo, a range of state-formation and peace-formation actors have used the state in order to mitigate power structures and negotiate a better form of peace.

A Summary

In summary, peace-formation processes run in many local, transversal, national and transnational layers and networks. They may be hidden, informal, critical of and resistant to a range of inequalities. These processes are embedded in socio-political and historical frameworks, or externalised strategies for stabilisation. They represent a current of social discourse and agency about what needs to be addressed and reformed if a positive, hybrid framework for peace and security is to be attained, from its micro-components in everyday life upwards to the state level. They may tend to appear passive, but in practice they send important signals to policymakers. They mitigate the insecurities of everyday life or indirectly shape political and economic structures and dynamics, as in Cyprus and Timor-Leste.

In every case where peace is slowly forming locally with its own characteristics, from Nepal to the intercommunal movements in Cyprus, the tribal elders in Liberia and the more hidden networks in Bosnia, they are concerned with everyday issues: security, mitigating power imbalances, land and resource distribution, pluralist identities, 'good neighbourliness', rights, representation, forming institutions, legal reform, gender equality and social justice. In other words, they span the range of issues that the core functions of the modern state are expected to deal with,[86] as well as internationally sponsored peace agreements. In their contextual locations, this means a renegotiation of the state and peace if an emancipatory framework for legitimate authority and progressive politics is to emerge. With this process the peace that is experienced in conflict-affected societies will be at best a negative hybrid peace.

Peace formation engages with identity, mitigates socio-economic and rights problems, and draws on contextual understandings of their specific geographic, political, social, economic and cultural environments, as in the Solomon Islands, Sierra Leone and Ghana. Peace formation and peace formers may be hidden to escape sanction or more simply because observers operate in a different register, as in most non-Western environments, including Somalia. They may operate more openly in informal customary or civil-society spaces and institutions, as in Afghanistan. They often do so by adopting the rationalities of the modern state and the vocabulary of internationals. They hold both to account, offer transparency, connect with historical identities and dynamics, identify their weaknesses, and encourage power holders, state actors and internationals to reform. They simultaneously learn and teach how order may be constructed.

Peace formers are concerned with a number of different aspects of a peace process. First, they locate the Western epistemology of peace in a broader social-cultural framework, as well as pointing to alternative forms of political and economic praxis. This has occurred in almost every case outside the global North, and even in the Balkans and Cyprus – that is, within the 'West' – local traditions as well as alternative political ideologies have been expressed. They may find low-level ways of improving security by making local agreements, as has been the case in Afghanistan or Somalia. They seem to preserve or improve processes by which economic resources are distributed in society, or political power is yielded, as has been observed in Timor-Leste and the Solomon Islands. They may deploy indigenous, customary or religious forms of political, social or economic organisation to confront locally embedded inequalities of power, or what they consider to be inappropriate external interventions, or to mitigate the effects of neoliberalism. They often operate in a register where social consensus is the aim, rather than political competition, focusing on communities rather than individuals. Where communities are opposed, are at odds with broader society or hold views that are exclusive and ethno-nationalist, peace formers tend to unpack the range of opinions in a broader perspective in order to build bridges and facilitate pluralism.

In many cases, such processes have found ways to marry themselves with democratic reform and the framework of the state, even where the latter has long been regarded as predatory. Sometimes they operate in parallel to the state, as in Kosovo before 1999, or in Cyprus, but occasionally they form part of state–society institutions, such as councils or ministries, as in Nepal or Ghana. They often rely on external assistance, but not always. They bring to the attention of elites and internationals alike the presence and significance of different life-worlds (meaning the world as conflict-affected societies experience it), political ideologies and human needs. They represent an agency that has surprised many observers (perhaps they are partly the reason why the concept of 'resilience'[87] has emerged).

Ultimately they endeavour to expose conflict's roots, and increasingly to realise a role in local, state and global governance.

These processes may remain separate to more formal peace processes or they may gradually connect with them. CSOs, local NGOs, and labour, political, religious and other movements may, however, coalesce in more formal peace processes, committees, councils and institutions, as with local peace councils, and eventually form institutions or even ministries within the state, as in Timor-Leste, Nepal, Kenya and Ghana. The development of these more formalised approaches may be externally supported, as with the work of the UNDP with peace committees and ministries, but often such external assistance draws on already existing local social discourses and practices. Gradually they may form an institutional architecture that reaches from the local to the global, as they are often locally and internationally networked. They represent, often very cost-effectively, local agencies that are well versed (though often stymied) by virtue of their proximity in opposing the forces of violence and predation, and also in dealing with a range of contextual factors that shape local politics. When they join peace processes and are supported by a range of international actors, they offer the possibility of local and international forms of legitimacy and so a more sustainable peace.

Encouragingly for liberal peacebuilding's supporters, local agents of peace formation often seek to develop relations with international donors. They draw on arguments close to, or in favour of, democracy, human rights, sometimes free markets and a rule of law, but also want to 'localise' these or connect them with reforming local practices. They do so in order to develop a positive, hybrid form of peace, not to mimic the liberal peace or neoliberal state. They are well aware of the deficiencies of their own power structures, and of both the state and the international community. This process requires exceptions and modifications to account for local contextual dynamics, sometimes confronting liberal norms, sometimes learning from them. Peace-formation actors seek to insert their own institutions, norms, identities and conceptions of law to mitigate and resolve conflict. International assistance is therefore still necessary, but it needs to be grounded in local legitimacy as well as in international norms, meaning it has to tread a difficult path between local traditions and Western or Northern understandings of peace. However, the positive, hybrid forms of peace that are emerging need to depend on deep 'local ownership' if local legitimacy and a viable peace are to be attained.

This is not to romanticise such local agency and organisation, or to reify a new form of 'native administration' and international trusteeship. To be clear, peace formation is directed at peace, not violence or self-interest; it works from the most marginalised position in terms of power relations, material resources and status. Even so, it appears to represent a significant force in terms of local legitimacy and agency. Peace formation may remain marginal to the political process because it does not conform to nationalist objectives, as in Cyprus; it may be coopted by the state, as in Nepal; it may partly endeavour to preserve existing and predatory customary or religious hierarchies, as in Afghanistan or Sierra Leone; but it also represents a significant social and political agency, more open to reform and, in the context of any rights-based or representational understanding of (liberal) peace, it cannot be ignored. The agency it signals has become formative of peace and the state in many cases over the last twenty years.

Comprehending these dynamics, as Chambers has argued in another context, involves 'putting the last first', a partial reversal, and certainly a refinement, of Western knowledge about peace.[88] In the cases discussed above, such peace-formation agency has eventually been integrated into the state and the state should as a result become more fully representative of all local identity groups in society. This blending of the formal and informal aspects of peace and governance is now perceived to be essential for a sustainable form of peace. These agendas are related to those long proposed by many scholars and some policymakers, and again more recently in the Busan agreement and by the G7+ (an organisation of so-called fragile states – the 'club that everyone wants to leave', including Timor-Leste, Somalia, Sierra Leone and fifteen others).[89] The Busan agreement on peacebuilding was influenced by this lobbying group, whose interest in achieving the MDGs, for example, is far more direct than that of many donors, for whom poverty and conflict are distant problems. Such developments have brought to the fore the notion that societies and their elites also build peace and states, not just donors or state elites. As a result, the peace that emerges should be locally shaped and based if it is to be legitimate, and not simply a product of an authoritarian state or trusteeship form of intervention. This means that any peace and process involved in its creation, and any resulting state or set of political institutions, laws, rights and needs frameworks, will be hybrid in character; the more consensual they are, the more likely it is that a positive form of hybrid peace will result.

Given the widespread nature of these peace-formation phenomena in many post-conflict environments around the world, and the interest of governments and civil-society actors in developing informal local peace committees into state institutions, from Kenya and Ghana to Nepal and Timor-Leste, it may well be that they represent a convergence between the Western, rational-legal state and more local, socio-historical processes of peacemaking. These dynamics endorse a common goal of the international, state and civil-society actors in creating an interwoven system to ensure peace. These dynamics underline how often they are at odds with each other currently. On the one hand, these dynamics may represent the translation of local aspirations for peace, security, development and identity into the state. On the other, they also represent the translation of the state into a more localised polity, less formal, less rational-legal and more contextual. This recent phenomenon of peace formation might indicate the emergence of a post-liberal peace depending on local forms of peace praxis as well as international capacity and enablement.

Conclusion: Towards a Positive Hybrid Peace

The emergence of a positive hybrid form of peace is a difficult but necessary part of any new agenda for peace. Peace formation offers local legitimacy, which may prevent the unintended consequences of external efforts, and it may be supported in order to overcome locally entrenched power asymmetries. Clearly, there are many more questions to be asked and answered about these processes, not least how they may be bridged and enabled without being instrumentalised. Furthermore, how might peace-formation signals be detected and fairly translated by external actors, and how might direct or governmental power be used to support these signals? How might subaltern sites of legitimacy, which seek a locally pluralist peace bridging the local, state and international scale, be aligned in favour of the subaltern and not contaminated by state or international interests? The turn to a more reflective understanding of international intervention and the local, the opening-up of critical agency and the recognition of the hybridity of any state or peace have offered a significant advance on older, monolithic narratives of peace, security and the state.

Peace formation and peace infrastructures offer the possibility of resolving the contradictions of an internationally perceived positive peace (as in liberal peacebuilding) which, in its transfer to different contexts, is converted into a negative hybrid peace or some form of neo-trusteeship or 'native administration'. It also offers the possibility that the state, with its dependence on state formation's negative agency, might offer more than a negative peace. Peace formation is essential for a positive hybrid form of peace.

It is from contextual and mediated, local, state, regional and international legitimacy that the agency for peacebuilding and peace formation arises in parallel. Legitimate authority arises from peace formation and peace infrastructures for a wide range of activities related to peace. Peace formation suggests a contextual framework of networks and relationships for peace, in which emancipation is often framed by culture and identity, material needs and some reference to international norms, but it also cannot engage the direct or structural forms of power that often block peace. The key object of peacemaking in general should be to build a consensus among peace formers in a given location and support them. This may lead to a more organic socio-political state framework, enabled by international actors and reflecting an international agreement reached equitably, rather than by a coalition of a few dominant actors.

International actors have long been aware of the legitimacy of such a move, making appeals for local participation, local ownership, community peacebuilding and bottom-up approaches, even if these appeals were mainly rhetorical. This is more than representing order in its absence, as Debrix argued the UN did with its traditional approach to peacekeeping, but less than engaging with the agency and aspirations of social actors and citizens in their local contexts and global networks.[90] Informal and social agencies are what make everyday life bearable in such difficult post-conflict environments, in practical ways and also in offering signals as to how internationals may facilitate the development of peace. The signals lie in critiques of, demands about, or resistance to certain strategies, in local acceptance or attempts to modify them, expressed through local leaders, NGOs, identity and religious groups, trade unions, professional groups, religious communities, media, peacebuilding and human-rights organisations, and women's and veterans' groups. They also lie in political and collective mobilisation for national unity and statehood, or to influence an externally constructed statebuilding project. The mere existence of such signals indicates that there are local peace-formational agencies already in operation.

These should be represented in the formation of political institutions, whether state or international. There have long been hints of this in related literatures, from Burton's focus on basic human needs in IR, to earlier Marxist literatures focusing on class and ownership issues, and general shifts in anthropology from cataloguing the exotic for the benefit of power to an understanding of social dynamics and alterity for their own sake, as well as in liberal aspirations for social contracts, law and rights.[91] Studies of peace matters have also long been aware of the need for bottom-up approaches, including local issues related to custom and society, whether or not theories were oriented to a more realist conflict-management approach or a more liberal-peacebuilding approach.[92] UN and World Bank policies, setting an example followed by many donors in the 1990s, also adopted such discourses. Reaching further back in time, policies and writings about the creation of peace and order have long recognised the basic capacities of individual agency and group mobilisation, and their tendency to be concerned with rights and needs, governance and international order.

The enablement of peace formation might increase the chances of dealing with root causes of conflict that impact on everyday life. Peace formation would need to be able to build relationships with citizens, subjects, the oppressed and the marginalised on their own terms, offering them a form of emancipation that they would recognise and embrace. This would mean bottom-up, subaltern agency rather than merely top-down agency, and empowerment of local and marginal actors, communities and individuals. It would mean exercising caution about institutional and state power and their ideologies' and biases' unintended consequences for rights and needs, and an attempt to connect with local epistemologies of peace. It would be a process of enablement and liberation rather than a process of intervention and governance (direct or governmental power).[93] Peace formation cannot achieve this without support from external actors, of course.

This means more than mere participation or local ownership representing externalised praxes of intervention seeking local support. This is not to inscribe the international, national or local with new forms of colonialism or with local power dynamics posing as 'local knowledge'.[94] Representation of the new citizens and their institutions in the international community would be vital, as would consideration of their situation and needs in the context of the developmental shortcomings of the global economy, not to mention their need to be able to move and trade freely across borders uninhibited by somewhat Orientalist visa regimes (as until recently in the case of Bosnia-Herzegovina and most other post-conflict countries such as Kosovo). This is not to see hybridity as mere mimicry. Peace formers have long bemoaned such injustices, and internationals have so far failed to respond, but clearly they should.

Positive hybridity is a site of radical possibilities for peace, representing a deeper legitimacy and democratic voice (just as much as it is a site of hegemony, power or disorder).[95] Peace formation enables a perspective of local and networked positive contributions to peace, drawing on a range of infrapolitical and infrastructural dynamics beyond the rational-legal and market-driven logic of liberal institutionalism. It sees power, norms, law and rights as working horizontally and from the bottom up as well as from the top down. Such strategies do not valorise or romanticise the local, or seek to place it solely in the context of Western knowledge, or claim that it is self-sufficient, that the West cannot help and that its multiple practices cannot be transformed, or that the state will disappear or cease to be predatory.[96] It is to claim that great efforts should be made to listen to such voices by both state and international actors if they are to develop or to retain a wider legitimacy.[97]

At the same time, peace-formation agencies should not be seen as ahistorical and eternally present, or solely resistant.[98] Instead, the local scale needs to be seen in the context of its divisions, contexts and networks, local, state, regional and global, and engaged with via a wide range of methodologies if the dynamics, agencies and potential of hybrid forms of politics are to be understood, and if a positive hybrid peace that is emancipatory and empathetic is to emerge. It needs to be understood in terms of its local, national and international networks and connections. International agencies and markets, as well as globalisation itself, need to critically appraised from the perspective of the local conditions required for a contextual, emancipatory and empathetic form of peace.[99] This acknowledges and recognises local and international agency and their impact on each other. It acknowledges differences over matters of rights, needs and inequality. It does not privilege, a priori, one form of knowledge over another. It may also not be useful to see the social as separate from the state if the needs, rights and identity of the local are to be reflected from the grassroots to the international, as hybridity would suggest. This is, rather, a case of parallel local, state and international structures forming as at present.

This basis for peace-formation processes requires an understanding of emancipation that goes beyond its Enlightenment roots and its modernist Marxist or liberal conceptualisations. In

Enlightenment terms, emancipation represented the application of scientific knowledge through rationalism to a particular problem of war, violence, need or oppression (as opposed to a dependence on god or king). It became associated with social justice and rights as civil-society movements developed in opposition to slavery, militarisation and class differentials (most notably in the work of Marx). In its modernist liberal conception, emancipation has been associated with democracy and human rights, as well as cosmopolitan norms and law at the international level to uphold them. A liberal conception of emancipation focuses on a form of peace inherent in state governance framed by democracy and rights. A critical version enables this via a wide variety of international interventions, whereas a post-structural understanding highlights the need of individuals and communities to emancipate themselves according to their identity and socio-historical value systems, avoiding international narratives of norms and rights as well as the state. Clearly, all of these versions are unsatisfactory alone, but what can be taken from them is that a post-liberal version would value autonomy, local agency and identity, equality, and international enablement of citizens in their own context and subjectivity (rather than through external intervention), indeed intersubjectivity, as well as a liberal state and a mixed economy. This may represent an ungainly balance, of course. Peace in reality does not offer elegance or simplicity. It is a recognition of a messy reality, contingency, diversity, pluralism and flexibility, and processes that are designed to facilitate, assist and transform themselves as well as the lives of those in post-conflict zones.

What emerges from the above analysis of the general tensions and contradictions of hybrid forms of peace and the pressures that are leading towards post-liberal forms is that there are two main categories of hybridity, both for peace and politics. The first is a hegemonic, negative form that is predicated on superficial mimicry and compliance with the liberal-peace system but with modifications in hidden spaces and around its fringes, mostly dependent on local, critical forms of agency. The second is a more radical, positive form where such critical agency might mobilise on a grander scale to take the lead in producing forms of peace that are more local than liberal or driven by state or international interests.[100] Accommodation is not the result of one model emerging to unite all, but the fusion of a range of different understandings of peace, politics, progress, rights, needs and institutions.

A more locally oriented form of hybridity may be radical if it offers local identity and needs as part of its basis. It will be less so if it involves any compromise on basic human rights, though their broadening and deepening could be envisaged. However, local forms of hybridity are often radical because they aspire to aspects of the liberal value system such as human rights and democracy. Local forms may also be hegemonic if they rest on the support of historical stratifications and elite power. An internationally oriented form of hybridity might be radical if it offers the local scale a range of rights and needs that have traditionally been the domain of elites alone. It may be hegemonic if it reflects those elites over the masses and their rights and needs. The determination of order according to these permutations of local or international hegemony or radicalism indicates the necessity of such radicalism in the search for contextual and universal rights and needs frameworks, which give rise to the institutions and dynamics of peace. It equates to a critical agency in which the politics of peace emerge from 'equaliberty', micro-solidarities, local-to-global networks and self-formation, as well as autonomy, resistance, identity and, of course, the liberal peace.

Positive, hybrid forms of peace do not fit neatly with state sovereignty or nationalistic understandings of political order, though hybrid forms of politics might. The latter may lead to a negative hybrid peace, dominated by predatory capital, elites and external rule. Equally, they may lead to a positive hybrid peace in which contextual conflict systems are countered by local peace systems, which are in turn supported by internationals. A positive hybrid peace transcends state borders and formal levels of analysis. Hybrid forms of politics also indicate a letting-go of colonial mindsets (even if unintended) within the donor, peacebuilding, statebuilding, international-community and foreign-policy establishments.[101] They may transcend traditional class distinctions and epistemic frameworks of thought. They transcend culture and identity but they also express them. They transcend foundationalism, are fluid and depend on the growing capacity of late modernity to empower fluidity, via technology and communication, in education and thought, and in politics, economics and society. Contextual as well as regional or international/transnational forms of agency are expressed through these processes; fragmented but mobile critical agency challenges embedded structures of power.

Peace formation does not offer a teleological framework of evolution as state formation does (from negative agency to a negative peace and a state formed by war). It does not offer a process whereby critical agency produces a positive peace and a state shaped by Enlightenment values and the liberal peace. Peace formers are normally a significant minority in society; they struggle to keep or develop existing or new processes of peace. They cannot engage with direct or structural power, and their subaltern responses to it or to governmentality are subtle. Instead, peace formation offers an uneven and low-level response to conflict, to imposed forms of peace and to the neoliberal state, and looks to local, hidden processes and the international community for support. Peace formers fade in and out of vision; sometimes they become instrumental in a peace process or a process that is formative of the state, but often peace formation provides indications of a way out of violence in everyday life, or signals about legitimacy and the nature of the state. Peace formation offers faint signals for the construction of a locally legitimate, necessarily hybrid, positive peace.

V

Peace Formation versus Intervention

Introduction

There are three sites or levels of peace and progressive politics, with differing norms, identities, institutions and types of power: the local and everyday, the state, and the international system. Aligning these, deciding which should lead, coordinating their complementary roles, resolving their tensions and dealing with the various aspects of conflict, requires an agreement on the nature of everyday peace, progressive politics, the state and the international. This is the key to a positive hybrid peace, which includes contextual resonance, reform, and equity across local and international scales.

All too often, high-level talks between leaders or warlords over territory and the state have dominated peace processes, at the expense of local peace, reconciliation and emancipation (as with the fifty-year-long – and still counting – high-level talks over the Cyprus Problem).[1] Peace praxis and theory have certain problem-solving limitations and international or state biases. Efforts are required to move beyond these blockages. A positive hybrid peace requires, as I have argued in previous chapters, that peace formation be understood in its local contexts and in its state and international networks, as well as in terms of debates around the conditions for progressive politics. It should be understood as a discursive formation, which may exercise agency to build a locally resonant peace, legitimacy, representation, rights and redistributions of resources. This also reflects what legitimate institutions and authority are for, and essentially what the state is for. In this sense, peace formation requires a confluence of direct, structural, governmental and normative, as well as subaltern, agencies.

However, peace-formation processes are often in opposition not only to localised or regional conflict dynamics, but also to the linkages between peace and statebuilding within the international peace architecture, aimed at creating a homogeneous state and mode of life. Furthermore, they are affected by global capital and dominant international interests. From a peace-formation and subaltern perspective, these processes aim at expunging local history, identity, culture, religion and society, and replacing them with a rational-legal administrative framework and a soft form of nationalism, in which individuals focus on consuming and producing ever more efficiently. This is the progressive version of politics that has, since the Cold War, been appended to high-level peace talks by internationals. This positive peace project has failed where it confronts key norms and values of society, as well as material needs in both a local and a global context.

Clearly, a positive peace is not perceived as such from below, because it is either a liberal peace or represents neoliberal statebuilding. From below, a positive hybrid peace would be more acceptable, and would involve active peace formation. However, the peace-formation project is also fragile, subsisting only because of great ingenuity and supportive networks, despite the fact that it offers a clear advance over older conflict-management, resolution, transformation and peacebuilding systems, or that it may well provide internationals with an avenue to enable peace. The problem is that internationals operate in a relatively parochial epistemological framework, which claims a universal ontological status that justifies a global perspective: it is rare that they accept the diversity of local political institutions (which they often exploit when it comes to identity). The inability of international actors to accept difference in terms of identity, local culture and institutions, as well as in modes and paces of development, has been noted over the years by the very civil-society actors that internationals claim to be empowering.[2] Yet peacebuilding and statebuilding praxis underlines the limits of both the will and the power of internationals to 'make' peace.

The reasons for this are complex, down to methodological limitations and blinkers, ontological hypocrisy, and an epistemology that enables sacrifices to be made through the exercise of executive power on behalf of voiceless others in the name of 'global' interests, 'universal norms' and economic power. Underlying this is a link with the West's colonial and imperial past (and, some would argue, its neocolonial present) and a now-challenged assumption that its norms, sciences, institutions, legal framework, military power and economic systems set it above emergent societies. From this rationality of governance – for security and prosperity – emerged the UN, IFI, donor and INGO architecture, which continues this process in liberal or neoliberal form, depending on the preferences of key donors and the IFIs. This approach is carried through all international policies aimed at 'the local'. It is a hierarchy of eradication and reform, and, in practice, of state-formation assumptions about endemic violence, a negative peace or, perhaps at best, a negative hybrid peace. Peacebuilding and statebuilding are merely assemblages of practices, policies and thinking used to deal with post-conflict zones – merely one type of ungoverned *terra nullis* in a world of many threats. They combat the external fear of 'ungovernmentality' in which local resistance and identity produces a less manageable web of 'many peaces'. They represent the soft edge of a sophisticated form of hegemony, a paternalistic and paradoxical attempt to solidify an international peace, and support rights and civil society, but also both to deny and to remake local peace systems.

On the one hand, no longer is 'peace' an abstract concept that cannot be created other than through historical chance, but, on the other hand, its very construction is fraught with many pitfalls. This has underlined the conceptual limitations of a literature and practice now dominated by peacebuilding, statebuilding and state-formation concepts, as previous chapters have described. Statebuilding has not become the antidote to state-formation dynamics of violence, nor has peacebuilding in its liberal form connected with local forms of political legitimacy, with their social, cultural, political and economic requirements. They have attempted to monopolise the local, and have thus become associated with Western paternalism, hypocrisy and insensitivity, raising the spectre of still-unaddressed legacies of colonialism and much 'hidden resistance'. Failed statebuilding has been the result of externalised states being based on blueprints determined by decontextualised and depoliticised agendas for states. Though they provide security, political rights and institutions, and market access, they offer little in the way of material political rights. Nor have they been proficient at developing a social contract, meaning that they have led to virtual forms of peace that have mainly benefited elites who have been able to occupy the state.

Remodelling this relationship to allow both local and international processes to meet their potential is necessary. This chapter sketches out how these various conceptual and policy frameworks relate and interact, and what their potential might be.

Relating the Four Conceptual Frameworks

The 'failed by design' type of statebuilding has come about because of confusion in the literature relating to the dynamics of state formation, and overly prescriptive and extravagant policy claims, particularly early on in the Iraq and Afghanistan missions. These focused on security, systems, processes, coordination, efficiency and the production of neoliberal subjects, rather than on the quality of the peace citizens might experience in everyday life. In this, it was heavily influenced by the realist perspective of a victor's peace, with its resultant understanding of the state. This contributed to a heavily and negatively romanticised version of local-agency and state structures, influenced by state-formation literature and the vestiges of a colonial attitude, and arrived at by removing the normative concerns liberal peacebuilding carried relating to civil societies' constitutive framework for the contractual state, instead perceiving civil society mainly as a subject of the state (and of international donors). The everyday has thus been ignored, causing an imbalance that has undermined the state and its structures, surprising internationals who believe that the state was mainly a rational-legal institution rather than a social framework. Indeed, internationals subscribing to liberal dogma tend to see society as problematic, and mired in custom, ethnicity, tribalism or ideology. Liberalism shows how such societies may be reformed and modernised by elites. This view has fed, and been fed by, ideological expediency and self-interest in international policy towards conflict-affected contexts, which in turn has infected the nature of peace and the state it has endeavoured to create. It has led to a focus on statebuilding and peacebuilding as a way of negating state formation through direct, structural and governmental power, while overlooking peace formation and its subaltern agency as crucial to local legitimacy.

Thus, it appears that conceptualising a positive hybrid peace – as a first stage towards better practices – requires a disaggregation and examination of the relationships between state formation, statebuilding, peacebuilding and peace formation. As this study has so far outlined, a far more balanced model than liberal peacebuilding or neoliberal statebuilding recognises four cornerstones:

(1) *State formation* describes the formation of the state through indigenous or internal violence between competing groups and their agendas, which often turn the state into a criminal and predatory elite racket, à la Tilly.[3] This leads ultimately to internal balances of power and power-sharing arrangements based on hierarchies and inequalities that perpetuate structural forms of violence. State formation is a mainly internal exercise of direct and structural power. Owing to the shifting alliances and kinds of force often associated with forms of identity, parochial or national, the nature of the resultant state is determined in favour of authoritarian elites. It also facilitates their control of security and capital. At best, states so formed are unstable and represent a negative or victor's peace. Attempts by internationals to intervene in this process have often simply dragged them into the dynamics of violence (Iraq and South Sudan being recent examples) or at best a superficial mitigation of its effects.

(2) *Statebuilding* is the resultant externalised process aimed at rectifying this situation. It is focused on the role of external actors, organisations, donors, IFIs, agencies and INGOs, and on building institutions for security, democracy and markets, and creating basic infrastructure and public services. Statebuilding is an exercise of direct, structural and governmental power. It requires

international technical expertise and capacity, and attempts to persuade or force local elites to comply with liberal or neoliberal institutions as they are under construction. Statebuilding's aim is to develop an institutional framework that will begin to tame the forces of violence and offer the possibility of a future neoliberal state as a constructive member of the international community. However, it is normally aimed at producing the basic framework of a neoliberal state in a procedural and technocratic sense, and is less concerned with norms or civil society, as with examples from Afghanistan to Liberia. Ultimately, neoliberal statebuilding indicates the development of a 'small' state with significant security capacity. This combination means the state that comes into being is externally dependent and subject to international capital, which often provokes some internal resistance. As a result, statebuilding tends to lead to a negative hybrid peace.

(3) *Peacebuilding* in its liberal guise focuses on external support for liberally oriented, rights-based institutions with a special and legitimating focus on norms and human rights, civil society and a social contract via representative institutions embedded in a rule of law. Peacebuilding exercises governmentality and its focus is more directly on building peace rather than building a state as a passport for peace in the future. This support is legitimated by international norms, assuming that these are universal and so widely acceptable. In its very early form, it was more focused on localised dynamics of peace. By the 1990s, it had come to focus on universal, liberal norms, as in democracy and human rights. It parallels statebuilding but is normatively broader, more focused on a rights-based peace than singular understandings of security and sovereignty, though these are inevitably intertwined. There are two alternative modes of liberal peace, in theory leading to different types of state. First, the liberal mode implies social democracy and so a strong/large and interven-

tionist state focused mainly on material redistribution and rights. Secondly, a trusteeship mode enables external oversight and control of liberal institutions, creating protectorate-style states, as with Bosnia-Herzegovina. Both tend to arouse much resistance, and therefore lead to a negative hybrid peace.

This much has been theorised to some degree in the existing literature, but there is a missing dimension at the local scale. That it has been ignored partly arises from the inherent biases of Northern, rational, compliance-oriented, problem-solving theory. The historical dominance of the West has been naturalised through such dominance. Any positive form of agency at the local scale has also been ignored because the types of agencies, networks and activities it represents are small-scale, fragmented and disaggregated, informal, ontologically different, sometimes non- or only partially liberal, rather than being representative of large-scale industrial mobilisation, and secular, rational-legal and official in nature. This is not to romanticise the capacity of individuals, families, communities, societies and their networks, or of liberation, emancipation and resistance, but to accept that they have a fundamental role to play in the dynamics of politics and the development of institutions and rights (especially under any deepening democratic framework). Statebuilding and state formation represent different ends of the same spectrum and liberal peacebuilding parallels statebuilding. They are all based on the application of force, liberal interventionism or softer forms of external agency, such as conditionality. Yet there is an obvious omission from an emerging four-sided matrix representing the architecture of both the contemporary state and peace praxis. This implies the following:

(4) *Peace-formation processes* can be defined as the mobilisation – formal or informal, public or hidden – of indigenous[4] or local agents of

peacebuilding, conflict resolution and development, or of peace actors in customary, religious, cultural, social or local political or local government settings. They exercise subaltern, critical agency though a range of local- to international-scale networks. They seek to find ways of establishing peace processes and the dynamics of local forms of peace in everyday conflict settings, in their social and historical context, from which political institutions, norms, law, rights and processes of redistribution may emerge. These are influenced by the international system as well as also being constitutive of state, regional and global positive hybrid forms of peace. They may operate in relation to local understandings of politics and institutions, welfare and economics, social and customary resonance, and identity, law and security, framed also by external praxes of intervention and their norms for state–society relations. This process occurs through non-violent, politicised processes, representing resistance and critical agency, as well as cooptation and compliance. They offer some socio-historical continuity but are also interested in transformation, drawing on external influences. Again, this is not to romanticise the local or its related peace-formation processes, but to accept the primacy of rights, democracy and needs, supported by institutions, politics, the economy and their epistemological basis.[5] From a peace-formation perspective, the role of the state and the international is to build peace, which has to be contextual if it is to be sustainable.[6] Peace formation represents a site in which the new and progressive politics of emancipation are being contested for the twenty-first century (extending the liberal-international, liberal-institutional and rights-based approach that shaped much of the twentieth century).

In an agonistic way, the four cornerstones of this matrix, representing several phases of an interdisciplinary and intermethodological dialogue about the international, state and peace spanning at least forty years, point to the same thing: the emergence of a peaceful and positive hybrid order. This order rests on harmony, pluralism and relative equality, rather than structural violence, identity discrimination, inequality or even a benign hegemony. Sociology, anthropology, development studies, post-colonial and subaltern studies, as well as economics, politics and IR, have all played a role in this debate and its interwoven methodologies.[7] It points to a hybridised epistemology for peace in simple terms. Positive hybrid peace requires 'unity and diversity, conflict and consent, integration and exclusion, substantial identity and openness to indefinite change', to quote Balibar.[8] Whichever of these four cornerstones is dominant will determine the character of that order, the state it creates and the quality of the 'peace' that emerges. Understanding peace formation in its relationship to the other three dynamics is probably key to the sustainability of any peace and state that emerges, yet it is also the most challenging aspect of the whole process of creating a viable and legitimate order or peace.

A peace dominated by the processes of local-scale peace formation also connected to externalised peacebuilding is likely to be more viable, particularly if they actively shape one another. A peace that is dominated by statebuilding or state formation is likely to be very conservative and security-oriented, and is unlikely to survive in the long term because it will lack both international and broad local legitimacy and resonance (as the state will tend to be elite-dominated and authoritarian). Eventually, such inequalities, whether in political structures, class and social hierarchies, or material resources, will cause enough tension for the system to lose its legitimacy. A peace dominated by liberal peacebuilding is likely to rest on external support and international rather than local legitimacy. It may survive for as long as the international normative consensus is supported in a material manner by IOs or external states, but it results in a poor-quality peace in the local context – as so many post-Cold War cases of intervention have shown. Peacebuilding and statebuilding may appear to offer an efficient shortcut to the neoliberal state and liberal peace, and connect with, and support, peace formation, but they should not do so at the expense of autonomy, identities and local ownership.[9] All the frameworks for peace, from the international to the local, require pluralism and equity.

The following diagrams (on pp. 184 and 185) outline these dynamics. They show the way state formation shapes external understandings of local agency as negative and how statebuilding and peacebuilding effectively become exercises of direct, structural and governmental power to prevent or remove this 'negative agency'. However, peace formation offers local knowledge and legitimacy, which no externalised approach can offer.

Statebuilding is a praxis mainly focused on technical and programmatic aspects of state design, based on rationalism, individualism and self-help, whereas peacebuilding has become far more focused on a normative framework for politics within the state, including rights and a social contract, and therefore some sense of community and legitimacy. To some degree, Figure 1 presents artificial distinctions between the four concepts – it is important to note the many connections and overlaps between them. These overlaps represent the synergies and relationships via which a hybrid form of peace may emerge.[10] However, the diagram also points to the problem of direct, structural and governmental power, which confronts peace formation, especially in the form of inequality, injustice and insecurity. The reality is that negative forms of hybrid peace have emerged from these interactions. A positive form of hybrid peace would require a shift from the discourses of 'intervention', 'development', 'building' and other validations of Northern power and legitimacy.

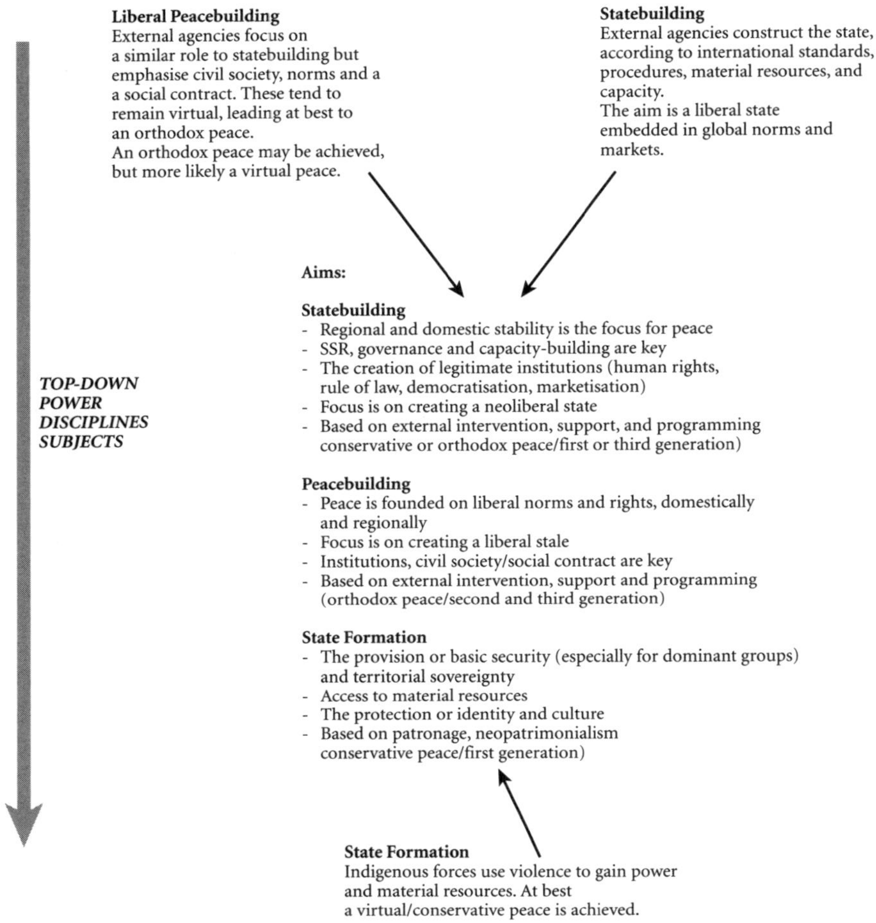

Figure 1. A historical matrix of conflict and peace

In practice, the presence of peace formation among the four cornerstones in Figure 2 on p. 185 prevents an elision of statebuilding and peacebuilding into a securitised, hegemonic or sometimes predatory model for politics. Peace formation preserves a focus on emancipation, empathy, rights and a social contract from the perspective of

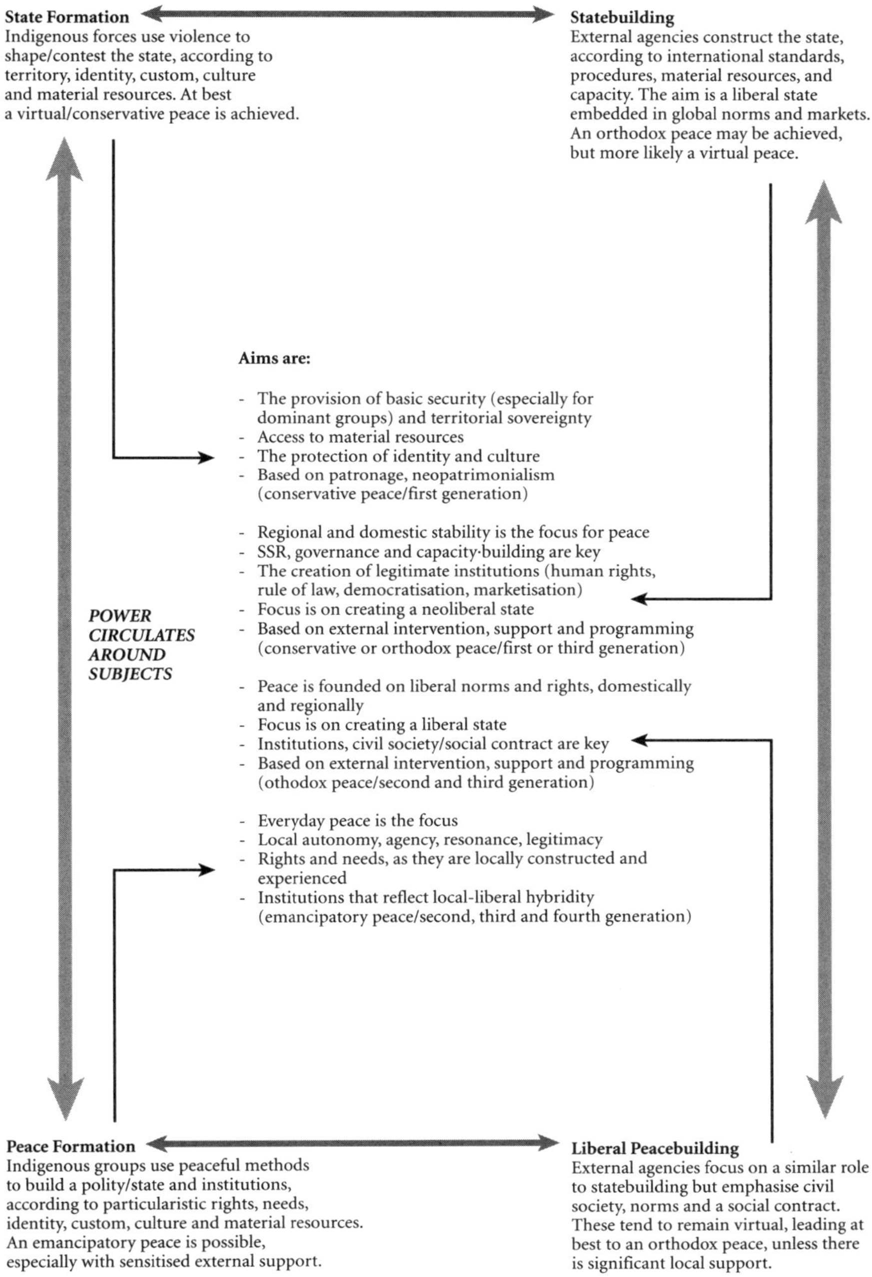

Figure 2. A contemporary matrix of conflict and peace

the subject in the conflict-affected environment, which ultimately points to a more emancipatory form of peace, one that is difficult to comprehend from the international perspective. It does so by making clear the significance of peace formation for statebuilding and peacebuilding as well as in opposing state formation. Each cornerstone implies a range of actors, interests, dynamics, institutions, structures and agencies. If they are taken together in the range of relationships the diagram implies, different forms of peace, state, politics and development may arise.

Statebuilding is a narrow version of peacebuilding, with its focus on institutions and security as a way of taming state formation, whereas peace formation is the essential source of local legitimacy for the international norms and interests that statebuilding and peacebuilding represent. It also offers the hope of a less naive approach to contextual forces of state formation, though, of course, on its own it may not be able to negate them. International norms and law have mainly been constructed on the basis of a Euro-Atlantic understanding of IR and the requirements for order since the early twentieth century (though this is now widening considerably in the post-colonial context). The greater the number of voices – from emerging states to citizens newly empowered in different ways – the more international legitimacy needs to be reconsidered and to be made more locally inclusive. It is in the process of peace formation that mediated forms of identity, custom, culture, political rights and economic needs emerge at an institutional level, shaping the state and making it both representative and resonant, and providing sufficient support and legitimacy from its citizens to enable a plausible and self-sustaining peace. It is from this understanding that a positive and hybrid peace may be externally facilitated, in the dual role of taming the violence of statebuilding processes and enabling a peace that reflects contextual needs, rights and identity.

Peace formation implies a reconstruction of political community, the state and international organisations from the ground up, if they are to be representative, democratic and responsive to the situations of their subjects in local, state, regional and global contexts. Ultimately, peace-formation processes also connect to a post-colonial civil society. Such resistance and critical agency can be seen as contributing to a local and international conversation about the impact of hegemony, colonial praxis, the global economy and the reconstitution of rights, needs and identity. This conversation is carried along transversal, transnational networks and connects both the liberal and the local, the global North and the global South. These are driving the emergence of new peace networks in subtle and unscripted ways.[11] These networks, in post-colonial and subaltern fashion, normally transcend the state as well as any Northern consensus, however, via dynamics of networked agency. They operate via the international system itself, through communications, trade, civil and global civil society, donors and agencies, IFIs, NGOs and even academia where such critical agency is now exercised on both a global and a local scale.[12] They are dynamic and offer legitimacy at both levels, in cultural, social, political and economic terms.[13] They draw on local and international forms of legitimacy and operate from platforms that the state – when not representing the consensus of its citizens or international norms – finds difficult to engage with or countermand. Increasingly, they critique the state, international organisations, and financial institutions and donors in a manner reminiscent of the subaltern critique of imperialism.[14] As has commonly occurred, the UN, World Bank and others react by adjusting their strategies and policies to reflect their intent to do more for those who need assistance, while doing no harm and ensuring local ownership rather than trusteeship emerges as a result of their involvement. Nevertheless, they are only partially successful, though what success emerges out of this process depends upon peace-formation dynamics as much as it does upon international engagement.

Yet since the early 2000s, policy and intellectual understandings of the relationship of state formation, statebuilding and liberal peacebuilding indicate that statebuilding is now the antidote for the often violent processes of state formation. Ironically, this also implies that peacebuilding in its liberal form acts as an antidote for peace formation where this achieves a form of peace that is not commensurate with liberal norms. This problematic understanding of peace in general undermines its legitimacy. Instead, as has now become clear, peacebuilding and statebuilding should align with, and support, peace formation. However, it is probably true to say that local processes of peace formation are often in partial opposition to statebuilding and liberal-peace processes, as well as to state formation. This is not to suggest that local agency represents an ideal subject, but that 'less is more' in terms of intervention. It may be preferable to focus on the enablement of local actors who have long-standing knowledge, legitimacy and capacity, and who do not exercise direct or governmental power. This would add legitimacy to the reform of the state and the nature of the peace, and relations between domestic actors as well as with international actors would rest within a local context. Executive decision-making power extruded from international donors, agencies, IFIs, the UN or foreign ministries for reasons of peacekeeping or humanitarian concern should not seep into political, identity, social, cultural or economic realms reserved for local peoples to determine. Internationals may, however, need to deal with local or state-level exercises of direct, structural and governmental power where they are producing direct and structural violence, in order to allow peace formation to prosper.

Clearly, peacebuilding should facilitate peace formation (and vice versa), and be very wary of prejudging it, on normative grounds especially. By contrast, state formation should probably not inform statebuilding. Mediating the state is a different matter as long as power relations are not brought to bear by external or elite actors, and the material needs, identity and culture of citizens are taken into account on their own terms. This means that the citizens or subjects represent their own understandings of peace formation and the way that peacebuilding can assist its various dynamics, and that they also do this in the knowledge of the possibilities peacebuilding represents (including its liberal and neoliberal ideological leanings).[15] This is not to inscribe the international, national or local with new forms of colonialism or with local power dynamics posing as 'local knowledge' – indicating new forms of trusteeship.[16] It is not to see hybridity as mere mimicry. Instead, hybridity is a site of possible radical possibilities for positive and emancipatory peace.[17]

It is notable that Tilly's work on state formation was a precursor to his later work on civil-society organisations. Similarly, many development-studies scholars, anthropologists and political theorists have tended to move from analysis of the failures of systemic, institutional, or state- or market-focused research to work on local, bottom-up agencies and organisations. They have even turned to counterorganisations of the sort partially envisaged by many sociologists and philosophers interested in social sources of power and agency, including Foucault and, later, Scott.[18] The following diagram on p. 190 illustrates the various issues, dynamics and actors involved in the 'formation' and 'building' approaches and illustrates how force, governance, government, actors and social dynamics are central to this quadripartite model of the basic elements of peace, order and violence, and how easily each element can be conflict- or peace-inducing. Figure 3 also aligns each of the elements of order and peace with the four generations of thinking about peace and conflict that I have outlined in an earlier work.

State Formation	**Statebuilding**
Violence/force	Governance
Territorial sovereignty	Soft sovereignty
Weberian State/nationalism	Weberian state embedded in regional and international security complex
State autonomy/security	International security complex; regional security
Elite governance	Elite but also representative governance
Highly stratified/class	Merit-based
Hegemony and domination	Emancipation through security and markets
Elites, military and militias, allies	Major regional powers, donors, UN, World Bank, agencies, INGOs, etc.
Communitarianism	Communitarianism
Structral/Direct Power	***Governmental Power/Ocassional Direct Power***
No conflict-resolution processes	Institutions and markets manage conflict
First-Generation Approach	***First-/Third-Generation Approach***
Peace Formation	**Peacebuilding (Liberal)**
Social dynamics/agency/capacity/identity	Government
Contextual and legitimate	International legitimacy
Harmony/difference/merit/patronage/patriarchy	Shared/norms/merit
Local agency and organisation for peace, including institutions, rules, norms, rights and needs	Cosmopolitan norms, institutions, law, social contract, civil society, humanitarianism, mainly rights
Localised understandings of emancipation	Liberal versions of emancipation
Contextual governance	Liberal government
Local actors, CSOs, NGOs, trade unions, religious groups, customary institutions	UN, World Bank, agencies, INGOs/NGOs, donors, etc
Contextual/customary conflict resolution	Conflict resolution derived from liberal norms
Pluralism	Universalism
Subaltern Agency: some direct and government power on a small scale	***Governmental Power***
Third-/Fourth-Generation Approach	***Second-/Third-Generation Approach***

Figure 3. Related issues, actors and dynamics

A first-generation conflict-management approach revolves around structural and direct power aimed at a victor's or negative peace, whereas a second-generation conflict-resolution approach brings in bottom-up, or subaltern, power, but within a liberal value system (a positive peace imagined from an internationalist perspective). A third-generation peacebuilding and statebuilding approach revolves mainly around governmental power, again within political liberalism (and once more a positive peace from an internationalist perspective). A fourth-generation approach brings in the subaltern in the context of its alterity, making clear the necessity of pluralism for a positive hybrid peace to emerge, viewed from either or both a local and an international perspective.[19]

The fourth-generation approach makes clear that the process of peace formation offers vital levels of legitimacy and understanding of context necessary for peacebuilding, as well as for the attempt via statebuilding to tame the processes of state formation, which should also strongly influence any externally led intervention or statebuilding process. It makes clear that statebuilding and peacebuilding are necessary parts of any peace process in the short, medium and long term, but also that they suffer from internal contradictions that limit their contributions without a concurrent engagement with the more contextual processes of peace formation. At the same time, peace formation may remain a 'subsistence peacebuilding' activity to a large degree, dependent on marginal but critical agency, and very few material resources, without international assistance. It may run parallel, and disconnected as a social process, to the state and international project of peace in its various forms, or it might integrate with them. It may do so while becoming coopted or it may do so while maintaining an independent identity.

Clearly, a positive hybrid peace is preferable, given that an internationally oriented positive or negative peace would lack local legitimacy, and a negative hybrid peace would probably lack both local and international legitimacy. The objective would be to find a progressive interrelationship between peace formation, peacebuilding and statebuilding that mitigates state-formation violence and other forms of local violence as well as creating a supportive international political and economic environment. Solving conflicts and making peace cannot only be carried out by focusing on the state or norms, but must also engage with local social practices and the injustices and inequalities maintained by the international system. Peace formation does not depend on idealised local subjects or on benevolent internationals. Instead, different political struggles interact to determine the nature of peace, institutions, norms, rights and the state, and run from the local to the global, forming key narratives of legitimacy. The smaller the gap between local and global narratives, the more the universalist impulse of the international is shaped by the multiple particularisms of the local and their interactions. Power relations determine the overall shape of the hybrid peace and the form of the state that emerges, but as power circulates and includes resistance, local agency plays an important role in shaping peace. This is not a matter of enabling hegemony to have its way (as in the liberal-peace and neoliberal-state model), but a method of understanding how the local-to-global architecture of peace is transforming and redefining the contemporary framework of emancipation.

The four-cornered understanding of the underlying dynamics of peace and order (as in Figure 2) has implications for the nature of democracy, rights, needs and civil society, and the construction of the rule of law and constitutions. Similarly, it affects the type of property rights and economic system that emerges in the form of the state, and the way in which consensus is made, resources are distributed and rights are maintained in the international system. While peace formation, and all of the cultural, historical, social, economic and political dynamics it implies, has an impact on, but is also mediated by, the state and the broader compromises any pluralist constitution entails, it also has a significant impact on the international. Witness the ways in which local ownership, poverty, crisis response, peacekeeping, peacebuilding and development have emerged in historical terms as responses to the international echoes of local problems. Thus, international practices shift as they learn about the local and their engagements' impacts and shortcomings on the ground. The state adjusts to both international and local pressures for legitimacy as well as to elites' power-sharing arrangements in the interests of placating them and holding them accountable.

Meanwhile, local understandings of legitimacy are communicated as local voices find ways of navigating upwards, towards the state and the international. This implies that peace formation in its multiple and diverse forms around the world influences the construction and form of the liberal peace (and its emerging reorganisation according to the interests of new donors and investors on the international stage). It includes IFIs, the diversifying groups of donors, and the increasingly diverse, transnational nature of NGOs and civil-society organisations. In effect, it implies the democratisation of the international as well as more direct forms of redistribution and a pluralist openness to difference in a more participatory, democratic, local context. This also creates a debate about any retrogressive aspects of the local (or overbearing aspect of the international). Yet, at the same time, it problematises many of the unitary concepts, actors and boundaries that an understanding of IR in late modernity implies. So the influence of peace formation is not merely significant for a replication of pre-existing institutions and norms, but also for a process of consensus-building whereby these are transformed, along with statebuilding, peacebuilding, peacekeeping or the role of the UN and donors more generally. Ultimately, what it illustrates are the

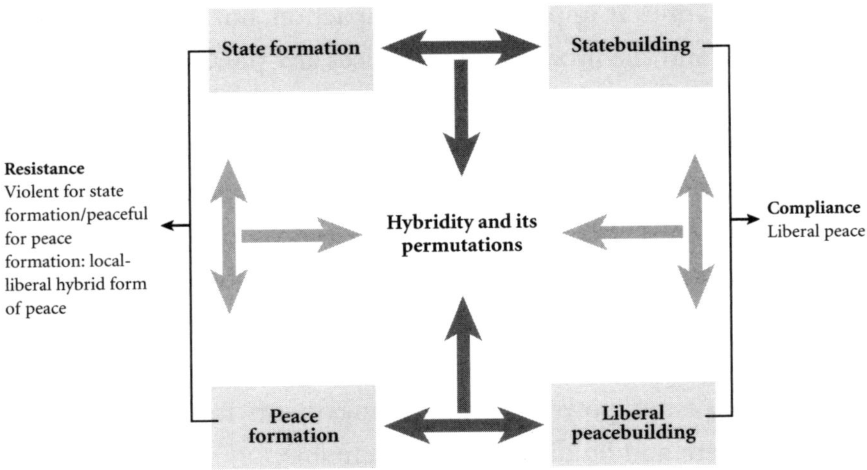

Figure 4. Dynamics of hybridity

multiple processes and agencies that produce a negative and positive hybrid peace as new structural, social, economic, political identity forms.

Figure 4 above illustrates how hybridity emerges and what its dominant form is depending on where its main influence arises – whether state formation, statebuilding, peacebuilding or peace formation. Figure 5 shows how international and local forces, broadly understood, produce peace through an agonistic interaction, which contests and reformulates legitimacy, authority, and the dynamics and institutions of peace. What this diagram also makes clear is that if local peace-formation dynamics align with international statebuilding and liberal peacebuilding, peacemaking should outweigh the violent processes of state formation. This tends not to occur, however, as the 'international' is so often the starting point for liberal peacebuilding and statebuilding because of Northern assumptions of normative and technical superiority and limited capacity to

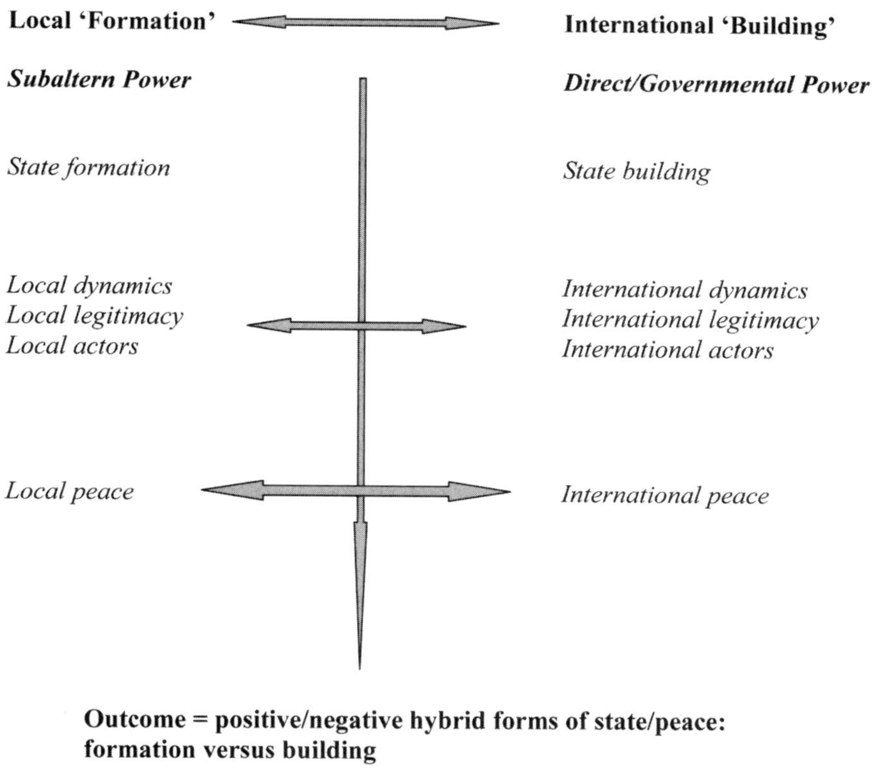

Figure 5. Formation of, and building, a hybrid peace

engage with the local. This deprives peace-formation agency of the structural power or capacity it requires to resist the local dynamics of conflict and maintain an autonomous place in the international architecture of peace. If this can be rectified so that peacebuilding is locally driven and externally supported, a local-liberal form of peace, or at least a local-regional/international form, might emerge. Such an outcome may represent a positive hybrid and post-liberal form of peace with high levels of local and international legitimacy.

Without a counterbalancing, context-sensitive understanding of peace formation and local forms of critical agency, international statebuilding and peacebuilding have little to guide them with regard to how local and international forms of peace and legitimacy interact to mitigate state-formation dynamics. Statebuilding strategies may mitigate state formation while peacebuilding should enable peace formation as an autonomous process resting on local socio-political and historical conceptions of legitimacy, which also encounter the international peace architecture and its own conceptions of legitimacy.

Conclusion

State-formation, statebuilding, peacebuilding and peace-formation approaches, when taken together, offer the possibility that an emancipatory peace can emerge from the constraint of predatory forms of power: the exercise of governance in the interests of the wider population; the refinement of international norms to be more widely inclusive; the improvement of instruments and policies to meet the identity, rights and needs claims of local populations; and the translation of the faint but vital signals of peace formation with regard to how legitimate forms of authority and an emancipatory peace should be configured. Taken together, they imply that an emancipatory and hybrid peace demands the reform of the overall system of relations, from the local to the global.

The realist strand of the literature on state formation has strongly influenced the statebuilding and peacebuilding literatures and policies. The historical, sociological and anthropological strands have more or less been ignored, because they contradict the right to executive and unaccountable authority of the internationals, as well as their romanticised perspectives of the dynamics of local agency (as mainly negative). The reason peacebuilding and statebuilding are externally driven and dependent is that there is a general perception that local agency is devious, that the state that emerges from its unalloyed development tends not to conform to liberal-democratic norms, and that its conflicts spill over into this international system. Indeed, similar perceptions are also often held of peace-formation or civil-society actors: they are apathetic, not innovative, and only express their peaceful agency because of the opportunities that external actors bring to the conflict environment. There is little appreciation among internationals, and even less among state-formation agents, of the risks of being part of civil-society and peace-formation activities, and of their inherent weight and legitimacy. There is little understanding of the ways in which pre-existing social networks, political systems, party systems, kinship systems, and custom and social hierarchies, may act to support or sanction those involved openly in peace formation. Likewise, there is little understanding of how, being embedded in these local, transnational and transversal frameworks, peace-formation agencies emerge and are able to operate. These bridge the liberal peace/neoliberal state with local, socio-political and historical frameworks, and mitigate direct, structural and governmental power so that, rather than invoking resistance, they are deployed to support subaltern agency. This is the reason peace formation is so often hidden and slow.

This implies a realisation of the potentialities of such networks in terms of how well they understand, and can countermand, power and violence, even subtly: how they navigate around difficult topics and themes, and how they maintain peace discourses and activism despite ill-matched external involvement and the intensely politicised environment and long-lasting range of sanctions the agents of conflicts can often bring to bear on those who deviate from the nationalist norm or from existing political hierarchies. All this makes it unsurprising that peace formation is often the great hope of international actors for progress, but is also little understood and often hardly visible. Indeed, it has become fashionable for international actors to penalise peace formation and to exert sanctions on its actors and organisations through various forms of conditionality more suited to international or national levels. Donors are withdrawing their funding for civil society in order to support states and small and medium sized business enterprises (SMEs) instead,[20] and arguing that civil society has to be 'leaner' and more productive, and that the global financial crisis makes it unlikely funding patterns can be sustained.

This paradox puts peace formation at the centre of peace processes in terms of legitimacy, but often last in terms of agency, because of the fact that internationals tend to ask for efficiency, observable outcomes and work on a short-term basis. Internationals want civil-society organisations to engage in self-help and become resilient, to operate and become sustainable in a funding marketplace, and place few expectations on the state to support such activities. Internationals do little to improve the structural conditions in which peace formation operates, contradicting international support for civil society and undermining its subtle but significant capacity for peace.[21] Given that peace-formation processes wield little direct or governmental agency, it may well be the case that external support is vital if they are to make the transition from a localised to a state-level process, which is also where peace formation may be modified to reflect a compromise on existing local and international norms and power structures (which may also be embedded in a conflict system), and a social contract.

The lack of understanding of civil-society and peace-formation capacities and limitations reflects a disciplinary ignorance on the part of many internationals, even though they also regard themselves as peace activists. This is often accepted by peace-formation actors, who develop a false consciousness about the expectations placed upon them, even though they are extremely aware of the political, economic, professional, social and personal sanctions and penalties they may face – penalties that elites or internationals rarely face, regardless of their success or failure. When pushed, however, increasing numbers of civil-society actors are moving outside external donor support, even at material cost to themselves, and this often has a beneficial impact on their local legitimacy, a fact that internationals should consider carefully. The latter are in danger of creating an agreement of sorts between recalcitrant elites who fear their loss of power if the liberal peace takes root, and otherwise supportive civil-society actors who tire of donor 'support' and conditionality, and increasingly see it as careless and naive in its expectations.

What is most urgent is to begin to understand the hybrid forms of politics and peace that emerge from the interaction of complex local formation processes and external building processes. The linkages between peace formation and external capacity and support may well be vital for the former's ability to counter violence in and around the state, and to create a framework for a locally legitimate and emancipatory peace to emerge.[22] What this means in practice is a range of both uncomfortable compromises between international norms and standards and local patterns of politics, as well as a range of often ignored opportunities for a positive hybrid peace.

CONCLUSION

International Peace Enablement

Introduction

PEACEBUILDING AND STATEBUILDING have been contaminated by mainstream state-formation theory's negative view of local agency, its fear of ungovernmentality and by external interests, norms and preferences. As a result, they veer towards trusteeship and counter-insurgency approaches. Local subjects of intervention quickly identify this tendency of the heuristic rule of experts who exercise locally unaccountable power. They may even begin to 'outgovern' and coopt external actors, as has occurred in Kosovo and Afghanistan.[1]

Realist state-formation arguments have strongly influenced modern peacebuilding and statebuilding praxis. They have positioned the state as the anti-liberal site and also the neoliberal outcome of violent contestation of local groups, intent on domination, following the inherency argument about human nature. The state is Hobbesian, Weberian, the site of legitimacy and of any hope for a negative peace – which is merely an interlude between periods of violence. This logic extends the realist line of thought from the violence inherent in human nature to the state and the international system, and back again. When transferred to peacebuilding and statebuilding, this has elevated international actors normatively, bureaucratically, politically, economically and socially, because they are thought to offer superior epistemologies for peace, order and the state. Their legitimacy derives from this. Thus, peace and the state are hierarchical, transferred from metropolitan centres, through their exercise of direct, structural and governmental power. Under this paradigm, military force shapes the state internally and through external intervention.

Historically, states that manage to amass military and economic resources and sufficient international cohesion to harness common direct, structural and governmental power have been relatively successful in meeting national interests over time. Power has determined politics, freedom and the subject. The modern state, global economy and liberal-peace system appear to have captured both peace and progressive politics, as most of the examples alluded to in this book attest. These have become authoritarian, vanguardist modes of peacebuilding and statebuilding, which preach rights and democracy. Yet they have tended to consolidate the order that emerged during, or because of, the conflict, and which thus lacks local legitimacy. At best they have brought about negative forms of hybrid peace in which local power structures and the illiberal aspects of international intervention have combined.

Over the last three hundred years of peace praxis and advocacy, there have been several sites of political mobilisation: where power gathers around society, around the state, its laws, constitution and military, and around the international, its organisation, peace talks and gatherings, institutions, and financial and legal frameworks.

The nineteenth and twentieth centuries focused in particular on state-constitutional, international-economic and international-organisation design, trying to perfect these in order to develop a more stable, legitimate and emancipatory peace. Yet there are many imperfections in this system of thought and design that remain to be addressed, though, of course, much progress has been made. Not least, the system of sovereignty, nationalism and particularism, the focus on the state, and the attempt to promote transnational norms, laws, courts, trade, cooperation and understanding are clearly contradictory. Solidarity and responsibility appear to merge into interests and power when subjects and interveners are separated by geographic distance, and ideological, socio-economic and identity differences. Internationalism becomes hegemonically universal and localism is perceived as anti-modern, unless it conforms to neoliberal notions of self-help. This unrealistic division is particularly problematic where international actors have to keep thinking of solutions to problems inherent in the international system and partly of their own making – the arms trade, colonialism, territorialism, nationalism, development and poverty – but without raising the prospect of radical reform.

If statebuilding leads, peace will be state-centric, bureaucratic, and security- and market-oriented. Inequality will drive competition over scarce resources, and thus peace will be very conservative, following both Hobbes's and Locke's understanding of government and property rights. As conflict so often centres on the distribution of resources, this peace will be fragile. The state will mainly focus on constraining local state-formation agency and guaranteeing regional peace and security. International actors will often have to provide the resources for security and for marketisation, as well as a modicum of 'good governance', but the focus will be on a 'light' international footprint. Statebuilding occurs when international actors have sufficient security and economic interests at stake to coalesce around an intervention. Its scale errs on the military side, so the resources put into it can be enormous, though such activity may have little impact on everyday life. It is a purely externalised and interventionary process until local power holders become its partners. States are vessels for regional security, domestic stability and market access. The state represents a power base to control society, as well as offering a framework for common security and rights. Ultimately, a negative peace is aimed at by statebuilding, but in actual fact a negative hybrid peace emerges out of a compromise between international and state elites, mainly over security and economic questions.

If liberal peacebuilding leads, peace will be driven by normative understandings of rights and democracy, developing along the lines suggested by Rousseau's work on the social contract. Furthermore, it will be positioned within a liberal-internationalist and institutionalist framework whereby the state is a carrier of rights and associated bureaucratic, developmental and egalitarian reforms. The international and its norms are the site of peacebuilding legitimacy, authority and agency, and within its hybrid of a cosmopolitan, imperial and bureaucratic framework, the social contract between state and citizens is key. It is an extension of the liberal-internationalist and institutionalist dream, drawn from Kant and nineteenth-century liberalism and Marxism. Peacebuilding implies some attempt to lessen tension over scarce resources, whether material, institutional or identity-oriented. It needs a very significant international presence on the ground – a heavy footprint – with trained local actors and institutions across the full range of political, social and economic institutions (capacity-building, in other words). Statebuilding and peacebuilding require significant external intervention and investment, and around these practices a very significant international architecture of military, bureaucratic, financial, political, legal and INGO actors have coalesced. Peacebuilding occurs when conflict, security and developmental issues attract the attention of international actors concerned about human rights and democracy, as well as regional stability. Its scale is potentially massive, but the resources put into it are limited, though mainly civilian. It may well have an impact on everyday life, if only to establish a set of standards for citizens, in principle if not in practice. It should be noted that peacebuilding is also concerned with legitimacy, the social contract and local ownership, but has had less success in promoting these at the local level than at the international level. At the local level, states have tended to be 'virtual' from the perspective of citizens. However, the shell of the state is built through cooperation between local liberal elites and the international civil service involved in extending peacebuilding from its normative roots into praxis, against the backdrop of historical configurations of power and international hierarchy. A positive peace (in liberal peace terms) is aimed at by liberal peacebuilding, but an international-local elite compromise over norms, as well as over security and economic deficiencies, often means a negative hybrid peace emerges. In effect, statebuilding and peacebuilding perceive the space of everyday life as a 'conquered country'.[2]

Both statebuilding and peacebuilding are dominated by hybrid politics. Yet from the international perspective, in the debate over what follows political liberalism and the liberal peace, neoliberalism and the neoliberal state appear to have won. This represents a step back from positive to negative peace, with little involvement of local actors unless they control direct, structural or governmental power. The subsequent loss of local-scale legitimacy can only be counteracted by peace formation and the development of preferably positive hybrid forms of peace – a far more emancipatory avenue for post-liberalism than neoliberalism offers. Peace formation bridges the empirical reality of the state, the nature of hybrid politics and peace (negative or positive), and the possibility of an emancipatory framework for peace emerging from the local-to-international-scale perspectives. The dynamics of peace formation, and emerging peace infrastructures, illustrate that conflict-affected citizens want more from their state and the international community in terms of security and stability: greater recognition of locally legitimate authority with its cultural, normative, historical, political and economic compromises, even if these operate outside of the modernising state; and greater material rather than merely technical support. They want less trusteeship, less expertise of an ideological nature, and more genuine support in the face of the structures of local and regional violence, and international inequality. However, they also often expect good governance and anti-corruption measures, and assume that human rights and democracy are essential, even if interpreted in a distinctively local way.[3]

Negative and Positive Hybrid Peace

A negative hybrid peace would tend to maintain or establish elite rule, following elite preferences, or it would be driven by an external pattern for state and peace. Structural violence from local, state and international sources would continue, although such a system would resonate with the host population as they may be historically embedded. A positive hybrid peace would see a mutual consensus achieved through which both host populations and external actors would agree on norms, values, institutions, law and rights in progressive terms resonant across the local and international scales. Equality, freedom, emancipation, identity and mutual assistance would be assured.

If hybrid forms are either of negative or positive form, then this raises three issues: (i) How might the obstacles that prevent external intervention from supporting peace formation be lifted, so avoiding a negative peace? (ii) How might the contextual conflict structures that produce a negative hybrid peace be dealt with? (iii) And how might the peace-formation potential that leads to the emergence of a positive hybrid form be enabled?

An approach that offers the possibility of a positive hybrid peace would have to be led by peace formation. Questions of authority, legitimacy and rights have always emerged, often promoted by subaltern forms of agency at the social level, and have been far more destabilising of top-down power and have promoted reform more effectively than such historical views suggest. The state and the international have tended to lose legitimacy where they have failed to offer rights and welfare to citizens, not merely as constituted in the modern liberal order, but also by contextual historical forms of identity and political order (thus producing hybrid forms of state, legitimacy and peace). In modernity, the expectation has been that power would restrain its negative facets and exercise itself in order to work for the rights and needs of societies around the world, and to form a stable and just peace, necessarily based on local epistemologies, supported by centralised power, whether at the state or international level. The subject would at least be 'partially self-constituting' and able to exercise – through a 'technology of the self' or self-formation – subaltern agency. The implication is that a better balance between the universal and the particular is required. The state and the international peace would be a reconciliation of these. Instead, significant gaps remain between the peace, order and legitimacy envisaged at all of these levels of analysis. A positive form of hybrid peace requires that the liberal and local reshape each other and move into a more emancipatory and post-liberal terrain.[4]

For IR, peace and conflict studies, and the disciplines that contribute to our understanding of peace, this means taking critical agency and subaltern power seriously. Peace-formation processes, and the dynamics, activities and possibilities that arise from them, including the various types of peace infrastructure, offer legitimate authority and consensus. This is relevant to the reform of the state and the role of the international community. If procedural forms of democratisation have shown themselves to be too limited to provide wide consent in practice, peace-formation processes provide more contextual routes towards the reconstitution of legitimate authority. Peace formation highlights dialogue as a basis for institutional development in a hybrid setting. It enhances social cohesion.[5] Yet the liberal egalitarian view of the international and the state as key sites of legitimate authority in which power may be exercised for peace (or at least against conflict), has failed to engage fully with the 'arrival' of the conflict-affected subject. Indeed, from this perspective, modernisation, development, peacebuilding and statebuilding discourses continue to reflect older imperial attitudes in relation to the way in which peace and progressive politics are conjoined. For these reasons, the liberal-peace architecture, the state, sovereignty and peace formation are not aligned comfortably, if at all. Indeed, the attempt to build a universal peace architecture appears from the conflict-affected subject's position to be an advancement of Northern hegemony designed to take control of everyday social relations. This indicates a loss of legitimacy for the international peacebuilding and statebuilding architecture, which now appears to be attached to two parochial but universal positions: that Western norms and ideology are best, and that the state is the only appropriate framework for peace and development.

Ultimately, the Anglo-American mix of plans for world organisation, including a contradictory mix of development, self-determination and a 'commonwealth', has dominated peace policy since 1945 (and with some notable successes), but cannot be reformed without an engagement with the modalities of peace formation. This requires, as Massey has suggested local-internationalism (heterogeneous as opposed to a homogenous internationalism) and what Escobar calls a 'pluriversality' as a response.[6] This indicates that what matters about these modern forms of intervention is the way in which such knowledge is used and applied, especially in the neoliberal context provided by the dominant ideological framework underpinning the wide range of interventionary practices that exist. By contrast, adopting a peace-formation perspective, and thinking about its implications for the connection between progressive forms of politics and everyday and emancipatory forms of peace, indicates that state-formation, statebuilding and peacebuilding approaches tend not to be conducive to advances in peacemaking, but are somewhat mired in currently inadequate nineteenth- and twentieth-century perspectives.

The Significance of Peace Formation

Peace formation is a counter to such parochial 'modernisation' narratives, whereby local-scale actors and processes, drawing on historical, customary and social as well as international sources of legitimacy, seek to manage and resolve local conflict dynamics, as has been the case in Afghanistan, Timor-Leste and other locations. Such actors mobilise in hidden spaces, as well as collectively in public spaces, try to ensure that local- and state-level politics are accountable and democratic, and advocate for human rights and more egalitarian economic systems and public services, as well as drawing on, coopting or resisting international sources of agency – as in Cyprus. This is an extension of the idea that autonomous individuals form communities, which in turn form institutions, states and international organisations to manage conflict (bottom up rather than vice versa). Furthermore, it indicates that relatively equitable development matters, from the local to the global, an issue that has arisen with liberal peacebuilding and neoliberal statebuilding from Cambodia to Afghanistan. Solidarity, cooperation and emancipation from oppressive power of any sort are its aims. Local, everyday, hidden or public action and mobilisation for a politics of emancipation have been historically derived from peace formation, and continue to be so. Peace formation wields subaltern agency, drawn from a nexus of different types of legitimacy: intimate local knowledge of conflict and peace systems, and an understanding of the benefits and deficiencies of the liberal-peace system, from which are drawn normative legitimacy and some material resources. Peace formation requires direct intervention to stop violence, as seen in both Bosnia-Herzegovina and Kosovo, but afterwards it requires empathy, sensitivity, listening, enablement and support from external actors rather than trusteeship, while it maintains its own autonomous authority. This was long understood by various theories related to the 'enabling state', social democracy and the views of the enabling state on the need for a strong civil society, and the role of the international community in the view of many UN and INGO workers.[7] Hybrid legitimacy emanates from such mediated approaches to peace. Polity, state and international cannot be legitimate without an *a priori* engagement from peace formers, of which they may be representative. Peace formation is internally driven by informal and formal networks of local actors contesting structural and direct violence. They seek international support and cooperation: partnership not compliance.

All of this implies that, in the circulation of the politics of power and peace between state formation, statebuilding, peacebuilding and peace formation, a positive hybrid peace, a hybrid state and a more representative politics, with greater distributive justice, are required and, indeed, may be emerging because of the agency that is being expressed. Hybridity, genealogy, critical agency and their encounters with power are establishing a growing 'right to politics' aimed at 'equaliberty': 'no equality without liberty: no liberty without equality', no transformation without civility, to quote Balibar.[8] This might be taken as a 'right to peace' and even of a 'right to intervention', where the rights and needs of individuals do not encroach upon the satisfaction of the rights and needs of others: 'life without war serves as the primary international prerequisite for the material well-being, development and progress of countries, and for the full implementation of the rights and fundamental human freedoms proclaimed by the United Nations'.[9] There can be no emancipation by a 'higher grace' but instead through the decision-making of subjects about how a peace process, the state and progressive politics are to be configured. This requires not just socio-economic equality, but relative equality and sustainability across broader local to international scales. If one part of the international system is conflict-affected, then conflict reverberates across the international architecture. Nevertheless, it must also be acknowledged, as Foucault pointed out, that emancipation, or liberty, produces new power relations, and therefore new claims for emancipation.[10] These would also have to be met. Peace praxis should not naturalise new asymmetries of power; the state and peace should be formed to liberate and emancipate across simultaneously universal and particular registers.[11] This is a long term process at local, state and international levels.

The liberal-internationalist and institutionalist, along with the liberal-democratic, dreams of peace have proven to be unable to achieve their goals without the involvement of society, individuals and the community. The state cannot support the liberal peace while it is connected so closely to territorial notions of security and sovereignty, or to neoliberalism, individualism, rationality, utilitarianism and industrial-scale mobilisation. Any system based on these qualities is inevitably going to favour the global North and the few states within it that control much of the global economy. These dreams have been used to build pluralist states around the results of nationalism, linked closely to the results of colonial governance. It has been hoped that external institutional design would overcome these contradictions, rather than in-depth and sympathetic knowledge of everyday life, context and history, in a peace and global-justice framework suggested by contemporary patterns of praxis about emancipation, liberation, self-determination and social justice, as well as identity. These frameworks of meaning cannot be resolved by ignoring them, nor can the state or the international be built without incorporating them. The critique of liberal peacebuilding, neoliberal statebuilding and the ontological assumptions behind state-formation theory implies the need for a very significant rethinking of the different scales of world order, including identity, institutions, law and economics, if an emancipatory peace – one that is positive and hybrid (pluriversal), and in tune with social and environmental factors (empathetic and promoting equaliberty) – is to be achieved.

A deeper examination of conflict-affected societies shows that there are significant, practised and able peace constituencies in such states. Their goals are at least related to some of those of the liberal peace. Criticism of the international community's engagement in post-conflict zones needs to be taken very seriously, especially in the spirit of democracy, rights and humanitarianism. Yet statebuilding and peacebuilding have fallen into the trap of ideological and interest-oriented strategies, rather than enabling localised peace formation. They have become extensions of direct, structural and governmental power, rather than peacemaking in an emancipatory and necessarily hybrid form. It is little surprise, therefore, that these conflicting dynamics have produced very unsatisfactory situations in every conflict zone today. One of the reasons for this is the very fragile position of citizens and peace formers in the context of governmental, direct and structural power, but clearly subaltern agency is very significant. Yet the current peacebuilding, statebuilding (and development) frameworks, through the UN system, the IFIs and donor system, are also partly a product of colonial liberal history.[12]

Project- or programme-based approaches also reflect this heritage, and are based upon conditionality, intervention and traditional, Western-versus-non-Western, official-versus-informal, sovereign-versus-non-sovereign sets of hierarchies. These are deployed by international planners to create a post-conflict 'governable-scape', according to the liberal-peace and neoliberal-state architecture. This is a space of pacification and neoliberalism, masquerading under the guise of human rights and representative democracy. At best such processes are illiberal (in previous political eras, stronger terms may have been used) and tend to rest on governmental and structural power rather than legitimacy and consent. State formation, statebuilding, and peacebuilding tend to view the development of a polity towards peace, development and order as teleological, drawing on 1950s modernisation theories, and probably benefiting from a relatively authoritarian external hand.[13] Such states remain sites of Northern extraction, however, dependent on donors and IFIs, and often victims rather than beneficiaries of globalisation. Indeed, the evolution of post-conflict states under such regimes may offer ominous warnings for the development of Northern states, from which such models are drawn.[14]

The Transformation of International Peacebuilding and Statebuilding

From the subject's perspective, peacebuilding and statebuilding are not a 'gift' or benign, but are part of the circulation of power, reflecting strategic and normative interests, a way of stabilising regional politics, cementing global governance and markets, validating the liberal peace by challenging otherness, and obscuring deeper issues of historical and global inequality and injustice. State formation suggests an epistemology in which power relations form all institutions, from the local to the international. Direct and structural forms of power are directed at social, political and economic partners and opponents. The international peacebuilding architecture, which projects both a liberal-peace and neoliberal-state scenario, suggests an externalised and normative vision of institutional and social reform. Governmental power is its mainstay in its relations with its subjects. Governmentality does not preclude sophisticated responses from its seemingly powerless subaltern subjects,[15] but it is easily subverted by local elites who may wield direct or structural power and seek to maintain it, albeit in a camouflaged way. Statebuilding's technocratic focus on state security and marketisation applies a blend of direct, structural and governmental power to the subject, which is aimed at shocking them out of a 'pre-modern' state of being (custom, subsistence, patrimonialism, tribalism or ethnicism) or isolating them. The exigencies of state formation require an 'assemblage of occupation'.[16]

As the years progressed, and problems began to arise with its grand vision, the project of peacebuilding became compressed into a narrower project of simply building a neoliberal state. It narrowed governance down to the state, whose role was merely technocratic, bureaucratic and determined by the rationalities of the neoliberal peace (the 'new' international model of peace for the twenty-first century). It was to play little role in peace and reconciliation, which would be left to an ironically mischaracterised and poorly supported civil society. Worse, civil society was seen to be dependent on the state and the international community, and not constitutive of either. Yet effectively radical social and political change was believed to be dependent on a state ill-equipped to maintain itself, and an international architecture of peacebuilding embedded in a Northern epistemology of peace and with extremely limited resources. The idea of engaging with root causes of conflict and of promoting reconciliation became more marginal as an increasing programmatic approach to statebuilding emerged among the growing international civil service. The state in these terms was not representative of its subjects, of their autonomy and identity, or even of their rights and needs; thus it lacked dignity and humanity. Peace became anchored to the hegemonic ideology that the developing areas and conflict sites of the world needed to be dragged, in a muscular manner, out of their failed states, institutions, norms and practices.

This happened, despite the fact that many internationals privately knew this was the wrong direction to take. Even though this shift, driven by IFIs and key donors, was strongly resisted inside the UN system,[17] it began to evoke significant responses – even resistance – on the ground. From the subaltern or local perspective this should hardly be surprising. Even at the state level, countries such as Sierra Leone, Liberia and Burundi, as well as Guatemala and Timor-Leste, began to resist UN peacebuilding and donor approaches publicly.[18] For this reason, the UN Secretary-General's 'Report on Peacebuilding in the Immediate Aftermath of Conflict' began to suggest a more positive peace, in emancipatory forms, reflecting its concern with social justice.[19] Furthermore, through the process the voices of Southern states, organisations and communities have begun to have a significant impact on peacebuilding and statebuilding, as well as on humanitarianism and development. In other words, peace formation has begun to intervene in peacebuilding and statebuilding praxis.

Peace formation provides a repository of capacities, techniques, networks, agency, resonance and legitimacy, and a natural network for peace enablement to replace the brusque and technocratic interventionary approaches of peacebuilding and statebuilding. Peacebuilding and statebuilding have generally not been guided by peace formation, but rather by state formation. This is counterintuitive, especially in the light of liberal norms, human rights and democracy, which would dictate that individuals and society should determine their own institutions, frameworks of meaning and laws. Peace formation is embedded in a local and transnational context, and aimed at promoting representation along historical, social and identity lines. It raises the issues of social justice and emancipation and combating the forces of state formation as well as the overbearing aspects of liberal peacebuilding and the reductionist aspects of statebuilding. Local actors – from national elites to rural leaders, politicians, elders and peace workers – have evolved their own forms of peacebuilding, in discourse and practice. This often occurs in private spaces, as opposed to the rational, public mobilisation the North expects. It is also less directly 'progressive', modernising or profit/interest-based than the 'Anglosphere's' positivist rationality of making, doing and building; it is more subtly and culturally directed.[20] This, as opposed to Western techniques of institutionalisation (meaning liberal peacebuilding or statebuilding in more or less bureaucratic forms), rests on local forms of politics and power, patterns of sustainability, agency and claims for autonomy. Some of these processes are viewed as dysfunctional from the West's perspective (and some quite obviously are because they represent ethnic, religious, gender, class, kin or age biases), while others are simply hidden from view but represent significant capacity for peacebuilding at the local level. Indeed, in small, isolated pockets of society a viable peace process often already exists, but in a different or hybrid epistemological setting, distinct from that of the formal process of peacebuilding or statebuilding. This is because the peacebuilding strategies they offer engage with local needs issues, with local forms of politics, representation and power. They represent historical, cultural or customary understandings of peace, often embedded in informal institutions related to these understandings. They resonate widely – in some respects at least – with populations and represent their own autonomy and agency, and their solidarity, in attempts to deal with injustice, poverty, conflict and oppression. Some of these dynamics may offer more grounded forms of reconciliation and legitimacy than those represented by the liberal-peace approach. Others, of course, perpetuate discrimination and oppression. They often reach out to the international peacebuilding architecture, which has only limited capacity to support them.

What is most crucial about this process is that it represents the dream of an international-society or state-peace system that the West has focused upon since the early twentieth century to deal with its systemic conflicts, while also representing the capacity of local actors in signalling the nature of an emancipatory peace, progressive politics and new designs for the state. In effect, these processes of renegotiation are making the liberal-peace system more democratic and representative as it is being influenced and remade outside the West, by others.

However, as a counterdynamic, the construction of the modern state in such contexts provides numerous opportunities for local elites to use it as a vehicle for predatory behaviour. In this situation, liberal peacebuilding and statebuilding provide the unfortunate stage upon which predatory behaviour occurs – the selling-off of customary lands and resources, the bypassing of localised systems that have provided equity, sustainability, representation and material capacity to the society, the introduction of alien political systems, market practices and so forth – which disorientates the very citizens who are expecting peace and a peace dividend. Other problems arise from the resources gained from controlling the state and institutions, or the deployment of the self-help rhetoric of IFIs, whose neoliberal approach to development and marketisation often makes citizens dependent on elite patronage. A partial reform syndrome[21] occurs in which new state elites modify the liberal-peace praxis to extract resources and maintain power hierarchies and systems of exclusion. Internationals resist this, of course, but also often appear to be complicit in it precisely because they prioritise the state, officialdom and Northern rationalities. The fact that statebuilding is so externalised and operates mainly in cooperation with the very local elites who may exploit it means that any constituencies, societies or populations not in direct contact with internationals are thoroughly marginalised, exactly as their elites often intend. This makes it all the more remarkable that local actors from within civil society, and indeed below it, have been able to have an impact on liberal peacebuilding at all.

A move away from Eurocentric understandings of peace in IR is hardly a post-colonial/subaltern idealisation of resistance, the marginalised or the oppressed. It requires an exploration of the complexity of peace-formation agency in juxtaposition with the hegemony of state-formation forces, and external actors and their elite status.[22] This means peace needs to be translated into a number of contexts: international institutions, global governance and international political economy, the state, history, society and culture in their local framings, and related power relations, of course. Rather than being utopian in liberal guise, it may be more accurate to expect post-liberal forms of peace to be 'heterotopian'.[23] But in an era of individualism, secularism, democracy and rights, this has become difficult because peace formation suggests significant variations on these Northern/Western assumptions in many cases, though not in all. In effect, the state and statebuilding in conflict-affected societies probably need to move away from the myths of Westphalian territorial sovereignty, and to institutionalise welfare and mitigate inequality, while promoting polycentrism, heterogeneity and plurality. Even fairly conservative liberal commentators are beginning to agree on the hybridity and necessity for external support that this requires.[24]

Peace Enablement rather than Intervention

One of the key implications of this understanding of the circulation of power around and between different types of formation and building activities relates to the nature of intervention. Rather than assuming the local is a blank slate offering automatic consent, as intervention does, as well as an absence of legitimate local opposition, enablement would work by piecing together and building on what is already there, led by peace-formation actors, rather than elite power holders or seekers implicated in conflict, or external actors embedded in a disconnected international system. Rather than an interventionary agenda for multinational forces, institutions, IFIs donors and agencies, this would rest on the external enablement of local peace formation, and a subsequent mediation of the liberal peace, neoliberal state and the position of the polity in the global economy. Peace enablement would always begin with a context-sensitive needs-and-rights assessment from a local perspective, rather than from an international perspective (which would anyway be part of any process given its external support).[25] This would mean an alignment of local, state and international legitimacy, and their respective capacities to exercise legitimate authority. It would mean recognising that the root causes of the conflict in historical, material, justice and institutional frameworks cannot be 'settled' without recognising a broad and diverse range of often mutually exclusive views.

It would be far better if local civil society, and the local-local behind it, where legitimacy, identity and the agency for peace formation may lie, could gradually create a peacebuilding agenda in the light of international norms, which – of course – international actors could then use to direct their own work with their local partners.[26] This might also be the case if strong government leadership at the recipient level reflected a local consensus and was determined to maintain control of peacebuilding, as with Paul Kagame's leadership in Rwanda (though this has, of course, been controversial, so far veering towards a negative rather than a positive hybrid peace). In the Rwandan case, the state that has emerged has been designed around local and international hybrid models related to how to deal with the specific issues the country has faced. In Kosovo, UNDP has tried to enhance local participation in governance to maximise representation and responsiveness, enhancing local legitimacy for the state. Of course, the Kosovan state already had very high levels of internal legitimacy. The UNDP has encouraged the government to establish local mechanisms for planning, monitoring and assessing its services.[27] These were to operate across community lines, as with trade, though this has been a less successful strategy. A positive hybrid peace has not yet arrived, but it does look to be possible. In Iraq, Afghanistan, Kosovo, Cambodia and Sierra Leone, UNDP has engaged directly with the peacebuilding capacity of local government, focusing on gender issues, civil-society consultation for mediation and conflict-resolution skills.[28] Even so, conflict is not just about disagreements over identity and rights, but also about resources and structural inequality and its perpetuation or rectification. Furthermore, as in Afghanistan, the internationally supported National Solidarity Programme also indicates the way in which internationals assume that there is a nation and a viable state waiting to be united or come into being. Without engaging with peace-formation networks, none of this would be remotely possible.

Of course, such attempts at enablement of peace formation might still be seen as representing an interventionary and biopolitical agenda, associated with enabling an indigenous 'resilience' conveniently paralleling Western interests.[29] Nevertheless, it has local legitimacy with the part of the population engaged in making peace in situ, and such a reframing of intervention might make it less coarse, with more democratic and participatory legitimacy. This would enable international and local agendas, and would perhaps be more accepting of the inevitability of a fusion of forms of peace, representing an actually existing process ongoing in many situations, from Afghanistan to Timor-Leste.

The questions the range of international actors may usefully engage with might be: What are the processes, dynamics and networks, and who are the actors involved in local politics, social stabilisation and economic redistribution, and cultural and historical continuity? Who could be united by a vision of peace, even if it is not yet a common vision? How do they envisage peace and its processes and goals, and how do they relate to its local and international contexts? Next, they would need to ask themselves: Which of these actors and processes are engaged in peace work, and how can they help? Clearly, financial resources are significant as well as technical expertise and moral support for peace work, especially for professionals who have contact with many individuals in everyday life, from public services to the media and education. But these resources should be deployed in accordance with the views of those local actors involved in peace work, rather than as directed by external actors.

Of course, to arrive at the point of peace enablement would require internationals to have significant local knowledge and contacts, as well as support, consensus and legitimacy, underlining the political nature of creating peace even through external enablement and partnership. Because peace formation is risky and often hidden, and internationals tend to approach local relationships in an instrumental manner, establishing a cooperative relationship not influenced by both sides' relative power would be extremely difficult. However, the best prevention and the best enablement would probably involve international personnel who have long-term grassroots networks already in place, are accepted by peace-formation networks, and are able to discern how legitimacy is framed and peace formation arises in each context, and which elites and institutional frameworks at the state level are truly representative of a progressive and pluralist rather than exclusive political agenda. Remaining autonomous and avoiding national or international pressure to place external priorities or constraints over local ones is important.

This would have the following implications. For security actors, whether involved in humanitarian intervention or UN peacekeeping, their goal would be to form cooperative partnerships to countermand direct and structural power that local actors cannot respond to; and to enable actors on the ground who are engaged in mitigating insecurity already through cooperative assistance, support and guidance. Preventing sources of insecurity (arms supplies, control of information and resources, inflammatory rhetoric and structural forms of violence) may be necessary. This would mean building relationships with a range of actors quickly, or building on pre-existing lines of communication and cooperation. Dealing with structural and social-justice deficits, though a long-term task, should be immediately on the agenda, but again through local systems of legitimacy associated with peacemaking and progressive politics. Of course, existing security, political, social and economic practices may well support existing hierarchies (neopatrimonial, identity and gender discrimination), so the potential would arise to mediate these to some extent, but the initial priority would be to support local agency and security, not to create more tension and insecurity through imposing external reforms as conditions for assistance. Pressure for this would probably be obvious through the local to international-scale networks that develop as a result.

Actors involved in institution-building and democratisation would start with local forms of representation and institutions, from the state down to the local level. They would not start from scratch with institutions planned in venues and offices in the global North, according to Northern interests, norms and epistemology. Refraining from forming natural alliances with elites who may then use them to buttress their neopatrimonial practices, so blocking local diversity, is important. This requires detailed local interaction and knowledge, as well as the capacity to understand localised institutional and political practices, and how they are representative and maintain social and political order, in a particular historical context. Again, the relationships created would provide an opportunity for the further discussion of inbuilt structural hierarchies in such pre-existing systems, perhaps in comparison to liberal understandings of human rights in first- or second-generation forms, but led by the requirement of maintaining local legitimacy and stability. Conditionality should be replaced by listening, which allows civil society and the local-local to debate how to develop their political institutions so that past conflicts and structural forms of violence are not repeated.[30]

As is better known, hybrid legal systems, and transitional justice systems and institutions, are indicative of the everyday capacity that already exists on the ground, the limited reach of the state and internationals, as well as the tensions between liberal and local conceptions of law. Rule-of-law programming and policy have long been cognisant of the positive and negative dynamics of hybridity and the capacity and legitimacy required from contextual locations. Civil-society work has lagged behind in this area. While it is vital to have a vibrant, politicised and capable civil society, it has often been the case that the type of civil society that has emerged has been weakly connected to local sources of legitimacy. Thus, civil society often looks more like a liberal and Westernised middle class, dissociated from the rest of society (which is deemed customary or 'uncivil'). This means that the broadest range of organisations, networks and processes that already exist, even if they have been damaged or modified by war, need to be supported by international actors. Thus, enablement in this sense must be sensitive to difference in both local and international dimensions. Internationals must be sensitive to local practices, while local actors need to be sensitive to liberal practices. Exclusionary practices on either side would be hard to sustain in the long term. This means that everyday and local social, customary, religious, labour, political, cultural, economic and family networks, and their conceptions of needs, rights, institutions, security and peace, need to be the starting point for peace enablement. Ultimately, needs and rights assessments need to work through local institutions at the grassroots level, and become quickly cognisant of the issues at this level.

This has implications for the reframing of donor policy, the language of international and humanitarian law, the use of human rights, rule-of-law programming and DDR/SSR, as well as democratisation strategies. For the UN, PBC, UNDPKO, the World Bank, major donors such as the EU and African Union, as well as international NGOs, this will often require a significant shift in policy formation and expression as well as in the way they relate to their partners in the field (rather than as subjects). Given the poor record of accomplishment of internationals in translating their concepts into local languages,[31] this will be an enormous hurdle in that it implies not just the translation of international concepts but that internationals work in 'local languages': meaning the contextual, socio-historical and political language of peace, security, stability, development, justice and authority. Every local actor knows what this language is, but it is rarely apparent to internationals, and it is not translated into English or any other key lingua franca. Peace enablement demands a cultural shift, a partial inversion of epistemic hierarchies and a recognition that knowledge, material capacity and expertise peace enaldement requires a global and local – trans-scalar – commons.[32] Successful enablement might be observed when local actors, from the local-local, to civil society, to the state, are able to explain politely to international actors that their assistance has been gratefully received but is no longer required, and when localised experiences of peace formation themselves become a basis for enablement in other conflict contexts. In these terms, power asymmetries would have then been overcome and a broad legitimacy attained.

This has significant implications for international concepts such as 'do no harm' in its OECD-DAC usage, local ownership and participation, and the Responsibility to Protect, all of which might be reframed in the context of local and global equality in rights, representation and needs. There is a long way to go before this is attained, especially as it is opposed to most neoliberal assumptions. This further raises the question of who would set the standards for intervention, especially in a world in which equality should be seen to be far more foundational to peace than it currently is. This shift would need to be commensurate with emancipatory peace thinking if it were not to repeat the same vices that liberal internationalism and its later variants of liberal institutionalism and neoliberal capitalism have fallen into.

Rather than via the normative framework of the liberal peace, the policy and practical architecture could be developed by the pre-existing localised architectures of peace formation, and in their 'trans-scalar'[33] contexts, which would also then draw upon the liberal-peace framework. Such international peace enablement would then offer a more hands-off, but also more supportive, form of assistance. It would connect with local institutions, activists, organisations and elites, who operate within the terrain of peace formation (rather than state formation), providing material and technical support, but also guidance in terms of the liberal-peace system and any hybrid possibilities that may be explored. Enablement does not imply the governmental 'building' of international blueprints, but instead locally directed, autonomous formations of peace, connected with international models. This connection may be more of a bridge than the result of assimilation, meaning power relations would need mitigation. This would develop early on in a peace process and would require that internationals shift from their prescriptive monoculture of peace and statebuilding. In translating the elements of liberal peace, such as democracy, rights, justice, development and security, and even issues relating to discrimination, they would be almost certain to find similar local processes and expectations about the need for a longer-term structural process of emancipation, relying on localised forms of hybrid legitimacy. There are hints of this shift in the mainstream literatures of the World Bank and UNDP, as well as in more radical corners, relating to rights for development, 'right to peace', new economic orders, and others.[34]

The evolution of peacebuilding and statebuilding, the emergence of a hybrid peace and the role of peace formation are depicted in the diagrams in Appendix 1. For a summary, see Figure 6 below.

1. There are diverse actors, opinions, needs, identities and networks across different scales.
2. Peace voices, peace-oriented actors and peace formers are widely ignored. They are often very quiet, being dangerously positioned, but are always present in the local scale. They provide important signals.
3. Peace practices, formal and informal, normally already exist to deal with conflicts but have been disrupted by the expansion of power.
4. Local actors are very sensitive to the exercise of unaccountable power (direct/structural, governmental).

5. The local exercises subaltern agency/power, which is often, but not always, easily countermanded by state/governmental and direct/structural power. Thus, the local scale tends to hide its agency.
6. Contestation at the local scale forms the peace/state in view of its knowledge of legitimacy, power and authority, and in view of contextual history and the international scale (that is, liberal-peace norms).
7. Wide-ranging evidence indicates the local scale will already include security, mediation, reconciliation and mobilisation/activist practices, as well as legal processes, government, material redistribution and environmental management. There will be informal and possibly formal institutions already in existence.
8. There may also be claims for liberation/self-determination, which the state and the international will be expected to respond to.
9. There will already be debates about the role of the state in dealing with local issues.
10. The framework of the territorial/sovereign state, now embedded in global capitalism as well as in human-rights regimes, is already subject to dangerous contradictions (for example, rights versus capital or territory versus identity) in the context of peacebuilding. These tensions are amplified in post-conflict environments.
11. Identity, rights, representation, needs, public services, political ideology, legitimacy and capitalism have already been debated.
12. Local-scale views of rights, needs, identity, community, gender, law, justice, the state, poverty and development, legitimate authority and representation, among many other things, often differ significantly from the international perspective, and even from that of the central state elites.
13. In some areas, there are commonalities with one or all of local/state/international sites of authority: for example, peace, justice, law, security, representation, rights may be agreed upon in general form. Local actors will commonly say institutions of this nature already exist in slightly different form but need to be strengthened.
14. Their interpretation in detail of these concepts differs because of contextual experiences/history. It may be different because of different world-views: for instance, customary, ideological, North/South, bureaucratic/problem-solving.
15. The local scale represents a series of political claims about material needs, identity, rights, justice and representation. Context, identity and history put a specific spin on these.
16. These are made in a range of different realms: access to resources, to public services, about identity and context, as well as about the local's positionality in the state and the international. For example, the 'industrial' scale of the developed state may not be a top priority in local contexts.

17. The local scale exercises a range of agencies, often weak, but hard to see, capture or respond to. Private or critical discourse is important in democracies.
18. The local scale is hard for external actors to engage with or 'see', but its involvement in the political projects of peacebuilding (that is, normative agreements on rights and representation) and statebuilding (constitutional/institutional agreements on state machinery) is essential for legitimacy and consent.
19. Legitimate authority of state and/or international agencies cannot be exercised without the involvement of local communities and populations.
20. The state and statebuilding need to be responsive to local claims and demands, despite the fact they are diverse, expressed in different registers and hard to detect. Decentralisation and representation are essential in order for the state and the international to be able to 'hear' and engage with local claims.
21. If the state cannot be responsive, the international community is expected to compensate. The state and the international must be accountable to the local. Accountability systems are required between the local and international, as well as state/government.
22. It is very easy for the state and the international to operate in parallel to, or disregard of, the local scale, because of the state/international's access to governmental or structural power, and the difficulty of engaging with the local scale. Decentralisation and representation are necessary so that the state represents the local, not so that the local conforms to the state.
23. It is difficult, but necessary, to bring the state/international into line with the local scale. Legitimate authority cannot arise without the local scale, the state cannot be stable, and internationals cannot claim success.
24. Even particularistic claims need to be taken seriously (for example, peace needs enemies to be reconciled, not ignored).
25. Global capital undermines peace agreements where material peace dividends are not distributed reasonably equally. The state must ensure this occurs if it is to bring legitimacy.
26. Democratic change occurs very slowly.

Figure 6. What we know about the local scale of peacebuilding and what it means for the state/peace to invert legitimate authority from the international to the local

A hidden danger of any resulting hybrid peace is that relations of power continue to be dressed up in peace-oriented language. This may occur in liberal-local form, or in any transversal, transnational relationship over the formation and building dynamics of peace and conflict. This is because the top-down colonial practice of trusteeship, of which much external liberal intervention is an echo, shapes bottom-up notions of emancipation, of which most grassroots and contextual agency/resistance arguments are taken to be indicative. Ultimately, outside actors can rarely be peace formers and respect the autonomy of that space. Thus, in reality a bottom-up logic of emancipation is often subtly and compliantly entwined with a top-down logic of imperial domination.[35] Nevertheless, enablement and peace formation indicate an empathetic relationship and an emancipatory peace.[36] Thus, external actors can be partners with local actors and enable them, but must do so with a full awareness of their own position in the international historical order, as well as of the power they exercise. This awareness would be reflexive and sociological, as well as ethnographically informed, and such perspectives place the realities of more conventional notions of peace in IR into an everyday, as well as a global, perspective. 'Knowing subjects' and transformative, cooperative relationships are the reality of most peace work in the context of the social complexities of everyday life, which in any (putative) democracy needs to be the focus of policymaking.[37] In other words, as the role of the international community is to make and support peace on behalf of other states, the role of the state is peace on behalf of its citizens. Peace formers lead in shaping this role, in cooperation with internationals and, eventually, the state.

Bringing local peace formers together with international peace enablers reveals that both types of actors exist at international, state and local scales, and that peace formers are not merely 'local' or peace enablers merely international. In fact, it presages the end of territorial forms of sovereignty, and the emergence of new relationships and networks from the local to the global in a rights, democratic and social context. It also presages the end of global hierarchies based on the control of sovereignty and domestic institutions, international institutions, material resources and notions of local, state and international. The local–international divide appears to be a useful way of disaggregating power from structure and agency in the international system, but in reality it does not stand up to scrutiny. Indeed, it preserves a power hierarchy partly displayed through the liberal-peace epistemology: in other words, through an international monopoly over the construction of peace and order. Critical forms of agency, exercised as peace formation (even in discursive form), offer a far more disruptive capacity, as well as forms of legitimacy that traditional power brokers can rarely disentangle, resist or accrue. Disaggregating them in the knowledge that emancipatory peace in an everyday form requires enablement, equality and sustainability to be made central to the 'international' and to its peace agencies, enhances the legitimacy of the state and peace, inevitably in a hybrid form. Levels of analysis in their more traditional sense are now hardly viable if one is to describe and understand the transnational, transversal and trans-scalar dynamics of contemporary peace approaches.

This means that the international and state architecture of peace (meaning the visible formal system of laws, institutions, bureaucracy, and political and economic practices) should be driven by peace formation and its local infrastructure – the infrapolitics of peace. This is leading to new forms of state, new conceptions of the positionality of the citizen, and new requirements for international institutions, and their legal and material architecture. It requires a more wide-ranging system of checks and balances, and a positioning of peace and citizens in a local and global context, in forms of polity not necessarily configured through traditional forms of territorial sovereignty or current international institutions. This development recognises a transcendence of these, as well as of polities, peace, and organisations and institutions in the making. It demands significant reform of the institutional frameworks that have developed in order to accommodate individual and social rights and needs.

Perhaps as important, this development shows how the nature of the state, political authority and local legitimacy, and any post-liberal notion of peace and citizenship, have to be constructed as a joint enterprise between international and local actors and societies, with the latter in the driving seat. There are no simple formulas for internationals to achieve this, other than a sustained commitment to supporting everyday life and peace-formation processes that bring about stable institutions based on a mixture of local and international legitimacy and consent. This has very significant implications for statebuilding as a neoliberal enterprise and for liberal peacebuilding; and offers a way out of state-formation dynamics at the local, state and regional level. It also shows how flexibility is needed over international conceptions of democracy, rule of law, human rights, development, secularism and gender equality. Identity, patronage and customary systems also carry their own order-producing frameworks and legitimacy, along with a range of power asymmetries.[38] The encounter between these will inevitably change all of these concepts. The shift from subjects to citizens, from conflict to peace, requires that citizens design their institutions, law, democracy, rights and needs – meaning their state. How this polity finds a place in the international order is a related but secondary matter. Furthermore, any peace-formation process that ultimately establishes new forms of governmentality or structural power will itself be subject to critique and held to account vis-à-vis its capacity for emancipation. Peace formers should be seen as the culmination of the possibilities emanating from peaceful relations at local levels around the world, rather than as representative of an anachronistic or marginal core of 'peace actors'. They must assist in creating the good life for all, not just for those within a specific territorial purview, if legitimate authority is to be achieved across local, state and international levels.

In reality, many of these reforms are discursively in place or have already been imagined (for example, in terms of the later generations of human rights). However, the political and economic architecture associated with twentieth-century liberalism and neoliberalism, as well as the elitist nature of state and international politics, have prevented the more significant reforms that are required (for example, the reform of the UN, systems of global and national redistribution, and environmental sustainability).

A post-liberal peace is unknown in many of its dimensions, but what is well known is that its polity or state needs to be stable, equal, redistributory, sustainable and just, and resonate with its subjects if a positive hybrid peace is to emerge. As Foucault once noted, the relationship between colonialism and the state means that governmental power is inevitably projected outwards and inwards.[39] Peace formation, its micro-solidarities, the equaliberty it proposes, the hybrid forms of peace and state, and new frameworks of legitimacy, are a vital response to various forms of domination and their flawed, and often authoritarian, projects for human improvement at home and abroad.

Appendix 1a. Peace Formation and the Architecture of Liberal Peace

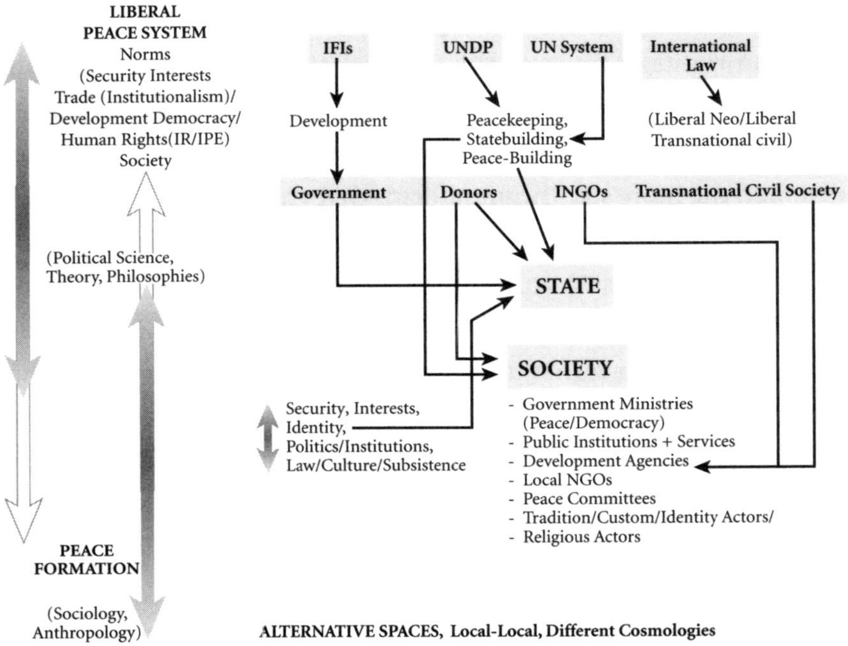

Appendix 1b. Hybrid Peace

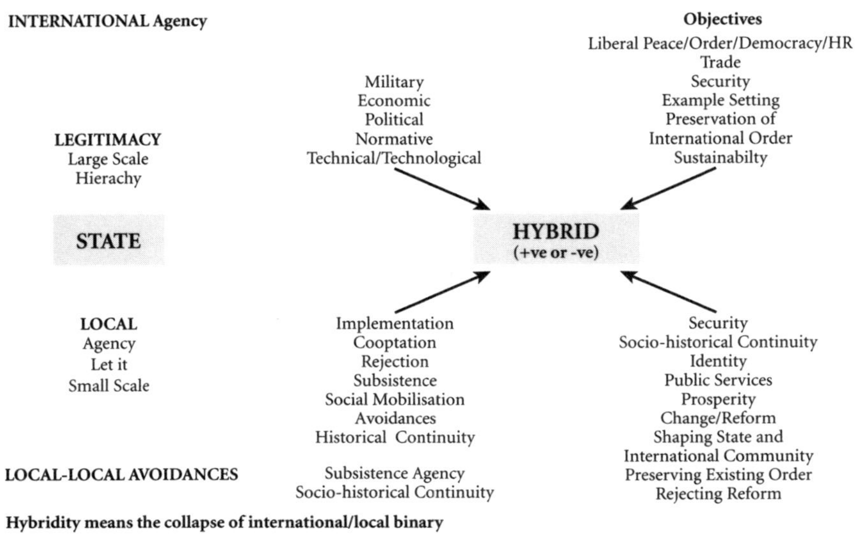

Appendix 1c. Peace Formation Dynamics

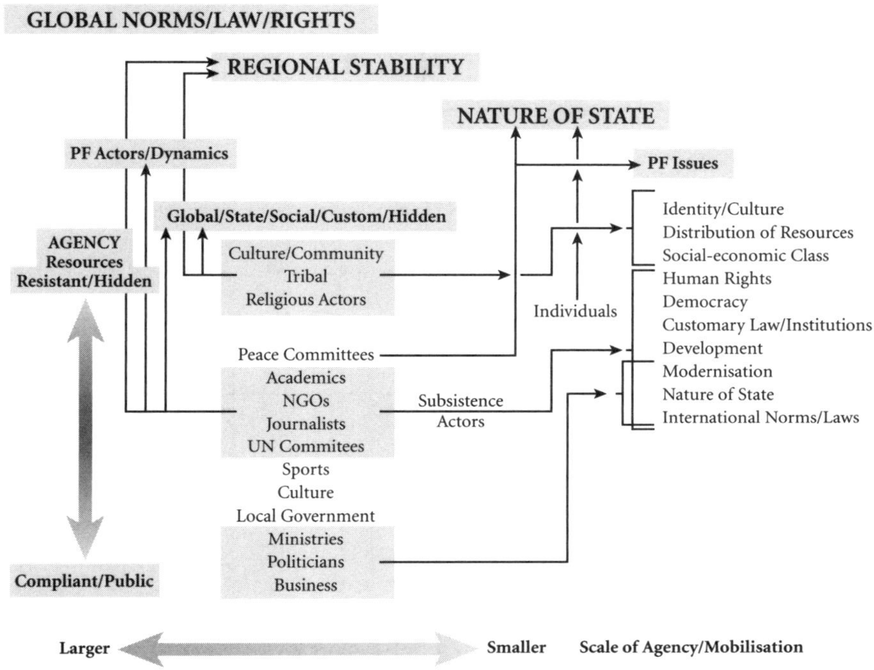

Appendix 1d. Peace Formation Rationalities

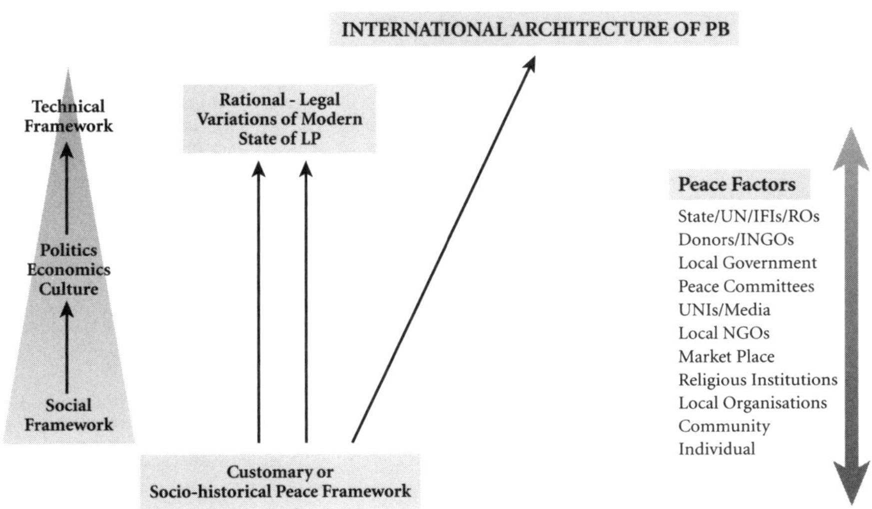

Appendix 2: Comparative Indices for Conflict-Affected Countries: From the End of Armed Conflict to the Present

HDI rank	Country (the end of armed conflict)	Date of HDI closest to the end of armed conflict	HDI closest to the end of armed conflict	HDI according to the HDR 2013	Results	Date of Gini Index closest to the end of armed conflict	Gini index closest to the end of armed conflict	Gini index according to the HDR 2013	Results
Very High Human Development									
31	Cyprus (1974)	1980	0.715	0.848	SI	N/A	N/A	N/A	N/A
47	Croatia (1995)	1995	0.719	0.805	I	1997-99	35.0	33.7	MI
High Human Development									
78	FYR of Macedonia (2001)	2005	0.711	0.740	MI	2002	38.8	43.2	D
72	Georgia (1995, reescalation 2008)	2005	0.713	0.745	MI	1996	37.1	41.3	D
81	Bosnia and Herzegovina (1995)	2005	0.724	0.735	MI	2001	26.2	36.2	SD
92	Sri Lanka (2009)	2010	0.705	0.715	MI	2009	41.1	40.3	MI
Medium Human Development									
107	El Salvador (1992)	1995	0.576	0.680	SI	1997	50.8	48.3	MI
114	Philippines (1990)	1990	0.581	0.654	I	1997	46.2	43.0	MI
125	Tajikistan (1996, with reescalation)	2000	0.529	0.622	I	1997–99	47.0	30.8	I
133	Guatemala (1996)	2000	0.523	0.581	I	1998	55.8	55.9	MD
128	Namibia (1988)	1990	0.569	0.608	MI	1993	70.7	63.9	I
134	Timor-Leste (1999)	2000	0.418	0.576	SI	N/A	N/A	31.9	N/A
138	Cambodia (1991)	1995	0.411	0.543	SI	1997	40.4	37.9	MI
Low Human Development									
142	DR Congo (ongoing)	ongoing	ongoing	0.304	N/A	ongoing	ongoing	44.4	N/A
143	Solomon Islands (2003)	2005	0.510	0.530	MI	N/A	N/A	N/A	N/A
146	Bangladesh (2000)	2000	0.433	0.515	I	2000	31.8	32.1	MD
156	Papua New Guinea (1998)	2000	0.415	0.466	I	N/A	N/A	N/A	N/A
157	Nepal (2006)	2010	0.458	0.463	MI	2010	32.8	N/A	N/A
161	Uganda (ongoing)	ongoing	ongoing	0.456	N/A	ongoing	ongoing	44.3	N/A
167	Rwanda (1994)	1995	0.214	0.434	SI	2000	46.8	53.1	D
168	Côte d'Ivoire (2004)	2005	0.405	0.432	MI	2008	41.5	N/A	N/A
171	Sudan (2005)	2005	0.390	0.414	MI	N/A	N/A	35.3	N/A
172	Zimbabwe (2008)	N/A	N/A	0.397	N/A	N/A	N/A	N/A	N/A
173	Ethiopia (2000)	2000	0.275	0.396	SI	2000	30.0	29.8	MI
174	Liberia (2003)	2005	0.301	0.388	I	N/A	N/A	38.2	N/A
175	Afghanistan (2001, reescalation 2003)	2005	0.322	0.374	I	2008	27.8	N/A	N/A
177	Sierra Leone (2000)	2000	0.244	0.359	SI	2011	35.4	42.5	SD
178	Burundi (2008)	2010	0.348	0.355	MI	N/A	N/A	33.3	N/A
185	Mozambique (1992)	1995	0.209	0.327	SI	1996-97	39.6	45.7	SD

Key: SI Significant Improvement; I Improvement; MI Marginal Improvement; NC No Changes; MD Marginal Deterioration; D Deterioration; SD Significant Deterioration.

HDI - Human Development Index -
Very high human development (HDI 0.900 and above);
High human development (HDI 0.800–0.899);
Medium human development (HDI 0.500–0.799);
Low human development (HDI below 0.500).

Gini Index - From 0 (absolute equality) to100 (absolute inequality).

Freedom rating - Free (1.0 to 2.5), Partly Free (3.0 to 5.0) or Not Free (5.5 to 7.0).

Failed State Index - From 0 (lowest intensity - most stabl 120 - (highest intensity - least stable)

Global Peace Index - From 1.000 (the most peaceful) to 5.000 (the least peaceful).

The data in the column 'HDI closest to the end of armed conflict' was compiled from the web page International Human Development Indicators http://hdr.undp.org/en/statistics/ due to the fact that

Date of Freedom rating closest to the end of armed conflict	Freedom rating closest to the end of armed conflict	Freedom rating in 2012	**Results**	Date of Failed state index closest to the end of armed conflict	Failed state index closest to the end of armed conflict	Failed state index in 2013	**Results**	Date of Global Peace Index closest to the end of armed conflict	Global Peace Index closest to the end of armed conflict	Global Peace Index 2013	**Results**	**Overal Results**
1974	4.0	1.0	SI	2006	70.5	67.0	MI	2007	1.915	1.840	MI	I
1995	4.0	1.5	SI	2006	61.9	54.1	MI	2007	2.030	1.571	I	I
2001	4.0	3.0	MI	2006	75.1	68.0	MI	2007	2.170	2.044	MI	MI
1995	4.5	3.0	MI	2006	82.2	84.2	MD	2009	2.736	2.511	MI	MI
1995	6.0	3.0	SI	2005	93.5	76.5	SI	2007	2.089	1.967	MI	MI
2009	4.0	4.5	D	2009	96.7	92.9	MI	2009	2.485	2.230	MI	MI
1992	3.0	2.5	MI	2005	75.5	73.2	MI	2007	2.244	2.240	MI	MI
1990	3.0	3.0	NC	2005	83.9	82.8	MI	2007	2.428	2.374	MI	MI
1996	7.0	6.0	MI	2005	86.7	85.2	MI	2011	2.272	2.282	MD	MI
1996	3.5	3.5	NC	2005	91.0	80.7	I	2007	2.285	2.221	MI	MI
1988	4.5	2.0	SI	2006	70.7	70.4	MI	2007	2.003	1.807	MI	MI
1999	5.0	3.5	MI	2007	94.9	91.5	MI	N/A	N/A	1.854	N/A	MI
1991	6.0	5.5	MI	2006	85.0	88.0	MD	2007	2.197	2.263	MD	MI
ongoing	ongoing	6.0	N/A	ongoing	ongoing	111.9	N/A	ongoing	ongoing	3.085	N/A	
2003	3.0	3.5	MD	2007	92.0	85.2	I	N/A	N/A	N/A	N/A	MI
2000	3.5	3.5	NC	2005	94.3	92.5	MI	2007	2.219	2.159	MI	MI
1998	2.5	3.5	MD	2006	84.6	84.9	MD	2007	2.223	2.126	MI	MI
2006	4.5	4.0	MI	2006	95.4	91.8	MI	2009	1.939	2.058	MD	MI
ongoing	ongoing	4.5	N/A	ongoing	ongoing	96.6	N/A	ongoing	ongoing	2.180	N/A	
1994	7.0	6.0	MI	2005	96.5	89.3	MI	2008	1.869	2.444	SD	MI
2004	6.0	5.0	MI	2005	106.0	103.5	MI	2007	2.638	2.732	MD	MI
2005	7.0	7.0	NC	2005	104.1	111.0	MD	2007	3.182	3.242	MD	MD
2008	6.5	6.0	MI	2008	112.5	105.2	MI	2008	2.385	2.696	SD	MI
2000	5.0	6.0	MD	2005	91.1	98.9	D	2007	2.479	2.630	MD	MD
2003	6.0	3.5	SI	2005	99.5	95.1	MI	2010	2.148	2.048	MI	MI
2001	7.0	6.0	I	2005	99.0	106.7	D	2009	3,285	3.440	D	D
2000	4.5	2.5	I	2005	102.1	91.2	I	2010	1.818	1.904	MD	MI
2008	4.5	5.0	MD	2008	94.1	97.6	MD	2009	2.529	2.593	MD	MI
1992	5.0	3.5	MI	2005	87.5	82.8	MI	2007	1.909	1.910	MD	MI

HDR methods have changed in 2010, which is why the data from previous reports was left unsuitable for comparison.

Sources:

UNDP - International Human Development Indicators http://hdr.undp.org/en/statistics/; Human Development Report (HDR) 1997; HDR 1999; HDR 2000; HDR 2001; HDR 2002; HDR 2007-08; HDR 2009; HDR 2013; Freedom House - Country ratings and status, FIW 1973-2013; The Failed States Index Rankings; 2007 GPI Results Report; 2008 GPI Results Report; 2009 GPI Results Report; 2010 GPI Results Report; 2011 GPI Results Report; 2013 GPI Results Report; Uppsala Conflict Data Program http://www.pcr.uu.se/research/ucdp/; The World Bank http://data.worldbank.org/indicator/SI.POV.GINI.

Notes

Preface

1. Keynes, John Maynard, *The Economic Consequences of the Peace*, London: Macmillan, 1920.

Introduction. The Limits of Peacebuilding and Statebuilding

1. Timothy Mitchell, *Rule of Experts*, Berkeley: University of California Press, 2002, p. 15.
2. Francis Fukuyama, *The Origins of Political Order*, Princeton: Princeton University Press, 2011, p. 459; Mark Mazower, *Governing the World*, London: Penguin, 2012, p. 21.
3. Douglass C. North, John Joseph Wallis and Barry R. Weingast, *Violence and Social Orders*, Cambridge: Cambridge University Press, 2009, pp. 11–12.
4. J. Galtung, 'Violence, Peace and Peace Research', *Journal of Peace Research*, Vol. 3, No. 5, 1970, pp. 167–91.
5. Samuel Huntington, *Political Order in Changing Societies*, New Haven: Yale University Press, 1968.
6. Mark Mazower, *No Enchanted Palace*, Princeton: Princeton University Press, 2009, pp. 30, 86.
7. Jean Comaroff and John L. Comaroff, *Theory from the South*, London: Paradigm, 2012, p. 86.
8. Michel Foucault, 'Governmentality', in Graham Burchell, Colin Gordon and Peter Miller (eds), *The Foucault Effect: Studies in Governmentality*, Hemel Hempstead: Harvester Wheatsheaf, 1991.
9. For more on the different components of peace and the different generations of approaches to peacemaking, see Oliver P. Richmond, *The Transformation of Peace*, London: Palgrave, 2005, and Oliver P. Richmond, *Maintaining Order, Making Peace*, London: Palgrave, 2002.

10. Huntington, *Political Order in Changing Societies.*
11. *Ibid.*, p. 4.
12. Kofi Annan, *A Life in War and Peace*, London: Allen Lane, 2012, p. 118.
13. Bertrand Badie, *The Imported State*, Redwood City, CA: Stanford University Press, 2000, p. 193.
14. *Ibid.*
15. This may be called a Eurocentric view in itself, but when scholars make such a claim they are often forced to fall back on rights and institutions within a liberal framework. See, for example, M. Sabaratnam, 'Avatars of Eurocentrism in the Critique of the Liberal Peace', *Security Dialogue*, Vol. 44, No. 3, 2013, p. 274.
16. See, among many, 'Declaration and Programme of Action on a Culture of Peace', A/RES/53/243, 6 October 1999; 'Declaration on the Establishment of a New International Economic Order', UNGA Res. 3201, 1 May 1974; 'Declaration on the Preparation of Societies for Life in Peace', UNGA Res. 33/74, 15 December 1978; 'Declaration on the Right of Peoples to Peace', UNGA Res. 39/11, 12 November 1984; 'Declaration on the Right to Development', UNGA Res. 41/128, 4 December 1986; 'Declaration on the Granting of Independence to Colonial Countries and Peoples', UNGA Res. 1514, 20 December 1960; 'Declaration on Social Progress and Development', UNGA Res. 2542, 11 December 1969; 'International Covenant on Economic, Social and Cultural Rights', UNGA Res. 2200, 19 December 1966.
17. UNDP, *Governance for Peace*, UNDP: New York, 2012, pp. 25 and 27.
18. *Ibid.*, p. 25.
19. United Nations, *Monitoring Peace Consolidation: UN Practitioners' Guide to Benchmarking*, New York: UN, 2010.
20. *Ibid.*, pp. 5–7.
21. See, for example, Toby Dodge, *Iraq: From War to a New Authoritarianism*, London: Routledge, 2013.
22. See, for example, Devesh Kapur, 'The State in a Changing World: A Critique of the 1997 World Development Report', *WCFIA Working Paper No. 98–02*, 1998, p. 4; World Bank, *The State in a Changing World*, Washington, DC: World Bank, 1997; Ajay Chhibber, 'The State in a Changing World', *Finance and Development*, September 1997, p. 17; US National Security Strategy, 2002, *www.state.gov/documents/organization/63562.pdf*; European Security Strategy, 2003, *www.consilium.europa.eu/uedocs/cmsUpload/78367.pdf*; US Department of Defense, 'National Defense Strategy', Washington, DC: DOD, 2008; Francis Fukuyama, 'The Imperative of Statebuilding', *Journal of Democracy*, Vol. 15, No. 2, 2004, p. 17; OECD-DAC, *Principles for Good International Engagement in Fragile States and Situations*, OECD-DAC, April 2007, *www.oecd.org/dataoecd/61/45/38368714.pdf.*
23. Homi K. Bhabha, *The Location of Culture*, London: Routledge, 1994, p. 25: E. Balibar, *Politics and the Other Scene*, London: Verso, 2002, p. 4.
24. See Ricardo Soares de Oliveira, 'Illiberal Peacebuilding in Angola', *Journal of Modern African Studies*, Vol. 49, No. 2, 2001, p. 305.
25. H. Eckstein, *Regarding Politics*, Berkeley: University of California, 1992, p. 188; Christian Reus-Smit, *The Moral Purpose of the State*, Princeton: Princeton University Press, 1999, p. 30; S.D. Krasner, *Sovereignty: Organized Hypocrisy*, Princeton: Princeton University Press, 1999.
26. Talal Asad (ed.), *Anthropology and the Colonial Encounter*, New York: Humanity Books, 1973, p. 17.
27. Paul van Tongeren, Former Secretary-General of Global Partnership for the Prevention of Armed Conflict (GPPAC), *Personal Interview*, Amsterdam, 17 December 2012.
28. Mark Malloch Brown, *The Unfinished Revolution*, London: Allen Lane, 2011, p. 94.
29. David Held, *Global Covenant: The Social Democratic Alternative to the Washington Consensus*, New York: Polity, 2004; M.M. Brown, *The Unfinished Revolution*, p. 13.

30. Sidney Tarrow, *Power in Movement: Collective Action, Social Movements and Politics*, Cambridge: Cambridge University Press, 1994; Adam Roberts and Timothy Garton Ash (eds), *Civil Resistance and Power Politics: The Experience of Non-violent Action from Gandhi to the Present*, Oxford: Oxford University Press, 2009.
31. Sam Marullo and John Lofland (eds), *Peace Action in the Eighties: Social Science Perspectives*, New Brunswick: Rutgers University Press, 1990.
32. P. Chabal, *The End of Conceit*, London: Zed, 2012, p. 136.
33. *Ibid.*, p. 99.
34. João Boavida, *Personal Interview*, CEPAD, Dili, 28 August 2012.
35. See, for example, Susan Strange, *States and Markets*, London: Pinter Publishers, 1988.
36. *Ibid.*
37. Foucault, 'Governmentality'.
38. Joseph Nye, *Soft Power: The Means to Success in World Politics*, New York: Public Affairs, 2004; Ian Manners, 'Normative Power Europe: A Contradiction in Terms?', *Journal of Common Market Studies*, Vol. 40, No. 2, 2002, pp. 235–58.
39. Oliver P. Richmond, 'Critical Agency, Resistance, and a Post-Colonial Civil Society', *Cooperation and Conflict*, Vol. 46, No. 4, December 2011, pp. 419–40.
40. Gayatri Chakravorty Spivak, 'Can the Subaltern Speak?', in C. Nelson and L. Grossberg (eds), *Marxism and the Interpretation of Culture*, Basingstoke: Macmillan, 1988, pp. 271–313; Oliver P. Richmond, 'A Pedagogy of Peacebuilding: Infrapolitics, Resistance, and Liberation', *International Political Sociology*, Vol. 6, No. 2, 2012.
41. See OECD, *The State's Legitimacy in Fragile Situations*, OECD, 2010, pp. 6–9.
42. Max Weber, 'The Three Types of Legitimate Rule' (trans. Hans Gerth), *Berkeley Publications in Society and Institutions*, Vol. 4. No. 1, pp. 1–11; Max Weber, *Political Writings*, Cambridge: Cambridge University Press, 1994.
43. For an elaboration of this concept in empirical terms, see Volker Boege, 'Bougainville Report: Addressing Legitimacy Issues in Fragile and Post-Conflict Situations to Advance Conflict Transformation and Peacebuilding', University of Queensland/ Berghof Foundation, January 2013, pp. 3–5.
44. Volker Boege, 'Legitimacy in Hybrid Political Orders – An Underestimated Dimension of Peacebuilding and State Formation', paper presented at the European Consortium of Political Research Conference, Potsdam, Germany, 10–12 September 2009, p. 10.
45. OECD, *The State's Legitimacy in Fragile Situations*, pp. 11 and 13.
46. *Ibid.*, p. 14.
47. For more on this from the perspective of the apogee of Western rationalism and power, see David Harvey, *The Condition of Post-Modernity*, Oxford: Blackwell, 1990, p. 40.
48. Boege, 'Bougainville Report', p. 23.
49. Michel Foucault, 'Of Other Spaces, Heterotopias' [1967], in *Architecture/mouvement/ continuité*, October 1984 (trans. Jay Miskowiec).
50. Carol Gilligan, *In a Different Voice*, Cambridge, M.A.: Harvard University Press, 1993.
51. Boutros Boutros-Ghali, *An Agenda for Peace: Preventative Diplomacy, Peacemaking and Peacekeeping*, New York: United Nations, 1992; International Commission on Intervention and State Sovereignty (ICISS), *Responsibility to Protect*, Ottawa: International Development Research Centre, December 2001.
52. For more on this 'fourth generation of peacemaking', see Oliver P. Richmond, *Maintaining Order, Making Peace*, conclusion; Oliver P. Richmond, *Peace in IR*, London: Routledge, 2008, conclusion.
53. *World Bank Development Report*, Washington, DC: World Bank, 2011.
54. See Oliver P. Richmond, *A Post-Liberal Peace*, London: Routledge, 2011.
55. See Victoria Fontan, *Decolonising Peace*, Doerzbach: Dignity Press, 2012.

56. James Clifford, 'Introduction', in James Clifford and George E. Marcus, *Writing Culture: The Poetics and Politics of Ethnography*, Berkeley, CA: University of California Press, 1986, p. 17.
57. This has occurred among a wide range of 'traditional donors' in the last ten years or so.
58. *World Bank Development Report*, 2001.
59. Confidential Source, *Personal Interview*, UN PBSO, New York, 6 February 2012.
60. Annan, *A Life in War and Peace*, pp. 214–15.
61. P. Mishra, *From the Ruins of Empire: The Revolt against the West and the Remaking of Asia*, London: Penguin, 2012.
62. See M. Foucault, *The Order of Things*, New York: Pantheon, 1970; M. Foucault, *Archaeology of Knowledge*, New York: Pantheon, 1972.
63. M. Foucault, 'Two Lectures', in Colin Gordon, (ed.), *Power/Knowledge: Selected Interviews*, New York: Pantheon, 1980; M. Foucault, *Society Must Be Defended*, New York: Picador, 2003.
64. See, for example, Paul van Tongeren, M. Brenk, M. Hellema and J. Verhoeven (eds), *People Building Peace II*, Boulder, CO: Lynne Rienner, 2005.
65. See, for example, Neil Harvey, *The Chiapas Rebellion: The Struggle for Land and Democracy*, Durham: Duke University Press, 1998.
66. Arjun Appadurai, *Modernity at Large*, Minneapolis: University of Minnesota Press, 1996, p. 178; Doreen Massey, 'A Global Sense of Place', in *Space, Place and Gender*, Minneapolis: Minneapolis University Press, 1994.
67. Doreen Massey, *World City*, Cambridge: Polity, 2007, p. 84.
68. *Ibid.*, p. 167.
69. Bruno Latour, 'On Actor-Network Theory: A Few Clarifications', *Soziale Welt*, Vol. 47, No. 4, 1996, p. 372.
70. Michel Foucault, *The History of Sexuality, Vol. 1: The Will to Knowledge*, London: Penguin, 1984 [1976].
71. See Richmond, *A Post-Liberal Peace*, introduction.
72. *Ibid.*, p. 13.
73. J.C. Scott, *Weapons of the Weak: Everyday Peasant Resistance*, Yale University Press, 1985.
74. Oliver P. Richmond, 'Eirenism and a Post-Liberal Peace', *Review of International Studies*, Vol. 35, No. 3, 2009.
75. Jens Bartelson, *The Critique of the State*, Cambridge: Cambridge University Press, 2001, p. ix.
76. Arturo Escobar, *Territories of Difference*, Durham: Duke University Press, 2008.
77. J. Habermas, *Between Facts and Norms*, Cambridge, MA: MIT Press, 1996.

Chapter I. The Legacy of State Formation

1. Antonio Gramsci, *Selections from the Prison Notebooks 1929–1935*, ed. and trans. Quintin Hoare and Geoffrey Nowell-Smith, New York: International Publishers, 1971, p. 52.
2. Charles Tilly, *Coercion, Capital and European States*, Oxford: Blackwell, 1990, p. 63; Scott, *Weapons of the Weak*.
3. Tilly, *Coercion, Capital and European States*, p. 117.
4. Max Weber, 'Politics as a Vocation', Lecture at the university in Munich, 1918.
5. Thomas Hobbes, *Leviathan*, Oxford: Oxford University Press, 2008 [1651], chapters 13 and 14.
6. See, for example, Rolf Schwarz, 'State Formation Processes in Rentier States: The Middle Eastern Case', Paper presented at the Fifth Pan-European Conference on International Relations, ECPR Standing Group on International Relations, The Hague, 9–11 September 2004.

7. For details of these, see Edward Newman, 'The Violence of Statebuilding in Historical Perspective', unpublished paper, 2011, pp. 8–13.
8. See Correlates of War Dataset, http://www.correlatesofwar.org/datasets.htm: the Failed States Index http://ffp.statesindex.org/; and the Uppsala/PRIO Dataset http://www.pcr.uu.se/research/ucdp/datasets/ucdp_prio_armed_conflict_dataset/. An alternative view is provided by the *Global Burden of Armed Violence* Reports.
9. *Ibid.*, pp. 13–15.
10. US Department of Defense, *National Defense Strategy*, Washington, DC: DOD, 2008; *European Security Strategy*, Brussels: December 2003; OECD-DAC, *Principles for Good International Engagement in Fragile States and Situations*, Paris: OECD: April 2007.
11. Annan, *A Life in War and Peace*, p. 316.
12. See Oliver P. Richmond, 'The Romanticisation of the Local: Welfare, Culture and Peacebuilding', *International Spectator*, Vol. 44, No. 1, 2009.
13. Karl Marx and Friedrich Engels, *The Communist Manifesto*, Oxford: Oxford University Press, 1998 [1848], p. 3: Karl Marx and Friedrich Engels, *The German Ideology*, London: Lawrence and Wishart, 1999 [1846].
14. Eric J. Hobsbawm, *Nations and Nationalism since 1780: Programme, Myth, Reality*, 2nd edn, Cambridge: Cambridge University Press, 1992.
15. Charles Tilly, *European Revolutions*, Oxford: Blackwell, 1993, p. 5; Tilly, *Coercion, Capital and European States*, p. 15.
16. See Charles Tilly (ed.), *The Formation of National States in Western Europe*, Princeton: Princeton University Press, 1975; Charles Tilly, *War Making and State Making as Organized Crime*, Cambridge: Cambridge University Press, 1985, pp. 169–91.
17. Barrington Moore Jr, *Social Origins of Dictatorship and Democracy*, London: Penguin, 1966.
18. J. Bayart, *The State in Africa: The Politics of the Belly*, London: Longman, 1993; C. Clapham, *Africa and the International System: The Politics of State Survival*, Cambridge: Cambridge University Press, 1993.
19. William Reno, *Warlord Politics and African States*, Boulder, CO: Lynne Rienner, 1999.
20. Yahia H. Zoubir (ed.), *North Africa in Transition: State, Society, and Economic Transformation in the 1990s*, Gainesville: University Press of Florida, 1999, p. 33.
21. Barry Buzan, Ole Waever and Jaap de Wilde, *Security: A New Framework for Analysis*, Boulder, CO: Lynne Rienner, 1998, p. 25.
22. For a superb critique of state formation along these lines, see Tony Day, *Fluid Iron: State Formation in Southeast Asia*, Honolulu: University of Hawai'i Press, 2002, esp. chapter 1.
23. For opposing views, see Kenneth Waltz, *Man, the State, and War*, New York: Columbia University Press, 1959; R.B.J. Walker, *Inside/Outside: International Relations as Political Theory*, Cambridge: Cambridge University Press, 1993.
24. Charles Tilly, 'Western State-Making and Theories of Political Transformation', in Tilly (ed.), *The Formation of National States in Western Europe*, p. 629.
25. Schwarz, 'State Formation Processes in Rentier States'; see also Tilly, *Coercion, Capital and European*, pp. 5–12.
26. Otto Hintze, 'The Formation of States and Constitutional Development', in Felix Gilbert (ed.), *The Historical Essays of Otto Hintze*, New York: Oxford University Press, 1975, p. 174.
27. Tilly, *The Formation of National States in Western Europe*, p. 42.
28. Michael N. Barnett, *Confronting the Costs of War: Military Power, State, and Society in Egypt and Israel*, Princeton: Princeton University Press, 1992, p. 7.
29. Schwarz, 'State Formation Processes in Rentier States', pp. 16–17.
30. Robert H. Jackson, *Quasi-States: Sovereignty, International Relations and the Third World*, Cambridge: Cambridge University Press, 1990.
31. Barnett, *Confronting the Costs of War*.

32. J.J. Linz and A. Stepan, *Problems of Democratic Transition and Consolidation: Southern Europe, South America, and Post-Communist Europe*, Baltimore, MD: Johns Hopkins University Press, 1996, p. 16.
33. Philip Corrigan and Derek Sayer, *The Great Arch: English State Formation as Cultural Revolution*, Oxford: Blackwell, 1985, pp. 2–3.
34. James C. Scott, Foreward, in Gilbert M. Joseph and Daniel Nugent (eds), *Everyday Forms of State Formation*, Durham, NC: Duke University Press, 1994, pp. ix and 65.
35. Richard Ashcraft, *Revolutionary Politics & Locke's Two Treatises of Government*, Princeton: Princeton University Press, 1986.
36. Scott, 'Introduction', p. 95.
37. Tilly, *Coercion, Capital and European States*.
38. Charles Tilly, 'War Making and State Making as Organised Crime', in P. Evans, D. Rueschemeyer and T. Skocpol (eds), *Bringing the State Back In*, Cambridge: Cambridge University Press, 1985, pp. 169–86.
39. Tilly, 'War Making and State Making as Organized Crime', pp. 161–91.
40. Richmond, 'The Romanticisation of the Local'.
41. North, Wallis and Weingast, *Violence and Social Orders*, pp. 11–12.
42. Tilly, 'Western State-Making and Theories of Political Transformation', p. 601.
43. Seymour Martin Lipset, 'Some Social Requisites of Democracy', *American Political Science Review*, Vol. 53, No. 1, 1959, pp. 69–105.
44. A.R. Radcliffe Brown, 'Preface', in M. Fortes and E.E. Evans-Pritchard (eds), *African Political Systems*, Oxford: Oxford University Press, 1955 [1940], p. xxiii.
45. Christian Krohn-Hansen and Knut G. Nustad (eds), *State Formation: Anthropological Perspectives*, London: Pluto Press, 2005, p. 5.
46. Michael Mann, *The Sources of Social Power: Volume 1, A History of Power from the Beginning to AD 1760*, Cambridge: Cambridge University Press, 1986; Mann, *The Sources of Social Power: Volume 2, The Rise of Classes and Nation States 1760–1914*, Cambridge: Cambridge University Press, 1993.
47. Krohn-Hansen and Nustard, *State Formation*, 2005, p. ix.
48. Tilly, *Coercion, Capital and European States*, p. 99.
49. P. Abrams, 'Notes on the Difficulty of Studying the State', *Journal of Historical Sociology*, Vol. 1, 1988, pp. 58–89 (74); M.R. Trouillot, 'The Anthropology of the State in the Age of Globalization: Close Encounters of the Deceptive Kind', *Current Anthropology*, Vol. 42, 2001, pp. 125–38.
50. Krohn-Hansen and Nustad, *State Formation*, p. 7.
51. J.F. Bayart, 'Finishing with the Idea of the Third World: The Concept of the Political Trajectory', in J. Manor (ed.), *Rethinking Third World Politics*, London and New York: Longman, pp. 52–53.
52. Krohn-Hansen and Nustad, *State Formation*, p. 9.
53. Michael Herzfeld, *The Social Production of Indifference: Exploring the Symbolic Roots of Western Bureaucracy*, Oxford: Berg, 1992, p. 62.
54. Clifford Geertz, *Negara: The Theatre State in Nineteenth-Century Bali*, Princeton: Princeton University Press, 1980, p. 136.
55. Katherine Verdery, *The Political Lives of Dead Bodies: Reburial and Postsocialist Change*, New York: Columbia University Press, 1999, p. 25.
56. Ana Maria Alonso, 'The Politics of Space, Time and Substance: State Formation, Nationalism and Ethnicity', *Annual Review of Anthropology*, Vol. 23, 1994, p. 390.
57. Trouillot, 'The Anthropology of the State in the Age of Globalization', p. 125.
58. Krohn-Hansen and Nustad, *State Formation*, pp. 11–14.
59. S. Ortner, 'Resistance and the Problem of Ethnographic Refusal', *Comparative Studies in Society and History*, Vol. 37, 1995, pp. 173–93.

60. Tilly, 'Western State-Making and Theories of Political Transformation', p. 618.
61. Cited in *ibid.*, p. 623.
62. Michael Foucault, *The Foucault-Chomsky Debate: On Human Nature*, New York: New Press, 2006, pp. 156–57.
63. Theda Skocpol, *States and Social Revolutions*, Cambridge: Cambridge University Press, 1979, p. 161.
64. Michael Lowy, *The Politics of Uneven and Combined Development*, London: Verso, 1981.
65. Jonathan Hill, 'Beyond the Other? A Postcolonial Critique of the Failed State Thesis', *African Identities*, Vol. 3, No. 2, 2005.
66. See, for example, Hisham Sharabi, *Neopatriarchy: A Theory of Distorted Change in Arab Society*, Oxford: Oxford University Press, 1988; Robert Cunningham and Yasin Sarayrah, *Wasta: The Hidden Force in Middle Eastern Societies*, New York: Praeger, 1993.
67. Jennifer Widner, 'States and Statelessness in Late-Twentieth-Century Africa', *Daedalus*, Vol. 124, No. 3, 1995, pp. 142–46; J.S. Migdal, *State in Society*, Cambridge: Cambridge University Press, 2001; see also Philip S. Khoury and Joseph Kostiner (eds), *Tribes and State Formation in the Middle East*, Berkeley: University of California Press, 1991, p. 4, and Schwarz, 'State Formation Processes in Rentier States', p. 20.
68. See http://www.isaf.nato.int/COIN; The Network of Concerned Anthropologists, *The Counter-Counterinsurgency Manual*, Chicago: Chicago University Press, 2009.
69. *Ibid.*, p. 629.
70. David Chandler, *International Statebuilding: The Rise of Post-Liberal Governance*, London: Routledge, 2010, p. 20.
71. Samuel P. Huntington, *The Clash of Civilizations and the Remaking of World Order*, London: Simon Schuster, 1997.
72. Robert I. Rotberg, 'The New Nature of Failed States', *The Washington Quarterly*, Vol. 25, No. 3, pp. 85–96.
73. Barry R. Posen, 'The Security Dilemma and Ethnic Conflict', *Survival*, Vol. 35, No. 1, pp. 27–47.
74. Tilly, 'Western State-Making and Theories of Political Transformation', p. 601.
75. Mann, *The Sources of Social Power, Vol. 2*, p. 55.
76. Kaplan, 'The Coming Anarchy'.
77. Khoury and Kostiner, *Tribes and State Formation in the Middle East*.
78. Barnett R. Rubin, *The Fragmentation of Afghanistan: State Formation and Collapse in the International System*, 2nd edn, New Haven, CT: Yale University Press, 2002.
79. The key text here is Ashraf Ghani and Claire Lockhart, *Fixing Failed States: A Framework for Rebuilding a Fractured World*, Oxford: Oxford University Press, 2008.
80. For a good review, see Caroline Hughes, *An Investigation of Conflict Management in Cambodian Villages: A Review of the Literature with Suggestions for Future Research*, Centre for Peace and Development Cambodia Development Resource Institute, Phnom Penh, October 2001.
81. K.D. Jackson, *Cambodia, 1975–1978: Rendezvous with Death*, Princeton: Princeton University Press, 1992.
82. United Nations Security Council, 'Agreement on Comprehensive Political Settlement of the Cambodia Conflict', Paris, 23 October 1991; UN Security Council Resolution 718, 31 October 1991.
83. United Nations Security Council Resolution 745, 28 February 1992.
84. Day, *Fluid Iron*.
85. Oliver P. Richmond and Jason Franks, 'Liberal Hubris: Virtual Peace in Cambodia', *Security Dialogue*, Vol. 38, No. 1, 2007; Sorpong Peou, *International Democracy Assistance for Peacebuilding: Cambodia and Beyond*, London: Palgrave Macmillan, 2007.

86. Volker Boege, Anne Brown, Kevin Clements and Anna Nolan, 'On Hybrid Political Orders and Emerging States: What Is Failing – States in the Global South or Research and Politics in the West?', in *Building Peace in the Absence of States: Challenging the Discourse on State Failure, Berghof Handbook Dialogue No. 8*, 2009.
87. Ben Moxham, 'State-Making and the Post-Conflict City: Integration in Dili, Disintegration in Timor-Leste', *Crisis States Working Paper No. 2*, Development Studies Institute, London School of Economics and Political Science, February 2008.
88. Jennifer Milliken and Keith Krause, 'State Failure, State Collapse and State Reconstruction: Concepts, Lessons and Strategies', *Development and Change*, Vol. 33, No. 5, 2002, pp. 753–72.
89. Svetlana Broz, Writer and Activist, *Personal Interview*, Sarajevo, 23 July 2012.
90. Linz and Stepan, *Problems of Democratic Transition and Consolidation*.
91. Kori Schake, 'The Dayton Peace Accords: Success or Failure?', in K.R. Spillmann and J. Krause, *International Security Challenges in a Changing World*, Peter Lang: Bern, 1999, p. 295.
92. Sumantra Bose, *Bosnia after Dayton: Nationalist Partition and International Intervention*, London: Hurst & Co, 2002, p. 3.
93. Arnaud Kurze, 'State, Society, and Globalization in the Balkans: Problems of Democratic Consolidation in Bosnia and Herzegovina, Kosovo, the Former Yugoslav Republic of Macedonia, and Serbia', *Working Papers in Global Studies*, No. 4, April 2009.
94. Besnik Pula, 'The Emergence of the Kosovo "Parallel State", 1988–1991', *Nationalities Papers: The Journal of Nationalism and Ethnicity*, Vol. 32, No. 4, 2004.
95. Oliver P. Richmond and Jason Franks, *Liberal Peace Transitions: Between Statebuilding and Peacebuilding*, Edinburgh: Edinburgh University Press, 2009, chapter 4.
96. Scott, *Weapons of the Weak*.
97. Tilly, *Coercion, Capital and European States*, p. 101.
98. Richmond, *A Post-Liberal Peace*, conclusion.
99. Tilly, *Coercion, Capital and European States*, p. 162.
100. For example, see World Bank, *World Bank Development Report 2011*, in which civil society and social compact make a return to its discussion of development.
101. Richmond, 'Eirenism and a Post-Liberal Peace'.

Chapter II. Statebuilding: Failed by Design

1. Immanuel Kant, 'Perpetual Peace: A Philosophical Sketch' (1795), from *Principles of Politics*, trans. W. Hastie, Edinburgh: Clark, 1891.
2. Henry David Thoreau, *On the Duty of Civil Disobedience* (or *Resistance to Civil Government*), CreateSpace Independent Publishing Platform, 2012 [1849], p. 1.
3. Fukuyama, *The Origins of Political Order*, p. 420.
4. See James Dobbins, Seth G. Jones, Keith Crane and Beth Cole DeGrasse, *The Beginner's Guide to Nation-Building*, Santa Monica: RAND, 2007.
5. Robert Jackson, *Quasi-States*, p. 262.
6. UNDP, *Governance and Peacebuilding*, New York: UNDP, 2012, p. 7. For a very useful collection of essays on state formation and statebuilding, see Berit Bliesemann de Guevara (ed.), *Statebuilding and State-Formation: The Political Sociology of Intervention*, London: Routledge, 2012.
7. Hobbes, *Leviathan*, chapters 13 and 14; John Locke, *Second Treatise on Government*, Cambridge: Cambridge University Press, 1988 [1689].
8. Confidential Source, *Personal Interview*, Washington, DC: World Bank, 2 February 2012.
9. Davesh Kapur, 'The IMF: A Cure of Curse?', *Foreign Policy*, No. 111, 1998, pp. 114–29; Joseph Stiglitz, *Globalization and its Discontents*, W.W. Norton & Company, 2003, p. 53.
10. Tilly, *Coercion, Capital and European States*, p. 194.

11. Diana Cammack *et al.*, 'Donors and the "Fragile States" Agenda', Report submitted to the Japan International Cooperation Agency, March 2006, p. 45.
12. Badie, *The Imported State*, p. 57.
13. Toby Dodge, 'Intervention and Dreams of Exogenous Statebuilding: The Application of Liberal Peacebuilding in Afghanistan and Iraq', *Review of International Studies*, October 2013.
14. These goals were established following the Millennium Summit of the UN in 2000 and the adoption of the United Nations Millennium Declaration. 189 United Nations member states committed to achieve them by 2015. They include eradicating extreme poverty and hunger, achieving universal primary education, promoting gender equality, reducing child mortality rates, improving maternal health, combatting HIV/AIDS, malaria, and other diseases, ensuring environmental sustainability, and developing a global partnership for development. Not one has so far been achieved. See http://www.un.org/millenniumgoals/.
15. Toby Dodge, 'Intervention and Dreams of Exogenous Statebuilding', p. 37.
16. OECD, *Do No Harm: International Support for Statebuilding*, OECD, 2010, pp. 9–11.
17. This is widely agreed across a range of literatures, but see David Harvey, 'Neoliberalism as Creative Destruction', *The Annals of the American Academy of Political and Social Science*, Vol. 610, No. 21, 2007.
18. Susan Woodward, 'Varieties of State-building in the Balkans: A Case for a Shifting Focus', in Martina Fischer, Hans Joachim Giessmann and Beatrix Schmelzle, (eds), *Berghof Handbook in Conflict Transformation, Volume 2*, Berlin: Berghof Center, 2010, p. 316.
19. Fukuyama, 'The Imperative of Statebuilding', p. 17.
20. Migdal, *State in Society*, pp. 22–23; Bayart, *The State in Africa*.
21. Brown, *The Unfinished Revolution*, pp. 101–03.
22. Asad, *Anthropology and the Colonial Encounter*.
23. Jack S. Levy, 'Domestic Politics and War', *Journal of Interdisciplinary History*, Vol. 18, No. 4, 1988, p. 662.
24. Francis Fukuyama, *Statebuilding*, Profile: New York, 2005.
25. Charles Tilly, *Democracy*, Cambridge: Cambridge University Press, 2007, p. 20.
26. *Ibid.*, p. 23.
27. Migdal, *State in Society*.
28. Oliver P. Richmond, 'UN Peace Operations and the Dilemmas of the Peacebuilding Consensus', *International Peacekeeping*, Vol. 10. No. 4, 2004.
29. Richmond and Franks, *Liberal Peace Transitions*; Richmond, *Transformation of Peace* and *A Post-Liberal Peace*.
30. See Appendix 2.
31. Confidential Source, *Personal Interview*, New York: UN PBSO, 10 February 2012.
32. World Bank, *World Bank Development Report 2011*.
33. Robin Luckham and Tom Kirk, 'The Two Faces of Security in Hybrid Political Orders', *Stability: International Journal of Stability and Development*, Vol. 2, No. 2, 2013, pp. 1–30.
34. P. Chabal and J.-P. Daloz, *Africa Works: Disorder as Political Instrument*, IAI African Issues series, Oxford/Bloomington, 1999; Paul Collier and Anke Hoeffler, 'On Economic Causes of Civil War', *Oxford Economic Papers*, Vol. 50, Issue 4, 1998, pp. 563–73.
35. Roger Mac Ginty, 'Indigenous Peace-Making versus the Liberal Peace', *Cooperation and Conflict*, Vol. 43, No. 2, 2008, pp. 139–63.
36. World Bank, *The State in a Changing World*, Washington, DC: World Bank, 1997.
37. Devesh Kapur, 'The State in Changing World: A Critique of the 1997 World Development Report', *WCFIA Working Paper*, No. 98-02, 1998, p. 5.
38. World Bank, *The State in a Changing World*, p. 15.
39. *Ibid.*, p. 19.
40. Confidential Source, *Personal Interview*, UN Peacebuilding Commission, 6 February 2012.

41. OECD-DAC, *Principles for Good International Engagement in Fragile States*, 2005, p. 2.
42. OECD-DAC, *Principles for Good International Engagement in Fragile States and Situations*, April 2007.
43. World Bank, *The State in a Changing World.*
44. Klaus Schlichte and Alex Veit, *Coupled Arenas: Why State Building Is So Difficult*, www2.hu-berlin.de/mikropolik/downloads/03-07_coupled_arenas.pdf.
45. World Bank, *The State in a Changing World*; Francis Fukuyama, 'Statebuilding: The Missing Dimension of Stateness', www.carnegiecouncil.org/media/Francis_Fukuyama_Handout.pdf.
46. W.W. Rostow, *The Stages of Economic Growth: A Non-Communist Manifesto*, Cambridge: Cambridge University Press, 1960; Lipset, 'Some Social Requisites of Democracy'; David McClelland, *The Achieving Society*, New York: Free Press, 1967.
47. Kapur, 'The State in a Changing World', p. 4.
48. *Ibid.*, pp. 21 and 24.
49. Confidential Source, *Personal Interview*, World Bank, Washington, DC, 2 February 2012.
50. Chhibber, 'The State in a Changing World', p. 17.
51. World Bank, *The State in a Changing World.*
52. Astri Suhrke, 'Exogenous Statebuilding: The Contradictions of the International Project in Afghanistan', in Whit Mason and Martin Krygier, *Rule of Law in Afghanistan*, Cambridge: Cambridge University Press, 2011.
53. US National Security Strategy, 2002; European Security Strategy, 2003.
54. US Department of Defense, *National Defense Strategy*, Washington, DC: DOD, 2008. The UK National Security Strategy of 2008 makes similar points, which are also found in many subsequent policy documents around the world, from DFID, 2006; High Level Panel, 2004; OECD, 2008.
55. Migdal, *State in Society.*
56. Rotberg, 'The New Nature of Nation-State Failure', p. 85.
57. Robert I. Rotberg, 'Failed States, Collapsed States, Weak States: Causes and Indicators', in Robert I. Rotberg (ed.), *State Failure and State Weakness in a Time of Terror*, Washington, DC: Brookings Institution Press, 2003, p. 5.
58. Jonathan Di John, 'The Concept, Causes and Consequences of Failed States', *European Journal of Development Research*, Vol. 22, 2010, pp. 10–30.
59. See http://ingo.worldbank.org/governance/wgi/index.asp.
60. See Cammack et al., 'Donors and the "Fragile States" Agenda', p. 27 for a review of these.
61. UNDP, *Governance and Peacebuilding*, 2012, p. 16.
62. Charles T. Call, 'The Fallacy of the "Failed State"', *Third World Quarterly*, Vol. 29, No. 8, 2008, pp. 1491–1507.
63. Fukuyama, 'The Imperative of Statebuilding', p. 17.
64. Kapur, 'The State in a Changing World: A Critique of the 1997 World Development Report', p. 17.
65. *Ibid.*, p. 19.
66. This term refers to specific economic prescriptions used for developing and conflict-affected countries since the 1980s by the International Monetary Fund (IMF) and World Bank, among other institutions, mainly focused on economic liberalisation and marketisation. See John Williamson, "What Washington Means by Policy Reform", in Williamson, John (ed.), *Latin American Readjustment*, Washington: Institute for International Economics, 1989.
67. Kapur, 'The State in a Changing World: A Critique of the 1997 World Development Report', pp. 22 and 27.
68. Michel-Rolph Trouillot, *Silencing the Past: Power and the Production of History*, Beacon Press: Boston, 1995; Krohn-Hansen and Nustard, *State Formation*, p. 9.

69. Chandler, *International Statebuilding*, p. 15; Christopher Clapham, *Africa and the International System*.
70. Confidential Sources, *Focus Group*, New York: PBSO, UN, 7 February 2012.
71. *Ibid.*
72. Chhibber, 'The State in a Changing World', p. 18.
73. Richmond, 'The Romanticisation of the Local'.
74. Chandler, *International Statebuilding*, p. 65.
75. Volker Boege, Anne Brown, Kevin P. Clements and Anna Nolan, 'States Emerging from Hybrid Political Orders – Pacific Experiences', The Australian Centre for Peace and Conflict Studies (ACPACS) Occasional Papers Series, 2008.
76. This is a reference to the novella *The Strange Case of Dr Jekyll and Mr Hyde* by Robert Louis Stevenson (1886), which famously investigated the phenomenon of a London doctor's 'split personality', between good (Jekyll) and evil (Hyde).
77. For a good discussion of the manifold dynamics of neoliberalism in Cambodia, see S. Springer, *Cambodia's Neoliberal Order: Violence, Authoritarianism and the Contestation of Public Space*, London: Routledge, 2010.
78. M. Turner, 'Completing the Circle: Peacebuilding as Colonial Practice in the Occupied Palestinian Territory', International Studies Association Annual Conference, San Diego, 1–4 March 2012.
79. *Ibid.*
80. World Bank, *Building the Palestinian State*, Washington, DC: World Bank, 13 April 2011.
81. Turner, 'Completing the Circle', pp. 6 and 15.
82. Graham Harrison, *Neoliberal Africa*, London: Zed Books, 2010.
83. Turner, 'Completing the Circle', p.10.
84. Susan Woodward, *A Balkan Tragedy*, Washington, DC: Brookings Institute, 1995.
85. Bose, *Bosnia after Dayton*, p. 3.
86. L. Montanaro, 'The Kosovo Statebuilding Conundrum', *FRIDE Working Paper No. 91*, October 2009, p. 1.
87. *Ibid.*, p. 14.
88. Richmond, *The Transformation of Peace*, chapter 5.
89. Joanne Wallis, "What Role Can Decentralisation Play in State-Building? Lessons from Timor-Leste and Bougainville', *Commonwealth and Comparative Politics*, Vol. 51, No. 4, 2013, p. 433.
90. United Nations, 'Report of the Secretary-General on Timor-Leste Pursuant to Security Council Resolution 1690', August 2006, p. 9. Undocs, S/2006/628.
91. *Ibid.*
92. Douglas Grenfell, 'Governance, Violence and Crises in Timor-Leste', in D. Mearns (ed.), *Democratic Governance in Timor-Leste*, Darwin: Charles Darwin University Press, 2008, p. 87.
93. 'Address by HE President Taur Matan Ruak on the Commemoration of the 13th Anniversary of the Referendum for the Self-Determination of the People of Timor-Leste', Dili, 30 August 2012.
94. Barnett Rubin, 'Constructing Sovereignty for Security', *Survival*, Vol, 47, No. 4, pp. 93–106.
95. Suhrke, 'Exogenous Statebuilding', p. 227.
96. Yalda Hakim, 'Afghanistan's Hamid Karzai Says NATO Caused "Great Suffering"', *BBC News*, 7 October 2013.
97. William Maley, 'Statebuilding in Afghanistan', *Central Asian Survey*, Vol. 32, No. 3, p. 266; Kim Gupta, 'US Envoy Says Mistakes of the West Prolonged Afghan War and Cost Lives', *Independent*, 1 November 2013.
98. Maley, 'Statebuilding in Afghanistan', p. 258.
99. Suhrke, 'Exogenous Statebuilding', pp. 263 and 264.

100. Andreas Wilde and Katja Mielke, 'Order, Stability and Change in Afghanistan', *Central Asian Survey*, Vol. 32, No. 3, p. 353.
101. Tim Sharan, 'The Dynamics of Informal Political Networks and Statehood in Post-2001 Afghanistan', *Asian Survey*, Vol. 32, No. 3, p. 336.
102. Suhrke, 'Exogenous Statebuilding', p. 229.
103. Maley, 'Statebuilding in Afghanistan', p. 266.
104. Abdulaziz Sachedine, *The Role of Islam in the Public Square: Guidance or Governance?*, Amsterdam: Amsterdam University Press, 2006.
105. Confidential Sources, *Personal Interviews*, New York: UN PBSO, 6 February 2012.
106. Antonia Giustozzi, 'Bureaucratic Façade and Political Realities of Disarmament and Demobilisation in Afghanistan', *Conflict, Security and Development*, Vol. 8, No. 2, 2008, p. 170.
107. Ken Menkhaus, 'Governance in the Hinterlands by Africa's Weak States: Towards a Theory of a Mediated State', Conference paper at APSA, Philadelphia, 31 August 2006, p. 103.
108. Richmond, *A Post-Liberal Peace*.
109. Luckham and Kirk, *The Two Faces of Security*, p. 30.
110. See a World Bank Draft Report, 'Institutions Taking Root: Building State Capacity in Challenging Contexts', unpublished, 2011. See also UNDP, *Governance and Peacebuilding*, 2012.
111. Charles Boix, 'Economic Roots of Civil Wars and Revolutions in the Contemporary World', *World Politics*, Vol. 60, 2008, pp. 390–437.
112. World Bank, *World Bank Development Report 2011*, p. 18.
113. *Ibid.*, p. 24.
114. *Ibid.*, p. 26.
115. UNDP, *Governance and Peacebuilding*, p. 18. See also Confidential Source, *Personal Interview*, New York: UNDP, 8 February 2012.
116. UNDP, *Governance and Peacebuilding*, p. 42.
117. Migdal and Schlichte, cited in Berit Bliesemann de Guevara, 'The State in Times of Statebuilding', *Civil Wars*, Vol. 10, No. 4, 2008, p. 361.
118. Evgeny Lebedev, 'Hamid Karzai: In the Shadow of Terror, a Meeting with the World's Loneliest President', *The Independent*, 17 September 2011.
119. *Ibid.*
120. Confidential Source, *Personal Interview*, New York: UNDP, 8 February 2012.
121. North, Wallis and Weingast, *Violence and Social Orders*, pp. 11–12.
122. David A. Lake and Christopher Faris, 'International Trusteeship', in Stephen D. Krasner and Thomas Risse (eds), *External Actors, Statebuilding, and Service Provision in Areas of Limited Statehood*, forthcoming.
123. Badie, *The Imported State*, p. 115.
124. *Ibid.*, pp. 194–95.
125. Christof P. Kurz, 'The Limitations of International Analyses of Post-Conflict Statebuilding in Sierra Leone', in Berit Bliesemann de Guevara (ed.), *Statebuilding and State-Formation: The Political Sociology of Intervention*, London: Routledge, 2012, p. 114; UNDP, *Sierra Leone Country Profile*, 2010.
126. Louise Riis Anderson, 'Statebuilding as Tacit Trusteeship', in Berit Bliesemann de Guevara (ed.), *Statebuilding and State-Formation*, pp. 132–33.
127. Richmond, *The Transformation of Peace*, conclusion.
128. Migdal, *State in Society*.
129. OECD, *Do No Harm: International Support for Statebuilding*, p. 15.
130. Bartelson, *The Critique of the State*, p. 138.
131. Mohammed Youssef, *Personal Interview*, International Peace Academy, New York, 16 February 2012.

132. Tilly, *Democracy*, p. 20.
133. John Heathershaw, 'Conclusions', in Bliesemann de Guevara (ed.), *Statebuilding and State-Formation*, p. 255.

Chapter III. Liberal Peacebuilding

1. Badie, *The Imported State*, p. 2.
2. Herman Schmid, 'Peace Research and Politics', *Journal of Peace Research*, Vol. 5, No. 3, 1968.
3. Roland Paris, *At War's End*, Cambridge: Cambridge University Press, 2004; Richmond, *The Transformation of Peace*; Vivienne Jabri, *War and the Transformation of Global Politics*, London: Palgrave, 2007; Michael Pugh, Neil Cooper and Mandy Turner (eds), *Whose Peace? Critical Perspectives on the Political Economy of Peacebuilding*, London: Palgrave, 2008; Richmond and Franks, *Liberal Peace Transitions*; Edward Newman, Roland Paris and Oliver P. Richmond (eds), *New Perspectives on Liberal Peacebuilding*, Tokyo: United Nations University Press, 2009.
4. Jean-Jacques Rousseau, *Discourse on the Origin and Foundation of Inequality among Mankind*, London: Penguin, 1984 [1755].
5. Alex Bellamy and Paul Williams, 'Peace Operations and Global Order', *International Peacekeeping*, Vol. 10, No. 4, 2004; Elizabeth M. Cousens and Chetan Kumar (eds), *Peacebuilding as Politics: Cultivating Peace in Fragile Societies*, Boulder, CO: Lynne Rienner, 2001.
6. UN Secretary General Report on 'Peacebuilding in the Immediate Aftermath of Conflict', A/63/881, 11 June 2009, p. 6.
7. Adam C. Smith, 'Understanding What We're Saying: Dilemmas of the UN's Peacebuilding Paradigm', *Civil-Military Working Papers*, No. 11, 2010.
8. Official Source, *Personal Interview*, New York: UN PBSO, 2 February 2012.
9. Confidential Official Source, *Personal Interview*, New York: UN PBSO, 6 February 2012.
10. Vanessa Wyeth, *Personal Interview*, New York: International Peace Academy, 7 February 2012.
11. Dodge, 'Intervention and Dreams of Exogenous Statebuilding'.
12. See Richard Caplan, *International Governance of War-Torn Territories*, Oxford: Oxford University Press, 2004, pp. 184–86.
13. See the World Bank's Good Governance Indicators, 2010: http://info.worldbank.org/governance/wgi/sc_country.asp.
14. Lipset, 'Some Social Requisites of Democracy'.
15. See, for example, the UNESCO Culture of Peace Programme in El Salvador, 1992.
16. Report of the UN Secretary General on 'Peacebuilding in the Immediate Aftermath of Conflict', A/63/881-S/2009/304, 11 June 2009, p. 6.
17. See Richard Ponzio, *Democratic Peacebuilding*, Oxford: Oxford University Press, 2011, p. 206.
18. 'Statement by Representative of Guatemala at the Open Meeting of the Security Council on Peacebuilding: A Comprehensive Approach', S/PV.4272, 5 February 2001.
19. There are varying estimates, but by 2008 110,000 personnel were deployed in countries populated by a total of 100 million people. Ponzio, *Democratic Peacebuilding*, p. 2.
20. Charles Call and Susan Cook, 'On Democratisation and Peacebuilding', *Global Governance*, Vol. 9, No. 2, 2003, pp. 233–34; Richmond and Franks, *Liberal Peace Transitions*.
21. Martin, *Enforcing the Peace*, p. 11.
22. See Johan Galtung, 'A Structural Theory of Imperialism', *Journal of Peace Research*, Vol. 8, 1971, pp. 81–117.
23. See Shahrbanou Tadjbakhsh and Anuradha M. Chenoy, *Human Security: Concepts and Implications*, London: Routledge, 2006.

24. John Burton, *World Society*, Cambridge: Cambridge University Press, 1972
25. E.A. Azar, 'Protracted International Conflicts: Ten Propositions', in J. Burton and E.A. Azar, *International Conflict Resolution: Theory and Practice*, Hemel Hempstead: Harvester Wheatsheaf, 1986.
26. David J. Dunn, *The First Fifty Years of Peace Research*, Aldershot: Ashgate, 2005, p. 78.
27. Richmond, 'Eirenism and a Post-Liberal Peace', pp. 576–77.
28. Richmond, *The Transformation of Peace*.
29. Charles T. Call and Elizabeth M. Cousens, 'Ending Wars and Building Peace: International Responses to War-Torn Societies', *International Studies Perspectives*, Vol. 9, 2008, pp. 1–21.
30. For more on this elision, see Richmond and Franks, *Liberal Peace Transitions*, 'Introduction'.
31. David Holiday, 'El Salvador's "Model" Democracy', *Current History*, Vol. 104, No. 679, February 2005, pp. 77–80.
32. *Ibid.*, p. 81.
33. See, for example, the range of essays included in Pugh, Cooper and Turner, *Whose Peace?* See also Richmond, *The Transformation of Peace*, conclusion.
34. UN Secretary General Report on 'Peacebuilding in the Immediate Aftermath of Conflict', A/63/881, 11 June 2009, p. 9.
35. General Assembly Document, A/64/868, 21 July 2010.
36. UN General Assembly Resolution 60/180, 20 December 2005.
37. Michael Doyle, 'Strategy and Transitional Authority', in Stephen John Stedman, Donald Rothchild and Elizabeth M. Cousens (eds), *Ending Civil Wars: The Implementation of Peace Agreements*, Boulder, CO/London: Lynne Rienner, 2002, p. 72.
38. Confidential Source, *Personal Interview*, New York: UN Peacebuilding Trust, 6 February 2012.
39. Michael Pugh, 'The Political Economy of Peacebuilding: A Critical Theory Perspective', *International Journal of Peace Studies*, Vol. 10, No. 2, 2005, pp. 23–42.
40. See, for example, the emancipatory and yet locally sensitised approaches expressed in General Assembly Resolution 3201, 'Declaration on the Establishment of a New International Economic Order', 1 May 1974; General Assembly Resolution 33/73, 'Declaration on the Preparation of Societies for Life in Peace', 15 December 1978; General Assembly Resolution A/Res/53/243, 'Declaration and Programme of Action on a Culture of Peace', 6 October 1999.
41. John Paul Lederach, *Building Peace*, Washington, DC: United States Institute of Peace, 1997, p. 39. See also Lederach, *Preparing for Peace: Conflict Transformation across Cultures*, Syracuse: Syracuse University Press, 1995.
42. See Fukuyama, *The Origins of Political Order*, p. 27.
43. Lederach, *Building Peace*, pp. 60–61.
44. Pugh, Cooper and Turner, *Whose Peace?*
45. Charles A. Reilly, *Peacebuilding and Development in Guatemala and Northern Ireland*, London: Palgrave, 2009, p. 65.
46. Among others, see Richmond and Franks, 'Liberal Hubris: Virtual Peace in Cambodia'.
47. James Galbraith, 'Inequality, Unemployment and Growth', *Journal of Economic Inequality*, Vol. 7, No. 2, June 2009, pp. 2 and 36. Robert Skidelsky, *Keynes: The Return of the Master*, London: Penguin, 2009, pp. 114–15 and 168; Cf. Richard Wilkinson and Kate Pickett, *The Spirit Level: Why More Equal Societies Almost Always Do Better*, London: Allen Lane, 2009; Frances Stewart, 'Horizontal Inequalities: A Neglected Dimension of Development', *Working Paper 81*, Oxford: University of Oxford, February 2002.
48. Asian Development Bank Factsheet, 31 December, 2009, http://www.adb.org/Documents/Fact_Sheets/CAM.pdf.
49. Call and Cook, *Ending Wars and Building Peace*, p. 235.

50. *Ibid.*, p. 238.
51. For more on this, see Chandra Sriram, 'Revolutions in Accountability', *American University International Law Review*, Vol. 19, No. 2, 2003; Charles O. Lerche, 'Truth Commissions and National Reconciliation: Some Reflections on Theory and Practice', *Peace and Conflict Studies*, Vol. 7, No. 1, 2000.
52. For an interesting discussion of these dimensions, see Soares de Oliveira, 'Illiberal Peacebuilding in Angola', p. 305.
53. See Beatrice Pouligny, *Peace Operations Seen from Below*, London: Hurst, 2006.
54. See, for a review of responses to such deficiencies, the UN Secretary-Genera Report on 'Peacebuilding in the Immediate Aftermath of Conflict'.
55. UN, 'From Rhetoric to Practice: Operationalizing National Ownership in Post-Conflict Peacebuilding. A Policy Workshop', New York: *UN Peacebuilding Support Office*, 14 March 2011.
56. Janine Natalya Clark, 'Bosnia's Success Story? Brčko District and the "View from Below"', *International Peacekeeping*, Vol. 17, No. 1, pp. 67–79; Janine Natalya Clark, 'From Negative to Positive Peace', *Journal of Human Rights*, Vol. 8, No. 4, pp. 360–84.
57. Turner, 'Completing the Circle'.
58. M. Turner, 'Peacebuilding as Counterinsurgency in the Occupied Palestinian Territory', ISA, San Francisco, 2–5 April 2013.
59. A. Suhrke, 'Exogenous Statebuilding: The Contradictions of the International Project in Afghanistan', in (eds), *Rule of Law in Afghanistan*, Whit Mason and Martin Krygier, Cambridge: Cambridge University Press, 2011, pp. 225–48.
60. A. Donini, 'Local Perceptions of Assistance to Afghanistan', *International Peacekeeping*, Vol. 14, No. 1, pp. 158–72, p. 160.
61. UNDP, *Governance and Peacebuilding*, p. 33.
62. Turner, 'Peacebuilding as Counterinsurgency'.
63. Jeremy Bentham, 'Panopticon', in Miran Bozovic (ed.), *The Panopticon Writings*, London: Verso, 1995, pp. 29–95.
64. Richard Ponzio, *Democratic Peacebuilding*, p. 219; for peace as governance, see Richmond, *Maintaining Order, Making Peace*, conclusion.
65. R.S. Manglapus, *Will of the People: Original Democracy in Non-Western Societies*, New York: Greenwood, 1987, p. 129; A. Adedeji, 'An Alternative for Africa', *Journal of Democracy*, Vol. 5, No. 4, 1994, p. 126.
66. See, for example, Roland Paris, 'Saving Liberal Peacebuilding', *Review of International Study*, Vol. 36, 2010, pp. 337–65; Richmond, 'Eirenism and a Post-Liberal Peace', pp. 576–77.
67. UN Secretary-General Report on 'Peacebuilding in the Immediate Aftermath of Conflict', p. 1.
68. *Ibid.*, pp. 18 and 22.
69. Richmond, *Maintaining Order, Making Peace*, conclusion.
70. United Nations, PBC/1/BDI/4, 30 July 2007.
71. United Nations, PBC/5/GUI/4, 23 September 2011.
72. UNDP, *Governance and Peacebuilding*, New York: UNDP, 2012, p. 20.
73. *Ibid.*, p. 22.
74. *Ibid.*, p. 31.
75. *Ibid.*, p. 28.
76. *Ibid.*, p. 41.
77. *Ibid.*, p. 46.
78. OECD-DAC, *The State's Legitimacy in Fragile States*.
79. *Ibid.*, pp. 50–51.
80. Mike Pugh, 'Review of UNDP Governance and Peacebuilding', *Peacebuilding*, Vol. 1, No. 1, 2013.

81. UNDP, *Governance and Peacebuilding*, p. 15.
82. For an excellent set of proposals including these, see Erskine Barton Childers, 'For a Democratic United Nations and the Rule of Law', *Development Dialogue*, No. 56, Dag Hammarskjold Foundation, June 2011.
83. North, Wallis and Weingast, *Violence and Social Orders*, pp. 11–12.

Chapter IV. The Dynamics of Peace Formation

1. Azar, *The Management of Protracted Social Conflict*; J. Burton and E.A. Azar, *International Conflict Resolution: Theory and Practice*, Hemel Hempstead: Harvester Wheatsheaf, 1990; R. Chambers, *Rural Development*, London: Longman, 1983; A. Curle, *Making Peace*, London: Tavistock, 1971; Kelman, 'The Problem-Solving Workshop in Conflict Resolution'; Lederach, *Building Peace*.
2. World Bank, *The State in a Changing World*; OECD-DAC, 'Principles for Good International Engagement in Fragile States and Situations', Vienna, April 2007; UN Secretary-General Report on 'Peacebuilding in the Immediate Aftermath of Conflict', A/63/881 (11 June 2009).
3. IMF, *Poverty Reduction Strategy Papers (PRSP)*, 19 April 2012, http://www.imf.org/external/np/exr/facts/prsp.htm.
4. Thania Paffenholz and Christoph Spurk, 'Civil Society, Civic Engagement, and Peacebuilding', *Social Development Papers*, World Bank, Paper No. 36, October 2006; Hideaki Shinoda, 'The Difficulty and Importance of Local Ownership and Capacity Development in Peacebuilding', *Hiroshima Peace Science*, Vol. 30, 2008, pp. 95–115.
5. Lederach, *Preparing for Peace*.
6. For an analysis and list of these and other examples, see Paul van Tongeren, 'Overview on Infrastructures for Peace', 2011, www.parliamentariansforconflictprevention.net. In a personal interview he mentioned at least thirty cases. *Personal Interview*, June 2012.
7. Andries Odendaal, *A Crucial Link: Local Peace Committees and National Peacebuilding*, Washington, DC: USIP, 2013, p. 35.
8. Bruno Latour, *Reassembling the Social*, Oxford: Oxford University Press, 2007, pp. 5 and 121.
9. See, for example, the UNESCO Culture of Peace Programme in El Salvador, 1992.
10. UNESCO and a Culture of Peace: Promoting a Global Movement (CAB-95/WS/1), 1995. Revised and reprinted in 1997 in Cultures of Peace Series (UNESCO, 1997).
11. Francisco Lacayo Parajon, Mirta Lourenco and David Adams, 'The UNESCO Culture of Peace Programme in El Salvador: An Initial Report', *International Journal of Peace Studies*, Vol. 1, No. 2, 1996, pp. 1–20.
12. *Ibid.*, p. 294.
13. Leslie Schuld, Director of Center for Exchange and Solidarity, *Personal Interview*, San Salvador, 17 January 2012.
14. George Williams, *Personal Interview*, Democracy Watch, Monrovia, 19 November 2009.
15. Richmond, *A Post-Liberal Peace*.
16. For example, see DFID, *The Politics of Poverty: Elites, Citizens and States*, London: DFID, 2011, pp. 61 and 62.
17. Richmond, 'The Romanticisation of the Local'.
18. Latour, *Reassembling the Social*, Oxford: Oxford University Press, 2005, p. 11.
19. Martina Fischer, 'Civil Society in Conflict Transformation', *Berghof Handbook for Conflict Transformation*, Berlin, 2011, p. 291.
20. Norbert Ropers, 'Civil-Society Peace Constituencies: NGO Involvement in Conflict Resolution – Areas of Activity and Lessons Learned', in G. Bachler (ed.), *Promoting Peace: The Role of Civilian Conflict Resolution*, Bern: Staempfli, pp. 97–126. Cited in Fischer, 'Civil Society in Conflict Transformation'.

21. Fischer, 'Civil Society in Conflict Transformation', p. 291.
22. W. Verkoren and M. van Leeuwen, 'Civil Society in Peacebuilding: Global Discourse, Local Reality', *International Peacekeeping*, Vol. 20, No. 2, p. 161.
23. *Ibid.*, p. 164.
24. *Ibid.*, p. 161.
25. Mazin Qumsiyeh, *Popular Resistance in Palestine: A History of Hope and Empowerment*, London: Pluto Press, 2011.
26. Leslie Schuld, Director of Center for Exchange and Solidarity, *Personal Interview*, San Salvador, 17 January, 2012.
27. Field Visit, San José, 27 January 2012.
28. Oliver P. Richmond, 'De-Romanticising the Local, Demystifying the International: Aspects of Liberal-Local Hybridity in Timor Leste and the Solomon Islands', *Pacific Review*, Vol. 24, No. 1, 2011.
29. Leslie Schuld, Director of Center for Exchange and Solidarity, *Personal Interview*, San Salvador, 17 January 2012.
30. Boege and Curth, 'Grounding the Responsibility to Protect', p. 12.
31. Fischer, 'Civil Society in Conflict Transformation', p. 302.
32. For example, see UNDP Discussion Paper, *Local Governance, Peacebuilding and Statebuilding*, New York: UNDP, 2010, p. 3.
33. Shahrbanou Tadjbakhsh, 'Liberal Peace and the Dialogue of the Deaf in Afghanistan', in Shahrbanou Tadjbakhsh (ed.), *Rethinking the Liberal Peace: External Models and Local Alternatives*, Milton Park: Routledge, 2011, pp. 206–20.
34. P. Johnson, 'Local vs. National Peacebuilding: The Richness of Somali Peacemaking', www.prio.no/peaceethics/PeacE-Discussions, 2010.
35. SIDA, 'Civil Society and Democracy in Cambodia: Changing Roles and Trends', The Fifth Report of the Sida Advisory Team on Democratic Governance, www.pnyx.se/docs/CambodiaI.pdf, 2003.
36. J. Plummer, *Voice, Choice and Decision 2: Local Basic Service Delivery*, Washington DC: World Bank Asia Foundation, 2013, p. 7.
37. Richmond and Franks, *Liberal Peace Transitions*, 2009.
38. For a detailed discussion of this concept, see Richmond, 'Eirenism and a Post-Liberal Peace' and *A Post-Liberal Peace*.
39. UNDP, 'Civil Society Index, Mozambique 2007', New York: UNDP, June 2008. Phil ya Nangoloh, 'The Role of Civil Society in the Socio-Economic Development of a Country', *Conference on Multipartyism and its Role in Democratization and Development*, organised by Forum for the Future, Council of Churches in Namibia (CCN) Hall, Katutura, Windhoek, 15–17 February 2010.
40. Oliver P. Richmond and Audra Mitchell, 'Peacebuilding and Critical Forms of Agency: From Resistance to Subsistence', *Alternatives*, Vol. 37, No. 1, 2011.
41. Stefanie Kappler and Oliver P. Richmond, 'Peacebuilding in Bosnia: Resistance or Emancipation?', *Security Dialogue*, Vol. 42, No. 3, 2011.
42. The Christian Council of Mozambique has run the 'Transforming Arms into Tools' project since 1995.
43. Kappler and Richmond, 'Peacebuilding in Bosnia: Resistance or Emancipation?'.
44. Susanne Jonas, *Of Centaurs and Doves: Guatemala's Peace Process*, Boulder: Westview Press, 1996, p. 167; Rachel Seder, 'Reframing Citizenship: Indigenous Rights, Local Power and the Peace Process in Guatemala, Accord', 1997, http://www.c-r.org/accord-article/reframing-citizenship-indigenous-rights-local-power-and-peace-process-guatemala; B. Warren Kay, 'The Indigenous Role in Guatemalan Peace', *Cultural Survival*, 1997, http://www.culturalsurvival.org/ourpublications/csq/article/the-indigenous-role-guatemalan-peace.
45. Benjamin Broome, 'The Cyprus Conflict: Root Causes and Implications for Peacebuilding', *Journal of Peace Research*, Vol. 44, 2007, pp. 349–65.

46. Maria Hadjipavlou, *Women and Change in Cyprus: Feminisms and Gender in Conflict*, London: I.B. Tauris, 2010.
47. Costas Constantinou, 'Aporias of Identity: Bicommunalism, Hybridity and the "Cyprus Problem"', *Cooperation and Conflict*, Vol. 42, No. 3, 2007, pp. 247–70.
48. Mehmet Ali Talat, Former President of the Turkish Republic of Northern Cyprus (TRNC), and George Vassiliou, Former President of the Republic of Cyprus, Public Debate, Home of Cooperation, Nicosia/Lefkosha, 8 October 2013.
49. See, for example, the work of PRIO's Cyprus Centre, which is internationally funded and locally staffed, and has developed a body of knowledge about the Cyprus conflict which perhaps shows the potential for reconciliatory praxis over the traditional ethno-nationalist legalism that has dogged Cypriot peace processes: http://cyprus.prio.org/.
50. Confidential Unofficial Source, *Personal Interview*, 20 April 2012.
51. Matthew Parish, 'Paradigms of State-Building: Comparing Bosnia and Kosovo', *Journal of Eurasian Law*, Vol. 3, No. 3, 2010.
52. Montanaro, 'The Kosovo Statebuilding Conundrum', p. 21.
53. See, for example, Paula M. Pickering, *Peacebuilding in the Balkans*, Ithaca, NY: Cornell University Press, 2007, pp. 2 and 6.
54. Wallis, 'What Role Can Decentralisation Play in State-Building?', p. 433.
55. Andrew McWilliam, 'Houses of Resistance in East Timor: Structuring of Sociality in the New National', *Anthropological Forum*, Vol. 15, No. 1, 2005; United Nations Development Assistance Framework, 'UNDAF Timor Leste 2009–2013'.
56. UNDP, *Human Development Report: Timor Leste*, Dili: Timor Leste, 2006; Lisa R. Palmer and Demetrio do Amaral de Carvalho, 'Nation Building and Resource Management: The Politics of Nature in Timor Leste', *Geoforum*, Vol. 39, 2008, pp. 1321–32.
57. Taur Matan Ruak, 'Address by HE President Taur Matan Ruak'; Josh Trindade, 'Reconciling Conflict Paradigms: An East Timorese Vision of the Ideal State', in D. Mearns, *Democratic Governance in Timor-Leste: Reconciling the Local and the National*, Darwin, Australia: Charles Darwin University, 2008.
58. Wallis, 'What Role Can Decentralisation Play in State-Building?', pp. 427 and 433.
59. *Ibid.*, p. 434.
60. Tom Woods, 'Informal Political System of Government in Solomon Islands', *Working Paper for the Constitutional Congress and the Eminent Persons Advisory Committee*, Soloman Islands: Honiara, 28 August 2008.
61. Laura Zanotti, 'Cacophanies of Aid: Failed Statebuilding and NGOs in Haiti', *Third World Quarterly*, Vol. 31, No. 5, 2010, p. 757.
62. *Ibid.*, pp. 762 and 768.
63. See, for example, EU External Action, EEAS Mediation Support Project, *Strengthening National Capacities for Mediation and Dialogue*, November 2012.
64. For an analysis and list of these and other examples, see Van Tongeren, 'Overview on Infrastructures for Peace'.
65. Odendaal, *A Crucial Link*, p. 7.
66. *Ibid.*, p. 41.
67. *Ibid.*, p. 42.
68. Lederach, *Building Peace*, pp. xvi and 49–51.
69. *Ibid.*, p. 51.
70. Andries Odendaal, 'An Architecture for Building Peace at the Local Level: A Comparative Study of Local Peace Committees', UNDP Discussion Paper, December 2010.
71. Chetan Kumar, 'Building National "Infrastructures for Peace": UN Assistance for Internally Negotiated Solutions to Violent Conflict', in Susan Allen Nan, Zachariah Cherian Mampilly and Andrea Bartoli (eds), *Peacemaking: From Practice to Theory, Volume 1*, Westport, CT: Praeger, 2011, p. 385.

72. Nepal Government, Ministry of Peace and Re-Construction, www.peace.gov.np.
73. National Peace Council in Ghana, http://www.undp-gha.org/mainpages.php?page=national%20peace%20council.
74. UNDP, http://www.sd.undp.org/projects/s_cp2.htm.
75. Swanee Hunt and William Jefferson Clinton, *This Was Not Our War: Bosnian Women Reclaiming the Peace*, Durham, NC: Duke University Press, 2004; UNESCO, *Women and Peace in Africa*, Paris: UNESCO, 2003.
76. Carolyn Hayman, 'Ripples into Waves: Locally Led Peacebuilding on a National Scale', New York: Peace Direct/Quakers UN Office, 2010, p. 3.
77. Ken Menkhaus, 'Governance without Government in Somalia', *International Security*, Vol. 31, No. 3, 2006, pp. 74–106.
78. See *Peace Agreement between the Government of Sierra Leone and the Revolutionary United Front of Sierra Leone*, November 1996.
79. For more details see Van Tongeren, 'Overview on Infrastructures for Peace', p. 17.
80. *Ibid.*
81. Kumar, 'Building National "Infrastructures for Peace"', p. 392.
82. EU, 'Development and Cooperation', http://ec.europa.eu/europeaid/where/asia/country-cooperation/afghanistan/afghanistan_en.htm. See also World Bank, 'Afghanistan Reconstruction Trust Fund (ARTF)', http://web.worldbank.org/.
83. Van Tongeren, 'Overview on Infrastructures for Peace', p. 22; National Solidarity Programme, http://www.nspafghanistan.org, Ministry of Rural Rehabilitation and Development; Cooperation for Peace and Unity, *Delivering the Impact of Peacebuilding*, policy paper by CPAU, http://www.cpau.org.af/docs/Peacebuilding%20Policy%20Paper%20Final%2013-10-09.pdf.
84. Torun Wimpelmann, 'Nexuses of Knowledge and Power in Afghanistan: The Rise and Fall of the Informal Justice Assemblage', *Central Asian Survey*, Vol. 32, No. 3, pp. 406–22 and 418.
85. Wilde and Mielke, 'Order, Stability and Change in Afghanistan', p. 353. See also Richmond and Franks, *Liberal Peace Transitions*.
86. OECD-DAC, 'Principles for Good International Engagement in Fragile States and Situations'.
87. OCHA Occasional Policy Briefing Series Brief No. 7: *Peacebuilding and Linkages with Humanitarian Action: Key Emerging Trends and Challenges*, August 2011, p. 5.
88. Chambers, *Rural Development*, p. 84.
89. 'Busan Partnership for Effective Development Co-Operation'; Vanessa Wyeth, 'Knights in Fragile Armour: The Rise of the G7+', *Global Governance*, Vol. 18, 2011, p. 11.
90. François Debrix, *Re-Envisioning Peacekeeping: The United Nations and the Mobilization of Ideology*, Minneapolis: University of Minnesota Press, 1999, p. 16.
91. Chambers, *Rural Development*; John Burton (ed.), *Conflict: Human Needs*, London: Palgrave, 1990; Asad, *Anthropology and the Colonial Encounter*.
92. I. William Zartman (ed.), *Traditional Cures for Modern Conflicts: African Conflict 'Medicine'*, Boulder, CO: Lynne Rienner, 2000, pp. 1–11.
93. Foucault, 'Governmentality'.
94. Giles Mohan, 'Beyond Participation: Strategies for Deeper Empowerment', in Bill Cooke and Uma Kothari (eds), *Participation: The New Tyranny*, London: Zed Books, 2001, p. 153.
95. Bhabha, *The Location of Culture*.
96. Mohan, 'Beyond Participation: Strategies for Deeper Empowerment', p. 163.
97. Mary B. Anderson, Dayna Brown and Isabella Jean, *Time to Listen: Hearing People on the Receiving End of International Aid*, Cambridge, MA: CDA, 2012.
98. Mohan, 'Beyond Participation: Strategies for Deeper Empowerment', p. 163.

99. *Ibid.*, p. 164; Oliver P. Richmond, *Peace in IR*, London: Routledge, 2008, conclusion.
100. Meera Sabaratnam, 'IR in Dialogue. But Can We Change the Subjects? A Typology of Decolonising Strategies for the Study of World Politics', *Millennium: Journal of International Studies*, Vol. 39, No. 3, 2011, pp. 781–803.
101. This is something that many, particularly in some foreign-policy establishments, are unwilling to do, and it even reaches as far as some quarters of the UN. It is often disguised by a paternalistic discourse of trusteeship, or a focus on counterfactual securitisation: i.e., the security threats that might arise if intervention does not occur.

Chapter V. Peace Formation versus Intervention

1. Odendaal, *A Crucial Link*, p. 19.
2. See, for example, Anderson, Brown and Jean, *Time to Listen*.
3. Tilly, 'War Making and State Making as Organised Crime'.
4. Mac Ginty, 'Indigenous Peacemaking versus the Liberal Peace'.
5. Richmond, 'The Romanticisation of the Local'.
6. Confidential Official Source, *Personal Interview*, New York: UNDP, 7 February 2012.
7. Clifford Geertz (ed.), *The Interpretation of Cultures*, New York: Basic Books, 1973; Asad, *Anthropology and the Colonial Encounter*; Arturo Escobar, *Encountering Development*, Princeton: Princeton University Press, 1995; Bhabha, *The Location of Culture*; Spivak, 'Can the Subaltern Speak?'; Ilan Kapoor, *The Post-Colonial Politics of Development*, London: Routledge, 2008.
8. Balibar, *Politics and the Other Scene*, p. x.
9. Odendaal, *A Crucial Link*, p. 7.
10. Thanks to Sandra Pogodda for reminding me of this point.
11. Richmond, 'Eirenism and a Post-Liberal Peace', p. 691.
12. See the collection of essays in Miles Kahler (ed.), *Networked Politics: Agency, Power, and Governance*, Ithaca, NY: Cornell University Press, 2009.
13. Bernhard Knoll, *The Legal Status of Territories Subject to Administration by International Organisations*, Cambridge: Cambridge University Press, 2008; Rodney S. Barker, *Political Legitimacy and the State*, Oxford: Clarendon Press, 1990.
14. Spivak, 'Can the Subaltern Speak?'; Bhabha, *The Location of Culture*.
15. Richmond, *A Post-Liberal Peace*.
16. Mohan, 'Beyond Participation: Strategies for Deeper Empowerment', p. 153.
17. Homi Bhabha, 'Of Mimicry and Man: The Ambivalence of Colonial Discourse', *October*, Vol. 28, spring 1984, pp. 125–33.
18. Scott, *Weapons of the Weak*; Brent L. Pickett, 'Foucault and the Politics of Resistance', *Polity*, Vol. 28, No. 4, 1996, pp. 445–47.
19. Richmond, *Maintaining Order, Making Peace*.
20. Numerous interviews working for the donor community attested to this shift around the world while I was conducting the research for this study.
21. For example, see the Cyprus example, Home of Cooperation, New York: UNDP, EU Commission, USAID, etc, *Personal Interviews and Field Notes*, Nicosia, November 2011.
22. Odendaal, *A Crucial Link*, p. 23.

Conclusion. International Peace Enablement

1. D. Killcullen, 'Deiokes and the Taliban', in W. Mason (ed.), *The Rule of Law in Afghanistan*, Cambridge: Cambridge University Press, 2011, pp. 35–50.
2. Henri Lefebvre, *Critique of Everyday Life, Vol. 3*, London: Verso, 2005, p. 128.
3. For similar conclusions from the perspective of development aid, see Anderson, Brown and Jean, *Time to Listen*.

4. See Richmond, *A Post-Liberal Peace*, conclusion.
5. Odendaal, *A Crucial Link*, p. 42.
6. Massey, *World City*, pp. 184 and 200; Escobar, *Territories of Difference*, pp. 11–12.
7. Skidelsky and Skidelsky, *How Much Is Enough?*, p. 189.
8. Bhabha, *The Location of Culture*, p. 25; Balibar, *Politics and the Other Scene*, pp. 4 and 35.
9. United Nations General Assembly 'Declaration on the Right of Peoples to Peace', General Assembly Resolution A/RES/39/11, 12 November 1984, www.un.org/documents/ga/res/39/a39r011.htm.
10. Michel Foucault, 'The Ethics of the Concern for Self as a Practice of Freedom', in Paul Rabinow (ed.), *Ethics, Subjectivity, and Truth*, The New Press: New York, 1997.
11. Balibar, *Politics and the Other Scene*, pp. 27 and 31.
12. Mazower, *No Enchanted Palace*, p. 68.
13. Comaroff and Comaroff, *Theory from the South*, p. 10.
14. *Ibid.*, p. 12.
15. Pickett, 'Foucault and the Politics of Resistance'.
16. Mark Duffield, *Development, Security and Unending War*, Cambridge: Polity Press, 2007. See also Laura Zanotti's excellent piece on NGOs in Haiti: 'Cacophanies of Aid: Failed State Building and NGOs in Haiti'.
17. Rob Jenkins, *Peacebuilding: From Concept to Commission*, London: Routledge, 2013, p. 92.
18. *Ibid.*
19. UN General Assembly Security Council, Report of the Secretary-General on Peacebuilding in the Immediate Aftermath of Conflict – A/63/881-S/2009/304, 11 June 2009, para. 16 – New York: UN Peacebuilding Support Office, 2009.
20. Srdjan Vucetic, *The Anglosphere: A Genealogy of a Racialized Identity in International Relations*, Palo Alto, CA: Stanford University Press, 2011.
21. N. van der Walle, *African Economies and the Politics of Permanent Crisis, 1979–1999*, Cambridge: Cambridge University Press, 2001.
22. For a discussion of these post-colonial dangers, see Alina Sajed, 'The Post Always Rings Twice', *Review of International Studies*, Vol. 38, No. 1, 2012, p. 141.
23. Foucault, 'Of Other Spaces, Heterotopias'.
24. Fukuyama, *The Origins of Political Order*, p. 478; North, Wallis and Weingast, *Violence and Social Orders*, pp. 144 and 269.
25. Woodward, 'Varieties of State-Building in the Balkans', p. 316.
26. Confidential Source, *Personal Interview*, UNPBSO, 7 February 2012.
27. UNDP, *Governance and Peacebuilding*, New York: UNDP, 2012, p. 53.
28. *Ibid.*, p. 55.
29. OECD, *Concepts and Dilemmas of State Building in Fragile Situations*, Vienna: OECD, 2008, p. 8.
30. Oliver P. Richmond, 'Beyond Local Ownership and Participation in the Architecture of International Peacebuilding', *Ethnopolitics*, Vol. 11, No. 4, 2012, pp. 354–75.
31. Confidential Source, *Personal Interview*, PBC, New York, 6 June 2010.
32. Jan Art Scholte, 'Reinventing Global Democracy', *European Journal of International Relations*, 29 May 2012.
33. *Ibid.*
34. Thomas Muhr, 'Bolivarian Internationalism', *Globalisations*, Vol. 9. No. 1, 2012.
36. Richmond, *Peace in IR*, conclusion.
37. J. Ann Tickner, 'Dealing with Difference', *Millennium*, Vol. 39, No. 3, 2011, p. 8.
38. Chabal and Daloz, *Africa Works*.
39. Foucault, *Society Must Be Defended*, p. 103.

Bibliography

Books and Articles

Abrams, Philip. 'Notes on the Difficulty of Studying the State', *Journal of Historical Sociology*, Vol. 1 (1988): 58–89.

Adedeji, Adebayo. 'An Alternative for Africa', *Journal of Democracy*, Vol. 5, No. 4 (1994): 119–32.

Alonso, Ana Maria. 'The Politics of Space, Time and Substance: State Formation, Nationalism and Ethnicity', *Annual Review of Anthropology*, Vol. 23 (1994).

Anderson, Louise Riis. 'Statebuilding as Tacit Trusteeship', in Berit Bliesemann de Guevara (ed.), *Statebuilding and State-Formation: The Political Sociology of Intervention*, London: Routledge, 2012, pp. 132–48.

Anderson, Mary B., Dayna Brown, and Isabella Jean. *Time to Listen: Hearing People on the Receiving End of International Aid*, Washington, DC: CDA Collaborative Learning Projects, 2012.

Annan, Kofi. *A Life in War and Peace*, London: Allen Lane, 2012.

Appadurai, Arjun. *Modernity at Large*, Minneapolis: University of Minnesota Press, 1996.

Asad, Talal (ed.). *Anthropology and the Colonial Encounter*, New York: Humanity Books, 1973.

Ashcraft, Richard. *Revolutionary Politics & Locke's Two Treatises of Government*, Princeton: Princeton University Press, 1986.

Azar, Edward E. *The Management of Protracted Social Conflict: Theory and Practice*, Hampshire, UK: Dartmouth Publishing, 1990.

Azar, Edward E. 'Protracted International Conflicts: Ten Propositions', in E. Azar and John W. Burton (eds), *International Conflict Resolution: Theory and Practice*, Hemel Hempstead: Harvester Wheatsheaf, 1986, pp. 27–39.

Badie, Bertrand. *The Imported State: The Westernisation of the Political Order*, Palo Alto, CA: Stanford University Press, 2000.

Balibar, Etienne. *Politics and the Other Scene*, London: Verso, 2002.
Barker, Rodney S. *Political Legitimacy and the State*, Oxford: Clarendon Press, 1990.
Barnett, Michael N. *Confronting the Costs of War: Military Power, State, and Society in Egypt and Israel*. Princeton: Princeton University Press, 1992.
Bartelson, Jens. *The Critique of the State*, Cambridge: Cambridge University Press, 2001.
Bayart, Jean-François. *The State in Africa: The Politics of the Belly*, London: Longman, 1993.
Bayart, Jean-François. 'Finishing with the Idea of the Third World: The Concept of the Political Trajectory', in James Manor (ed.), *Rethinking Third World Politics*, London and New York: Longman, 1992, pp. 51–71.
Bellamy, Alex, and Paul Williams. 'Peace Operations and Global Order', *International Peacekeeping*, Vol. 10, No. 1 (2004).
Bentham, Jeremy. 'Panopticon', in Miran Bozovic (ed.), *The Panopticon Writings*, London: Verso, 1995, pp. 29–95.
Bhabha, Homi. 'Of Mimicry and Man: The Ambivalence of Colonial Discourse', *October*, Vol. 28 (spring 1984): 125–33.
Bhabha, Homi K. *The Location of Culture*, London: Routledge, 1994.
Bliesemann de Guevara, Berit. 'The State in Times of Statebuilding', *Civil Wars*, Vol. 10, No. 4 (2008): 348–68.
Bliesemann de Guevara, Berit (ed.). *Statebuilding and State-Formation: The Political Sociology of Intervention*, London: Routledge, 2012.
Boege, Volker. 'Legitimacy in Hybrid Political Orders – An Underestimated Dimension of Peacebuilding and State Formation'. Conference paper presented at the European Consortium of Political Research Conference, Potsdam, Germany, 10–12 September 2009, p. 17.
Boege, Volker. 'Bougainville Report: Addressing Legitimacy Issues in Fragile and Post-Conflict Situations to Advance Conflict Transformation and Peacebuilding', University of Queensland/Berghof Foundation, January 2013.
Boege, Volker, Anne Brown, Kevin P. Clements and Anna Nolan. 'States Emerging from Hybrid Political Orders – Pacific Experiences', The Australian Centre for Peace and Conflict Studies (ACPACS) Occasional Papers Series (ACPACS Occasional Paper No. 11). Brisbane: ACPACS, 2008.
Boege, Volker, Anne Brown, Kevin Clements and Anna Nolan. 'On Hybrid Political Orders and Emerging States: What Is Failing – States in the Global South or Research and Politics in the West?', in *Building Peace in the Absence of States: Challenging the Discourse on State Failure, Berghof Handbook Dialogue No. 8*, 2009.
Boege, Volker, and Jodie Curth. 'Grounding the Responsibility to Protect: Working with Local Strengths for Peace and Conflict Prevention in the Solomon Islands', Paper presented at the ISA Asia Pacific Conference, Brisbane, 29–30 September 2011.
Boix, Charles. 'Economic Roots of Civil Wars and Revolutions in the Contemporary World', *World Politics*, Vol. 60 (2008): 390–437.
Bose, Sumantra. *Bosnia after Dayton: Nationalist Partition and International Intervention*, London: Hurst & Co, 2002.
Boutros-Ghali, Boutros. *An Agenda for Peace: Preventative Diplomacy, Peacemaking and Peacekeeping*, New York: United Nations, 1992.
Broome, Benjamin. 'The Cyprus Conflict: Root Causes and Implications for Peacebuilding', *Journal of Peace Research*, Vol. 44 (2007): 349–65.
Brown, Mark Malloch. *The Unfinished Revolution*, London: Allen Lane, 2011.
Burton, John. *World Society*, Cambridge: Cambridge University Press, 1972.
Burton, John (ed.). *Conflict: Human Needs*, London: Palgrave, 1990.
Burton, John W., and Edward E. Azar. *International Conflict Resolution: Theory and Practice*, Hemel Hempstead: Harvester Wheatsheaf, 1990.

Buzan, Barry, Ole Waever and Jaap de Wilde. *Security: A New Framework for Analysis*, Boulder, CO: Lynne Rienner, 1998.
Call, Charles T. 'The Fallacy of the "failed State"', *Third World Quarterly*, Vol. 29, No. 8 (2008): 1491–1507.
Call, Charles T., and Susan Cook. 'On Democratisation and Peacebuilding', *Global Governance*, Vol. 9, No. 2 (2003): 233–46.
Call, Charles T., and Elizabeth M. Cousens. 'Ending Wars and Building Peace: International Responses to War-Torn Societies', *International Studies Perspectives*, Vol. 9 (2008): 1–21.
Cammack, Diana et al. 'Donors and the "Fragile States" Agenda', Report submitted to the Japan International Cooperation Agency, March 2006.
Caplan, Richard. *International Governance of War-Torn Territories*, Oxford: Oxford University Press, 2004.
Chabal, Patrick. *The End of Conceit*, London: Zed, 2012.
Chabal, Patrick, and Jean-Pascal Daloz, *Africa Works: Disorder as Political Instrument*, IAI African Issues series, Oxford: James Currey/Bloomington: Indiana University Press, 1999.
Chambers, Robert. *Rural Development: Putting the Last First*, London: Longman, 1983.
Chandler, David. *International Statebuilding: The Rise of Post-Liberal Governance*, London: Routledge, 2010.
Chhibber, Ajay. 'The State in a Changing World', *Finance and Development*, September 1997.
Childers, Erskine Barton. 'For a Democratic United Nations and the Rule of Law', *Development Dialogue*, No. 56, Dag Hammarskjold Foundation (June 2011).
Clapham, Christopher. *Africa and the International System: The Politics of State Survival*, Cambridge: Cambridge University Press, 1993.
Clark, Janine Natalya. 'From Negative to Positive Peace', *Journal of Human Rights*, Vol. 8, No. 4 (2009): 360–84.
Clark, Janine Natalya. 'Bosnia's Success Story? Brčko District and the "View from Below"', *International Peacekeeping*, Vol. 17, No. 1 (2010): 67–79.
Clifford, James. 'Introduction', in James Clifford and George E. Marcus (eds), *Writing Culture: The Poetics and Politics of Ethnography*, Berkeley: University of California Press, 1986, pp. 1–26.
Collier, Paul, and Anke Hoeffler. 'On Economic Causes of Civil War', *Oxford Economic Papers*, Vol. 50, No. 4 (1998): 563–73.
Comaroff, Jean, and John L. Comaroff. *Theory from the South*, London: Paradigm, 2012.
Constantinou, Costas. 'Aporias of Identity: Bicommunalism, Hybridity and the "Cyprus Problem"', *Cooperation and Conflict*, Vol. 42, No. 3 (2007): 247–70.
Corrigan, Philip, and Derek Sayer. *The Great Arch: English State Formation as Cultural Revolution*, Oxford: Blackwell, 1985.
Cousens, Elizabeth M., and Chetan Kumar (eds). *Peacebuilding as Politics: Cultivating Peace in Fragile Societies*, Boulder, CO: Lynne Rienner, 2001.
Cunningham, Robert, and Yasin Sarayrah. *Wasta: The Hidden Force in Middle Eastern Societies*, New York: Praeger, 1993.
Curle, Adam. *Making Peace*, London: Tavistock, 1971.
Day, Tony. *Fluid Iron: State Formation in Southeast Asia*, Honolulu: University of Hawai'i Press, 2002.
Debrix, François. *Re-Envisioning Peacekeeping: The United Nations and the Mobilization of Ideology*, Minneapolis: University of Minnesota Press, 1999.
Department for International Development. *Saving Lives, Preventing Suffering and Building Resilience*, London: DFID, 2011.
Dobbins, James, Seth G. Jones, Keith Crane and Beth Cole DeGrasse. *The Beginner's Guide to Nation-Building*, Santa Monica: RAND, 2007.

Dodge, Toby. 'Intervention and Dreams of Exogenous Statebuilding: The Application of Liberal Peacebuilding in Afghanistan and Iraq', *Review of International Studies*, Vol. 39, No. 5 (2013): 1189–1212.
Dodge, Toby. *Iraq - From War to a New Authoritarianism*, London: Routledge, 2013.
Donini, Antonio. 'Local Perceptions of Assistance to Afghanistan', *International Peacekeeping*, Vol. 14, No. 1 (2007): 158–72.
Doyle, Michael. 'Strategy and Transitional Authority', in Stephen John Stedman, Donald Rothchild and Elizabeth M. Cousens (eds), *Ending Civil Wars: The Implementation of Peace Agreements*, Boulder, CO/London: Lynne Rienner, 2002, pp. 71–88.
Duffield, Mark. *Development, Security and Unending War*, Cambridge: Polity Press, 2007.
Dunn, David J. *The First Fifty Years of Peace Research*, Aldershot: Ashgate, 2005.
Eckstein, H. *Regarding Politics*, Berkeley: University of California, 1992.
Escobar, Arturo. *Encountering Development*, Princeton: Princeton University Press, 1995
Escobar, Arturo. *Territories of Difference*, Durham, NC: Duke University, 2008.
Fischer, Martina. 'Civil Society in Conflict Transformation', *Berghof Handbook for Conflict Transformation*, Berlin, 2011.
Fontan, Victoria. *Decolonising Peace*, Doerzbach: Dignity Press, 2012.
Foucault, Michel. *The Order of Things*, New York: Pantheon, 1970
Foucault, Michel. *Archaeology of Knowledge*, New York: Pantheon, 1972.
Foucault, Michel. 'Two Lectures', in Colin Gordon (ed.), *Power/Knowledge: Selected Interviews*, New York: Pantheon, 1980, pp. 78–108.
Foucault, Michel. *The History of Sexuality Vol. 1: The Will to Knowledge*, London: Penguin, 1984 [1976].
Foucault, Michel. 'Of Other Spaces, Heterotopias' [1967], trans. Jay Miskowiec, in *Architecture/mouvement/ continuité*, October 1984.
Foucault, Michel. 'Governmentality', in Graham Burchell, Colin Gordon and Peter Miller (eds), *The Foucault Effect: Studies in Governmentality*, trans. Rosi Braidotti and revised by Colin Gordon, Chicago: University of Chicago Press, 1991, pp. 87–104.
Foucault, Michel. 'The Ethics of the Concern for Self as a Practice of Freedom', in Paul Rabinow (ed.), *Ethics, Subjectity, and Truth*, New York: New Press, 1997, pp. 281–301.
Foucault, Michel. *Society Must Be Defended*, New York: Picador, 2003.
Foucault, Michel. *Security, Territory, Population*, London: Penguin, 2004.
Foucault, Michel. *The Foucault-Chomsky Debate: On Human Nature*, New York: New Press, 2006.
Fukuyama, Francis. *The Origins of Political Order*, Princeton: Princeton University Press, 2011.
Fukuyama, Francis. *Statebuilding*, Profile: New York, 2005.
Fukuyama, Francis. 'The Imperative of Statebuilding', *Journal of Democracy*, Vol. 15, No. 2 (2004): 17–31.
Fukuyama, Francis 'Statebuilding: The Missing Dimension of Stateness', www.carnegie-council.org/media/Francis_Fukuyama_Handout.pdf. (Undated.)
Galbraith, James. 'Inequality, Unemployment and Growth', *Journal of Economic Inequality*, Vol. 7, No. 2 (2009): 189–206.
Galtung, Johan. 'Violence, Peace and Peace Research', *Journal of Peace Research*, Vol. 3, No. 5 (1970): 167–91.
Galtung, Johan. 'A Structural Theory of Imperialism', *Journal of Peace Research*, Vol. 8, No. 2 (1971): 81–117.
Geertz, Clifford (ed.). *The Interpretation of Cultures*, New York: Basic Books, 1973.
Geertz, Clifford. *Negara: The Theatre State in Nineteenth-Century Bali*, Princeton: Princeton University Press, 1980.
Ghani, Ashraf, and Claire Lockhart. *Fixing Failed States: A Framework for Rebuilding a Fractured World*, Oxford: Oxford University Press, 2008.
Gilligan, Carol. *In a Different Voice*, Cambridge, MA: Harvard University Press, 1993.

Giustozzi, Antonia. 'Bureaucratic Façade and Political Realities of Disarmament and Demobilisation in Afghanistan', *Conflict, Security and Development*, Vol. 8, No. 2 (2008): 169–92.
Gramsci, Antonio. *Selections from the Prison Notebooks 1929–1935*, ed. and trans. by Quintin Hoare and Geoffrey Nowell-Smith, New York: International Publishers, 1971.
Grenfell, Douglas. 'Governance, Violence and Crises in Timor-Leste', in David Mearns (ed.), *Democratic Governance in Timor-Leste*, Darwin: Charles Darwin University Press, 2008, pp. 85–97.
Gupta, Kim. 'US Envoy Says Mistakes of the West Prolonged Afghan War and Cost Lives', *Independent*, 1 November 2013.
Habermas, Jürgen. *Between Facts and Norms*, Cambridge, MA: MIT Press, 1996.
Hadjipavlou, Maria. *Women and Change in Cyprus: Feminisms and Gender in Conflict*, London: I.B. Tauris, 2010.
Hakim, Yalda. 'Afghanistan's Hamid Karzai Says NATO Caused "Great Suffering"', *BBC News*, 7 October 2013.
Harrison, Graham. *Neoliberal Africa*, London: Zed Books, 2010.
Harvey, David. *The Condition of Post-Modernity*, Oxford: Blackwell, 1990.
Harvey, David. 'Neoliberalism as Creative Destruction', *The ANNALS of the American Academy of Political and Social Science*, Vol. 610, No. 21 (2007): 22–44.
Harvey, Neil. *The Chiapas Rebellion: The Struggle for Land and Democracy*, Durham, NC: Duke University Press, 1998.
Hayman, Carolyn. 'Ripples into Waves: Locally Led Peacebuilding on a National Scale', New York: Peace Direct/Quaker UN Office, 2010.
Heathershaw, John. 'Conclusions', in Berit Bliesemann de Guevara (ed.), *Statebuilding and State-Formation: The Political Sociology of Intervention*, London: Routledge, 2012, pp. 246–59.
Held, David. *Global Covenant: The Social Democratic Alternative to the Washington Consensus*, New York: Polity Press, 2004.
Herzfeld, Michael. *The Social Production of Indifference: Exploring the Symbolic Roots of Western Bureaucracy*, Oxford: Berg, 1992.
Hill, Jonathan. 'Beyond the Other? A Postcolonial Critique of the Failed State Thesis', *African Identities*, Vol. 3, No. 2 (2005): 139–54.
Hintze, Otto. 'The Formation of States and Constitutional Development', in Felix Gilbert (ed.), *The Historical Essays of Otto Hintze*, New York: Oxford University Press, 1975, pp. 157–77.
Hobbes, Thomas. *Leviathan*, Oxford: Oxford University Press, 2008 [1651].
Hobsbawm, Eric J. *Nations and Nationalism Since 1780: Programme, Myth, Reality*, 2nd edn, Cambridge: Cambridge University Press, 1992.
Hobson, John M. 'Is Critical Theory Always for the White West and for Western Imperialism? Beyond Westphalian to a Post-Racist Critical IR', *Millennium*, Vol. 33 (2007): 91–116.
Holiday, David. 'El Salvador's "Model" Democracy', *Current History*, Vol. 104, No. 679 (February 2005): 77–80.
Hughes, Caroline. *An Investigation of Conflict Management in Cambodian Villages: A Review of the Literature with Suggestions for Future Research*, Centre for Peace and Development, Cambodia Development Resource Institute, Phnom Penh, October 2001.
Hunt, Swanee, and William Jefferson Clinton. *This Was Not Our War: Bosnian Women Reclaiming the Peace*, Durham, NC: Duke University Press, 2004.
Huntington, Samuel. *Political Order in Changing Societies*, New Haven, CT: Yale University Press, 1968.
Huntington, Samuel P. *The Clash of Civilizations and the Remaking of World Order*, London: Simon Schuster, 1997.

International Commission on Intervention and State Sovereignty (ICISS). *Responsibility to Protect*, Ottawa: International Development Research Centre, December 2001.
Jabri, Vivienne. *War and the Transformation of Global Politics*, London: Palgrave, 2007.
Jackson, Karl D. *Cambodia, 1975–1978: Rendezvous with Death*, Princeton: Princeton University Press, 1992.
Jackson, Robert H. *Quasi-States: Sovereignty, International Relations and the Third World*, Cambridge: Cambridge University Press, 1990.
Jenkins, Rob. *Peacebuilding: From Concept to Commission*, London: Routledge, 2013.
John, Jonathan Di. 'The Concept, Causes and Consequences of Failed States', *European Journal of Development Research*, Vol. 22 (2010): 10–30.
Johnson, P. 'Local vs. National Peacebuilding: The Richness of Somali Peacemaking', www.prio.no/peaceethics/PeacE-Discussions, 2010.
Jonas, Susanne. *Of Centaurs and Doves: Guatemala's Peace Process*, Boulder, CO: Westview Press, 1996.
Kahler, Miles (ed.). *Networked Politics: Agency, Power, and Governance*, Ithaca, NY: Cornell University Press, 2009.
Kant, Immanuel. 'Perpetual Peace: A Philosophical Sketch' (1795), in *Principles of Politics*, trans. W. Hastie, Edinburgh: Clark, 1891.
Kaplan, Robert D. 'The Coming Anarchy', *The Atlantic Monthly*, Vol. 273, No. 2 (February 1994): 44–76.
Kapoor, Ilan. *The Post-Colonial Politics of Development*, London: Routledge, 2008.
Kappler, Stefanie, and Oliver P. Richmond. 'Peacebuilding in Bosnia: Resistance or Emancipation?', *Security Dialogue*, Vol. 42, No. 3 (2011): 261–78.
Kapur, Devesh. 'The IMF: A Cure of Curse?' *Foreign Policy*, No. 111 (1998): 114–29.
Kapur, Devesh. 'The State in a Changing World: A Critique of the 1997 World Development Report', *WCFIA Working Paper*, No. 98-02, 1998.
Kay, B. Warren. 'The Indigenous Role in Guatemalan Peace', *Cultural Survival*, 1997, http://www.culturalsurvival.org/ourpublications/csq/article/the-indigenous-role-guatemalan-peace.
Kelman, Herbert C. 'The Problem-Solving Workshop in Conflict Resolution', in R.L. Merrit (ed.), *Communication in International Politics*, Urbana: University of Illinois Press, 1972, pp. 168–204.
Khoury, Philip S., and Joseph Kostiner (eds). *Tribes and State Formation in the Middle East*, Berkeley: University of California Press, 1991.
Killcullen, D. 'Deiokes and the Taliban', in Whit Mason (ed.), *The Rule of Law in Afghanistan*, Cambridge: Cambridge University Press, 2011.
Knoll, Bernhard. *The Legal Status of Territories Subject to Administration by International Organisations*, Cambridge: Cambridge University Press, 2008.
Krasner, Stephen D. *Sovereignty: Organised Hypocrisy*, Princeton: Princeton University Press, 1999.
Krohn-Hansen, Christian, and Knut G. Nustard (eds). *State Formation: Anthropological Perspectives*, London: Pluto Press, 2005.
Kumar, Chetan. 'Building National "Infrastructures for Peace": UN Assistance for Internally Negotiated Solutions to Violent Conflict', in Susan Allen Nan, Zachariah Cherian Mampilly and Andrea Bartoli (eds), *Peacemaking: From Practice to Theory, Volume 1*, Westport, CT: Praeger, 2011, pp. 384–99.
Kurz, Christof P. 'The Limitations of International Analyses of Post-Conflict Statebuilding in Sierra Leone', in Berit Bliesemann de Guevara (ed.), *Statebuilding and State-Formation: The Political Sociology of Intervention*, London: Routledge, 2012, pp. 114–31.
Kurze, Arnaud. 'State, Society, and Globalization in the Balkans: Problems of Democratic Consolidation in Bosnia and Herzegovina, Kosovo, the Former Yugoslav Republic of Macedonia, and Serbia', *Working Papers in Global Studies*, No. 4 (April 2009).

Lake, David A., and Christopher Faris. 'International Trusteeship', in Stephen D. Krasner and Thomas Risse (eds), *External Actors, Statebuilding, and Service Provision in Areas of Limited Statehood*, forthcoming.
Latour, Bruno. *Reassembling the Social: An Introduction to Actor-Network-Theory*, Oxford: Oxford University Press, 2005.
Latour, Bruno. 'On Actor-Network Theory: A Few Clarifications', *Soziale Welt*, Vol. 47, No. 4 (1996).
Lebedev, Evgeny. 'Hamid Karzai: In the Shadow of Terror, a Meeting with the World's Loneliest President', *Independent*, 17 September 2011.
Lederach, John Paul. *Preparing for Peace: Conflict Transformation across Cultures*, Syracuse: Syracuse University Press, 1995.
Lederach, John Paul. *Building Peace: Sustainable Reconciliation in Divided Societies*, Washington, DC: United States Institute of Peace, 1997.
Lefebvre, Henri. *Critique of Everyday Life, Volume III*, trans. John Moore with a preface by Michel Trebitsch, London: Verso, 2002.
Lerche, Charles O. 'Truth Commissions and National Reconciliation: Some Reflections on Theory and Practice', *Peace and Conflict Studies*, Vol. 7, No. 1 (2000): 2–23.
Levy, Jack S. 'Domestic Politics and War', *Journal of Interdisciplinary History*, Vol. 18, No. 4 (1988): 653–73.
Linz, Juan J., and Alfred Stepan. *Problems of Democratic Transition and Consolidation: Southern Europe, South America, and Post-Communist Europe*, Baltimore, MD: Johns Hopkins University Press, 1996.
Lipset, Seymour Martin. 'Some Social Requisites of Democracy: Economic Development and Political Legitimacy', *American Political Science Review*, Vol. 53, No. 1 (1959): 69–105.
Locke, John. *Second Treatise on Government*, Cambridge: Cambridge University Press, 1988 [1689].
Lowy, Michael. *The Politics of Uneven and Combined Development*, London: Verso, 1981.
Luckham, Robin, and Thomas Kirk. 'The Two Faces of Security in Hybrid Political Orders: A Framework for Analysis and Research', *Stability: International Journal of Security and Development*, Vol. 2, No. 2 (2013): 1–30.
Mac Ginty, Roger. 'Indigenous Peace-Making Versus the Liberal Peace', *Cooperation and Conflict*, Vol. 43, No. 2 (2008): 139–63.
Maley, William. 'Statebuilding in Afghanistan', *Central Asian Survey*, Vol. 32, No. 3 (2013): 255–70.
Manglapus, Raúl S. *Will of the People: Original Democracy in Non-Western Societies*, New York: Greenwood, 1987.
Mann, Michael. *The Sources of Social Power: Volume 1, A History of Power from the Beginning to AD 1760*, Cambridge: Cambridge University Press, 1986.
Mann, Michael. *The Sources of Social Power: Volume 2, The Rise of Classes and Nation States 1760–1914*, Cambridge: Cambridge University Press, 1993.
Manners, Ian. 'Normative Power Europe: A Contradiction in Terms?', *Journal of Common Market Studies*, Vol. 40, No. 2 (2002): 235–58.
Marten, Kimberly Zisk. *Enforcing the Peace: Learning from the Imperial Past*, New York: Columbia University Press, 2004.
Marullo, Sam and John Lofland (eds). *Peace Action in the Eighties: Social Science Perspectives*, New Brunswick: Rutgers University Press, 1990.
Marx, Karl, and Friedrich Engels. *The Communist Manifesto*, Oxford: Oxford University Press, 1998, [1848].
Marx, Karl, and Friedrich Engels. *The German Ideology*, Lawrence and Wishart, 1999 [1846].
Massey, Doreen. 'A Global Sense of Place', in Doreen Massey, *Space, Place and Gender*, Minneapolis: University of Minnesota Press, 1994, 146–56.

Massey, Doreen. *World City*, Cambridge: Polity Press 2007.
Mazower, Mark. *No Enchanted Palace*, Princeton: Princeton University Press 2009.
Mazower, Mark. *Governing the World*, London: Penguin, 2012.
McClelland, David. *The Achieving Society*, New York: Free Press, 1967.
McWilliam, Andrew. 'Houses of Resistance in East Timor: Structuring of Sociality in the New National', *Anthropological Forum*, Vol. 15, No. 1 (2005): 27–44.
Menkhaus, Ken. 'Governance in the Hinterlands by Africa's Weak States: Towards a Theory of a Mediated State', Conference paper at APSA, Philadelphia, 31 August 2006.
Menkhaus, Ken. 'Governance without Government in Somalia', *International Security*, Vol. 31, No. 3 (2006): 74–106.
Migdal, Joel S. *State in Society: Studying How States and Societies Transform and Constitute One Another*, Cambridge: Cambridge University Press, 2001.
Migdal, Joel S., and Klaus Schlichte. 'Re-thinking the State', in Klaus Schlichte (ed.), *The Dynamics of States: The Formation and Crises of State Domination*, Burlington, VT: Ashgate, 2005, pp. 1–40.
Milliken, Jennifer, and Keith Krause. 'State Failure, State Collapse and State Reconstruction: Concepts, Lessons and Strategies', *Development and Change*, Vol. 33, No. 5 (2002): 753–72.
Mishra, Pankaj. *From the Ruins of Empire: The Revolt against the West and the Remaking of Asia*, London: Penguin, 2012.
Mitchell, Timothy. *Rule of Experts*, Berkeley: University of California Press, 2002.
Mohan, Giles. 'Beyond Participation: Strategies for Deeper Empowerment', in Bill Cooke and Uma Kothari (eds), *Participation: The New Tyranny*, London: Zed Books, 2001, pp. 153–67.
Montanaro, Lucia. 'The Kosovo Statebuilding Conundrum: Addressing Fragility in a Contested State', FRIDE Working Paper No. 91, 2009.
Moore, Barrington, Jr. *Social Origins of Dictatorship and Democracy*, London: Penguin, 1966.
Moxham, Ben. 'State-Making and the Post-Conflict City: Integration in Dili, Disintegration in Timor-Leste', *Crisis States Working Paper No. 2*, London: Development Studies Institute, London School of Economics and Political Science, February 2008.
Muhr, Thomas. 'Bolivarian Internationalism', *Globalisations*, Vol. 9. No, 1 (2012): 145–59.
Nangoloh, Phil ya. 'The Role of Civil Society in the Socio-Economic Development of a Country', Paper given at Conference on Multipartyism and its Role in Democratization and Development, organised by Forum for the Future, Council of Churches in Namibia (CCN) Hall, Katutura, Windhoek, 15–17 February 2010.
Network of Concerned Anthropologists. *The Counter-Counter Insurgency Manual*, Chicago: Chicago University Press, 2009.
Newman, Edward. 'The Violence of Statebuilding in Historical Perspective', Unpublished paper, 2011.
Newman, Edward, Roland Paris and Oliver P. Richmond (eds). *New Perspectives on Liberal Peacebuilding*, Tokyo: United Nations University Press, 2009.
North, Douglass C., John Joseph Wallis and Barry R. Weingast. *Violence and Social Orders*, Cambridge: Cambridge University Press, 2009.
Nye, Joseph. *Soft Power: The Means to Success in World Politics*, New York: Public Affairs, 2004.
Odendaal, Andries. 'An Architecture for Building Peace at the Local Level: A Comparative Study of Local Peace Committees', New York: UNDP Discussion Paper, December 2010.
Odendaal, Andries. *A Crucial Link: Local Peace Committees and National Peacebuilding*, Washington, DC: USIP, 2013.
Organisation for Economic Cooperation and Development. *The State's Legitimacy in Fragile Situations*, Paris: OECD, 2010.

Organisation for Economic Cooperation and Development's Development Assistance Committee. 'Principles for Good International Engagement in Fragile States and Situations', Vienna: April 2007.
Office for the Coordination of Humanitarian Affairs (UN). *Peacebuilding and Linkages with Humanitarian Action: Key Emerging Trends and Challenges*, Occasional Policy Briefing Series Brief No. 7, August 2011.
Ortner, Sherry B. 'Resistance and the Problem of Ethnographic Refusal', *Comparative Studies in Society and History*, Vol. 37 (1995): 173–93.
Paffenholz, Thania, and Christoph Spurk. 'Civil Society, Civic Engagement, and Peacebuilding', *Social Development Papers*, Paper No. 36, Washington DC: World Bank, October 2006.
Palmer, Lisa, and Demetrio do Amaral de Carvalho. 'Nation Building and Resource Management: The Politics of Nature in Timor Leste', *Geoforum*, Vol. 39 (2008): 1321–32.
Parajon, Francisco Lacayo, Mirta Lourenco and David Adams. 'The UNESCO Culture of Peace Programme in El Salvador: An Initial Report', *International Journal of Peace Studies*, Vol. 1, No. 2 (1996): 1–20.
Paris, Roland. *At War's End*, Cambridge: Cambridge University Press, 2004.
Paris, Roland. 'Saving Liberal Peacebuilding', *Review of International Study*, Vol. 36 (2010): 337–65.
Parish, Matthew. 'Paradigms of State-Building: Comparing Bosnia and Kosovo', *Journal of Eurasian Law*, Vol. 3, No. 3 (2010).
Peou, Sorpong. *International Democracy Assistance for Peacebuilding: Cambodia and Beyond*, London: Palgrave Macmillan 2007.
Pickering, Paula M. *Peacebuilding in the Balkans*, Ithaca, NY: Cornell University Press, 2007.
Pickett, Brent L. 'Foucault and the Politics of Resistance', *Polity*, Vol. 28, No. 4 (1996): 445–66.
Plummer, Janelle, Gavin Tritt and Joakim Öjendal. *Voice, Choice and Decision 2: Local Basic Service Delivery*, Asia Foundation, 2013.
Ponzio, Richard. *Democratic Peacebuilding*, Oxford: Oxford University Press, 2011.
Posen, Barry R. 'The Security Dilemma and Ethnic Conflict', *Survival*, Vol. 35, No. 1 (1993): 27–47.
Pouligny, Beatrice. *Peace Operations Seen from Below*, London: Hurst, 2006.
Pugh, Michael. 'The Political Economy of Peacebuilding: A Critical Theory Perspective', *International Journal of Peace Studies*, Vol. 10, No. 2 (2005): 23–42.
Pugh, Michael. 'Review of UNDP Governance and Peacebuilding', *Peacebuilding*, Vol.1, No.1 (2013).
Pugh, Michael, Neil Cooper and Mandy Turner (eds). *Whose Peace? Critical Perspectives on the Political Economy of Peacebuilding*, London: Palgrave, 2009.
Pula, Besnik. 'The Emergence of the Kosovo "Parallel State", 1988–1991', *Nationalities Papers: The Journal of Nationalism and Ethnicity*, Vol. 32, No. 4 (2004): 797–826.
Qumsiyeh, Mazin. *Popular Resistance in Palestine: A History of Hope and Empowerment*, London: Pluto Press, 2011.
Radcliffe-Brown, A. R. 'Preface', in M. Fortes and E. E. Evans-Pritchard (eds), *African Political Systems*, London: Oxford University Press, 1955 [1940], pp. xi-xxiii.
Reilly, Charles A. *Peacebuilding and Development in Guatemala and Northern Ireland*, London: Palgrave, 2009.
Reno, William. *Warlord Politics and African States*, Boulder, CO: Lynne Rienner, 1999.
Reus-Smit, Christian. *The Moral Purpose of the State*, Princeton: Princeton University Press, 1999.
Richmond, Oliver P. *Maintaining Order, Making Peace*, London: Palgrave, 2002.
Richmond, Oliver P. 'UN Peace Operations and the Dilemmas of the Peacebuilding Consensus', *International Peacekeeping*, Vol. 10, No. 4 (2004): 83–101.

Richmond, Oliver P. *The Transformation of Peace*, London and Basingstoke: Palgrave, 2005.
Richmond, Oliver P., and Jason Franks. 'Liberal Hubris: Virtual Peace in Cambodia', *Security Dialogue*, Vol. 38, No. 1 (2007): 27–48.
Richmond, Oliver P. *Peace in IR*, London: Routledge, 2008.
Richmond, Oliver P. 'Eirenism and a Post-Liberal Peace', *Review of International Studies*, Vol. 35, No. 3 (2009): 557–80.
Richmond, Oliver P. 'The Romanticisation of the Local: Welfare, Culture and Peacebuilding', *International Spectator*, Vol. 44, No. 1 (2009): 149–69.
Richmond, Oliver P. 'Critical Agency, Resistance, and a Post-Colonial Civil Society', *Cooperation and Conflict*, Vol. 46, No. 4 (2011): 419–40.
Richmond, Oliver P. 'De-Romanticising the Local, Demystifying the International: Aspects of Liberal-Local Hybridity in Timor Leste and the Solomon Islands', *Pacific Review*, Vol. 24, No. 1 (2011): 115–36.
Richmond, Oliver P. *A Post-Liberal Peace*, London: Routledge, 2011.
Richmond, Oliver P. 'Beyond Local Ownership and Participation in the Architecture of International Peacebuilding', *Ethnopolitics*, Vol. 11, No. 4 (2012): 354–75.
Richmond, Oliver P. 'A Pedagogy of Peacebuilding: Infrapolitics, Resistance, and Liberation', *International Political Sociology*, Vol. 6, No. 2 (2012): 115–31.
Richmond, Oliver P., and Jason Franks. *Liberal Peace Transitions: Between Statebuilding and Peacebuilding*, Edinburgh: Edinburgh University Press, 2009.
Richmond, Oliver P., and Audra Mitchell. 'Peacebuilding and Critical Forms of Agency: From Resistance to Subsistence', *Alternatives*, Vol. 37, No. 1 (2011): 326–44.
Roberts, Adam, and Timothy Garton Ash (eds). *Civil Resistance and Power Politics: The Experience of Non-Violent Action from Gandhi to the Present*, Oxford: Oxford University Press, 2009.
Ropers, Norbert. 'Civil-Society Peace Constituencies: NGO Involvement in Conflict Resolution – Areas of Activity and Lessons Learned', in Günther Baechler (ed.), *Promoting Peace: The Role of Civilian Conflict Resolution*, Bern: Staempfli, 2002, pp. 97–126.
Rostow, W.W. *The Stages of Economic Growth: A Non-Communist Manifesto*, Cambridge: Cambridge University Press, 1960.
Rotberg, Robert I. 'The New Nature of Nation-State Failure', *Washington Quarterly*, Vol. 25, No. 3 (2002): 85–96.
Rotberg, Robert I. 'Failed States, Collapsed States, Weak States: Causes and Indicators', in Robert I. Rotberg (ed.), *State Failure and State Weakness in a Time of Terror*, Washington, DC: Brookings Institution Press, 2003.
Rousseau, Jean-Jacques. *Discourse on the Origin and Foundation of Inequality among Mankind*, London: Penguin, 1984 [1755].
Ruak, Taur Matan, 'Address by HE President Tour Matan Ruak on the Commemoration of the 13th Anniversary of the Referendum for the Self-Determination of the People of Timor-Leste', Dili, Timor-Leste, 30 August 2012.
Rubin, Barnett R. *The Fragmentation of Afghanistan: State Formation and Collapse in the International System*, 2nd edn, New Haven, CT: Yale University Press, 2002.
Rubin, Barnett R. 'Constructing Sovereignty for Security', *Survival*, Vol. 47, No. 4 (2005): 93–106.
Sabaratnam, Meera. 'IR in Dialogue: But Can We Change the Subjects? A Typology of Decolonising Strategies for the Study of World Politics', *Millennium: Journal of International Studies*, Vol. 39, No. 3 (2011): 781–803.
Sabaratnam, Meera. 'Avatars of Eurocentrism in the Critique of the Liberal Peace', *Security Dialogue*, Vol. 44, No. 3 (2013): 259–78.
Sachedine, Abdulaziz. *The Role of Islam in the Public Square: Guidance or Governance?* Amsterdam: Amsterdam University Press, 2006.

Sajed, Alina. 'The Post Always Rings Twice', *Review of International Studies*, Vol. 38, No. 1 (2012): 141–63.
Schake, Kori. 'The Dayton Peace Accords: Success or Failure?', in Kurt R. Spillmann and Joachim Krause (eds), *International Security Challenges in a Changing World*, Peter Lang: Bern, 1999, pp. 281–95.
Schlichte, Klaus, and Alex Veit, *Coupled Arenas: Why State Building Is So Difficult*, www2.hu-berlin.de/mikropolik/downloads/03-07_coupled_arenas.pdf.
Schmid, Herman. 'Peace Research and Politics', *Journal of Peace Research*, Vol. 5, No. 3 (1968): 217–32.
Scholte, Jan Art. 'Reinventing Global Democracy', *European Journal of International Relations* (May 2012): 1–26.
Schwarz, Rolf. 'State Formation Processes in Rentier States: The Middle Eastern Case', Paper presented at the Fifth Pan-European Conference on International Relations, ECPR Standing Group on International Relations, The Hague, 9–11 September 2004.
Scott, James C. *Weapons of the Weak: Everyday Peasant Resistance*, New Haven, CT: Yale University Press, 1985.
Scott, James C. 'Foreword', in Gilbert M. Joseph and Daniel Nugent (eds), *Everyday Forms of State Formation*, Durham, NC: Duke University Press, 1994, pp. vii–xii.
Seder, Rachel. 'Reframing Citizenship: Indigenous Rights, Local Power and the Peace Process in Guatemala, Accord', 1997, http://www.c-r.org/accord-article/reframing-citizenship-indigenous-rights-local-power-and-peace-process-guatemala.
Sharabi, Hisham. *Neopatriarchy: A Theory of Distorted Change in Arab Society*, Oxford: Oxford University Press, 1988.
Sharan, Tim. 'The Dynamics of Informal Political Networks and Statehood in Post-2001 Afghanistan', *Asian Survey*, Vol. 32, No. 3 (2013): 336–52.
Shinoda, Hideaki. 'The Difficulty and Importance of Local Ownership and Capacity Development in Peacebuilding', *Hiroshima Peace Science*, Vol. 30 (2008): 95–115.
Skidelsky, Robert. *Keynes: The Return of the Master*, London: Penguin, 2009.
Skidelsky, Robert, and Edward Skidelsky. *How Much Is Enough? Money and the Good Life*, London: Penguin, 2012.
Skocpol, Theda. *States and Social Revolutions*, Cambridge: Cambridge University Press, 1979.
Smith, Adam C. 'Understanding What We're Saying: Dilemmas of the UN's Peacebuilding Paradigm', *Civil-Military Working Papers*, No. 11, 2010.
Soares de Oliveira, Ricardo. 'Illiberal Peacebuilding in Angola', *Journal of Modern African Studies*, Vol. 49, No. 2 (2001): 287–314.
Spivak, Gayatri Chakravorty. 'Can the Subaltern Speak?', in Cary Nelson and Lawrence Grossberg (eds), *Marxism and the Interpretation of Culture*, Basingstoke: Macmillan, 1988, pp. 271–313.
Springer, Simon. *Cambodia's Neoliberal Order: Violence, Authoritarianism and the Contestation of Public Space*, London: Routledge, 2010.
Sriram, Chandra. 'Revolutions in Accountability', *American University International Law Review*, Vol. 19, No. 2 (2003): 301–429.
Stevenson, Robert Louis. *The Strange Case of Dr Jekyll and Mr Hyde*, London: Longman, 1886.
Stewart, Frances. 'Horizontal Inequalities: A Neglected Dimension of Development', *Working Paper 81*, University of Oxford: Queen Elizabeth House, February 2002.
Stiglitz, Joseph. *Globalization and its Discontents*, New York and London: W.W. Norton & Company, 2003.
Strange, Susan. *States and Markets*, London: Frances Pinter, 1988.
Suhrke, Astri. 'Exogenous Statebuilding: The Contradictions of the International Project in Afghanistan', in Whit Mason and Martin Krygier (eds), *Rule of Law in Afghanistan*, Cambridge: Cambridge University Press, 2011, pp. 225–48.

Swedish International Development Cooperation Agency (SIDA), 'Civil Society and Democracy in Cambodia: Changing Roles and Trends', The Fifth Report of the Sida Advisory Team on Democratic Governance, www.pnyx.se/docs/CambodiaI.pdf, 2003.

Tadjbakhsh, Shahrbanou. 'Liberal Peace and the Dialogue of the Deaf in Afghanistan', in Shahrbanou Tadjbakhsh (ed.), *Rethinking the Liberal Peace: External Models and Local Alternatives*, Milton Park: Routledge, 2011, pp. 206–20.

Tadjbakhsh, Shahrbanou, and Anuradha M. Chenoy. *Human Security: Concepts and Implications*, London: Routledge, 2006.

Tarrow, Sidney. *Power in Movement: Collective Action, Social Movements and Politics*, Cambridge: Cambridge University Press, 1994.

Thoreau, Henry David. *On the Duty of Civil Disobedience (or Resistance to Civil Government)*, [1849], Heraklion Press, 2013.

Tickner, J. Ann. 'Dealing with Difference', *Millennium*, Vol. 39, No. 3 (2011): 1–12.

Tilly, Charles (ed.). *The Formation of National States in Western Europe*, Princeton: Princeton University Press, 1975.

Tilly, Charles. 'Western State-Making and Theories of Political Transformation', in Charles Tilly (ed.), *The Formation of National States in Western Europe*, Princeton: Princeton University Press, 1975, pp. 601–86.

Tilly, Charles. 'War Making and State Making as Organised Crime', in Peter B. Evans, Dietrich Rueschemeyer and Theda Skocpol (eds), *Bringing the State Back In*, Cambridge: Cambridge University Press, 1985, pp. 169–91.

Tilly, Charles. *Coercion, Capital and European States, AD 990–1992*, Oxford: Blackwell, 1990.

Tilly, Charles. *European Revolutions*, Oxford: Blackwell, 1993.

Tilly, Charles. *Democracy*, Cambridge: Cambridge University Press, 2007.

Trindade, Josh. 'Reconciling Conflict Paradigms: An East Timorese Vision of the Ideal State', in David J. Mearns (ed.), *Democratic Governance in Timor-Leste: Reconciling the Local and the National*, Darwin, Australia: Charles Darwin University, 2008, pp. 160–85.

Trouillot, Michel-Rolph. *Silencing the Past: Power and the Production of History*, Boston: Beacon Press, 1995.

Trouillot, Michel-Rolph. 'The Anthropology of the State in the Age of Globalization. Close Encounters of the Deceptive Kind', *Current Anthropology*, Vol. 42 (2001): 125–38.

Turner, Mandy. 'Completing the Circle: Peacebuilding as Colonial Practice in the Occupied Palestinian Territory', paper given at ISA Convention, San Diego, 1–4 March 2012.

Turner, Mandy. 'Peacebuilding as Counterinsurgency in the Occupied Palestinian Territory', paper given at ISA Convention, San Francisco, 2–5 April 2013.

United Nations. *Monitoring Peace Consolidation: UN Practitioners' Guide to Benchmarking*, New York: UN, 2010.

United Nations Development Programme. *Governance and Peacebuilding*, New York: UNDP, 2012.

United Nations Development Programme. *Governance for Peace*, New York: UNDP, 2012.

United Nations Educational, Scientific and Cultural Organization. *Women and Peace in Africa*, Paris: UNESCO, 2003.

Van der Walle, Nicolas. *African Economies and the Politics of Permanent Crisis, 1979–1999*, Cambridge: Cambridge University Press, 2001.

Van Tongeren, Paul. 'Overview on Infrastructures for Peace', 2011, www.parliamentarians-forconflictprevention.net.

Van Tongeren, Paul, M. Brenk, M. Hellema and J. Verhoeven (eds). *People Building Peace II*, Boulder, CO: Lynne Rienner, 2005.

Verdery, Katherine. *The Political Lives of Dead Bodies: Reburial and Postsocialist Change*, New York: Columbia University Press, 1999.
Verkoren, Willemijn, and Mathijs van Leeuwen. 'Civil Society in Peacebuilding: Global Discourse, Local Reality', *International Peacekeeping*, Vol. 20, No. 2 (2013): 159–72.
Vucetic, Srdjan. *The Anglosphere: A Genealogy of a Racialized Identity in International Relations*, Palo Alto, CA: Stanford University Press, 2011.
Walker, R.B.J. *Inside/Outside: International Relations as Political Theory*, Cambridge: Cambridge University Press, 1993.
Wallis, Joanne. 'What Role Can Decentralisation Play in State-Building? Lessons from Timor-Leste and Bougainville', *Commonwealth and Comparative Politics*, Vol. 51, No. 4 (2013): 424–46.
Waltz, Kenneth. *Man, the State, and War*, New York: Columbia University Press, 1959.
Weber, Max. 'Politics as a Vocation', Lecture at the University in Munich, 1918, Indiana: Hackett Publishing, 2004.
Weber, Max. 'The Three Types of Legitimate Rule', trans. Hans Gerth, *Berkeley Publications in Society and Institutions*, Vol. 4. No. 1 (1958): 1–11.
Weber, Max. *Political Writings*, Cambridge: Cambridge University Press, 1994.
Widner, Jennifer. 'States and Statelessness in Late-Twentieth-Century Africa', *Daedalus*, Vol. 124, No. 3 (1995): 129–53.
Wilde, Andreas, and Katja Mielke, 'Order, Stability and Change in Afghanistan: From Top-Down to Bottom-Up State-Making', *Central Asian Survey*, Vol. 32, No. 3 (2013): 353–70.
Wilkinson, Richard, and Kate Pickett, *The Spirit Level: Why More Equal Societies Almost Always Do Better*, London: Allen Lane, 2009.
Wimpelmann, Torun. 'Nexuses of Knowledge and Power in Afghanistan: The Rise and Fall of the Informal Justice Assemblage', *Central Asian Survey*, Vol. 32, No. 3: 406–22.
Woods, Tom. 'Informal Political System of Government in Solomon Islands', Working Paper for the Constitutional Congress and the Eminent Persons Advisory Committee, Honiara, 28 August 2008.
Woodward, Susan. *A Balkan Tragedy*, Washington, DC: Brookings Institute, 1995.
Woodward, Susan. 'Varieties of State-building in the Balkans: A Case for a Shifting Focus', in Martina Fischer, Hans Joachim Giessmann and Beatrix Schmelzle, (eds), *Berghof Handbook in Conflict Transformation, Volume 2*, Berlin: Berghof Center, 2010.
World Bank, *The State in a Changing World*, Washington, DC: World Bank, 1997.
World Bank, *World Bank Development Report*, Washington, DC: World Bank, 2001.
World Bank, 'Afghanistan Reconstruction Trust Fund (ARTF)', 2002, http://web.worldbank.org/.
World Bank, *World Bank Development Report*, Washington, DC: World Bank, 2011.
Wyeth, Vanessa. 'Knights in Fragile Armour: The Rise of the G7+', *Global Governance*, Vol. 18 (2011): 7–12.
Zanotti, Laura. 'Cacophanies of Aid, Failed State Building and NGOs in Haiti', *Third World Quarterly*, Vol. 31, No. 5 (2010): 755–71.
Zartman, I. William (ed.). *Traditional Cures for Modern Conflicts: African Conflict 'Medicine'*. Boulder, CO: Lynne Rienner, 2000.
Zoubir, Yahia H. (ed.). *North Africa in Transition: State, Society, and Economic Transformation in the 1990s*, Gainesville: University Press of Florida, 1999.

Interviews

Boavida, João. *Personal Interview*, CEPAD, Dili, 28 August 2012.
Broz, Svetlana. *Personal Interview*, Writer and Activist, Sarajevo, 23 July 2012.
'Busan Partnership for Effective Development Co-Operation', 2011.

Confidential Official Source, *Personal Interview*, UNDP, New York, 7 February 2012.
Confidential Official Source. *Personal Interview*, UN PBSO, New York, 6 February 2012.
Confidential Source. *Personal Interview*, World Bank, Washington, 2 February 2012.
Confidential Sources. *Personal Interviews*, UN PBSO, New York, 6 February 2012.
Confidential Source. *Personal Interview*, UN Peacebuilding Commission, 6 February 2012.
Confidential Sources. *Focus Group*, UN PBSO, New York, 7 February 2012.
Confidential Source. *Personal Interview*, UNDP, New York, 8 February 2012.
Confidential Source. *Personal Interview*, UN PBSO, New York, 10 February 2012.
Confidential Source. *Personal Interview*, PBC, New York, 6 June 2010.
Confidential Unofficial Source. *Personal Interview*, 20 April 2012.
Official Source. *Personal Interview*, UN PBSO, New York, 2 February 2012.
Personal Interviews and Field Notes, Nicosia, November 2011.
Schuld, Leslie, Director of Center for Exchange and Solidarity. *Personal Interview*, San Salvador, 17 January 2012.
Van Tongeren, Paul, Former Secretary-General of Global Partnership for the Prevention of Armed Conflict (GPPAC). *Personal Interview*, Amsterdam, 17 December 2012.
Wyeth, Vanessa. *Personal Interview*, International Peace Academy, New York, 7 February 2012.
Youssef, Mohammed. *Personal Interview*, International Peace Academy, New York, 16 February 2012.

Official Documents

DFID. *Saving Lives, Preventing Suffering and Building Resilience*, London: DFID, 2011.
European Council. *A Secure Europe in a Better World-European Security Strategy*, Brussels December 2003.
OECD. *High Level Panel, 2004*, OECD, 2008.
OECD. *Do No Harm: International Support for Statebuilding*, Paris: OECD, 2010.
OECD-DAC. *Principles for Good International Engagement in Fragile States*, 2005.
OECD-DAC. *Principles for Good International Engagement in Fragile States and Situations*, Paris: OECD, April 2007. http://www.oecd.org/dac/incaf/38368714.pdf.
Talat, Mehmet Ali, Former President of the TRNC, and George Vassiliou, Former President of the Republic of Cyprus. Public Debate, Home of Cooperation, Nicosia/Lefkosha, 8 October 2013.
UNDP. *Human Development Report: Timor Leste*, 2006.
UNDP. 'Civil Society Index, Mozambique 2007', UNDP, June 2008.
UNDP. *Sierra Leone Country Profile*, 2010.
UNDP. *Governance for Peace*, New York: UNDP, 2012.
UNDP. *Governance and Peacebuilding*, New York: UNDP, 2012.
UNESCO, *Culture of Peace Programme in El Salvador*, 1992.
UNESCO, *Women and Peace in Africa*, Paris: UNESCO, 2003.
United Nations. *Monitoring Peace Consolidation: UN Practitioners' Guide to Benchmarking*, New York: UN, 2010.
United Nations Development Assistance Framework. 'UNDAF Timor Leste 2009–2013'.
United Nations General Assembly. 'Declaration on the Granting of Independence to Colonial Countries and Peoples', UNGA Res. 1514, 20 December 1960.
United Nations General Assembly. 'International Covenant on Economic, Social and Cultural Rights', UNGA Res. 2200, 19 December 1966.
United Nations General Assembly. 'Declaration on Social Progress and Development', UNGA Res. 2542, 11 December 1969.
United Nations General Assembly. 'Declaration on the Establishment of a New International Economic Order', UNGA Res. 3201, 1 May 1974.

United Nations General Assembly. 'Declaration on the Preparation of Societies for Life in Peace', UNGA Res. 33/74, 15 December 1978.
United Nations General Assembly. 'Declaration on the Right of Peoples to Peace', UNGA Res. 39/11, 12 November 1984.
United Nations General Assembly. 'Declaration on the Right to Development', UNGA Res. 41/128, 4 December 1986.
United Nations General Assembly. 'Declaration and Programme of Action on a Culture of Peace', A/RES/53/243, 6 October 1999.
United Nations Security Council. 'Agreement on Comprehensive Political Settlement of the Cambodia Conflict', Paris, 23 October 1991.
United Nations Security Council. 'United Nations Security Council Resolution 718', 31 October 1991.
United Nations Security Council. 'United Nations Security Council Resolution 745', 28 February 1992.
United Nations Security Council. 'Statement by Representative of Guatemala at the Open Meeting of the Security Council on Peacebuilding: A Comprehensive Approach', S/PV.4272, 5 February 2001.
United Nations Security Council. 'Report of the Secretary-General on Timor-Leste Pursuant to Security Council Resolution 1690', Undocs, S/2006/628, August 2006.
United Nations Security Council. 'Report of the UN Secretary-General on Peacebuilding in the Immediate Aftermath of Conflict', A/63/881-S/2009/304, 11 June 2009.
United States Department of Defense. *European Security Strategy*, Brussels: December 2003.
United States Department of Defense. *National Defense Strategy*, Washington, DC: DOD, 2008.
United States National Security Strategy. 'US National Security Strategy', Washington, DC: The White House, 2002.
World Bank. *The State in a Changing World*, Washington, DC: World Bank 1997.
World Bank. *Building the Palestinian State*, Washington, DC: World Bank, 13 April 2011.
World Bank. 'Institutions Taking Root: Building State Capacity in Challenging Contexts', draft report, 2011.
World Bank. *World Bank Development Report 2011: Conflict, Security, and Development*. Washington, DC: World Bank, 2011.

Websites

Afghanistan International Security Assistance Force, http://www.isaf.nato.int/
Correlates of War dataset, www.correlatesofwar.org/datasets.htm
EU Commission, ec.europa.eu/index_en.htm
EU 'Development and Cooperation', http://ec.europa.eu/europeaid/where/asia/country-cooperation/afghanistan/afghanistan_en.htm
The Failed States Index, http://ffp.statesindex.org/
Global Burden of Armed Violence Reports, http://www.genevadeclaration.org/measurability/global-burden-of-armed-violence.html
Home of Cooperation, http://www.home4cooperation.info/
Prio Cyprus Centre, http://cyprus.prio.org/
UNDP, www.undp.org/
Uppsala Dataset, http://www.pcr.uu.se/research/ucdp/datasets/
USAID, www.usaid.gov/
World Bank's Good Governance Indicators, 2010, http://info.worldbank.org/governance/wgi/sc_country.asp

Index